PROBLEM EMPLOYEES

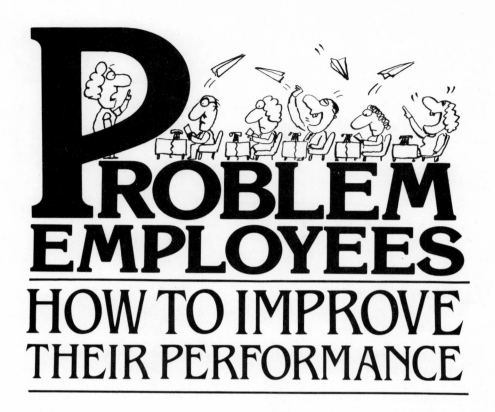

PROBLEM EMPLOYEES

HOW TO IMPROVE THEIR PERFORMANCE

Dr. Peter Wylie and Dr. Mardy Grothe

Pitman Management and Training, a division of PITMAN LEARNING, INC. Belmont, California

To Linda (P.B.W.)

———

To Lorna, Ted, Hilary,
and
Jordan (M.S.G.)

ACKNOWLEDGMENTS

We'd like to thank the following people for helping to make this book a reality:

Arlene Preisick and John Thiesmeyer for their thoughtful comments on the manuscript;

The hundreds of participants in our workshops who've contributed so many ideas to the book;

All of our friends who've offered us encouragement, support, and enthusiasm;

Bettie Richardson, who carefully typed much of the manuscript and endured the jokes we inserted on the tapes she transcribed; and

Linda Margolis-Wylie, whose experience as a supervisor helped inspire the book and who *nudjed* and supported us all along the way.

Editorial director: *Joan Wolfgang*
Editor: *Bonnie Bernstein*
Production manager: *Patricia Clappison*
Design manager: *Eleanor Mennick*
Cover and interior designer: *Ruth Scott*
Illustrator: *David Sipress*

ISBN–0–8224–9373–X

Library of Congress Catalog Card Number: 81-82032
Printed in the United States of America.

1.9 8 7 6 5 4 3 2 1

CONTENTS

PREFACE

The influx of new groups of people into the labor force, along with the erosion of our acceptance of traditional standards and rules, have combined to make most workers more of a challenge to their managers and supervisors than they would have been as recently as twenty-five years ago. In a sense, all of us have become problem employees for the people we work for. And all of us have problem employees who work for us.

As management consultants, we've had about a decade's worth of exposure to scores of different organizational settings and to many different types of managers and supervisors:

☐ Foremen and section supervisors in machine shops;
☐ Executive vice-presidents of large and small corporations;
☐ Head nurses and department heads of hospitals;
☐ Owner-operators of small family businesses, such as restaurants, dry cleaners, variety stores, and catering services;
☐ Principals and department heads in schools and colleges;
☐ Directors of personnel or of human resource development in private industry; and
☐ Department managers in retail stores.

We've consistently found that most people who become supervisors and managers achieve these levels of responsibility because they have demonstrated considerable technical or conceptual ability, not because they have the skills to motivate people or to handle the predictable people problems that they encounter in their positions. Such problems include:

☐ An employee who challenges a supervisor's authority in a group situation;
☐ A worker who maintains that, as a member of a minority group, he or she can't be fired;
☐ An employee who is obviously an alcoholic;
☐ A technician whose skills are superb but who frequently alienates coworkers and customers;
☐ A secretary who can't spell or distinguish a sentence from a phrase;
☐ A worker who's been on the job for twenty-five years and whose performance is on a gradual but steady decline;
☐ A young worker who is completely unwilling to stay after five o'clock and come in on weekends, even during peak periods when the crunch is on; and
☐ An overly dependent employee who seems to have no initiative and won't start any project without being told specifically to do so.

Our purpose in writing this book is to provide managers and supervisors with a simple, practical, and straightforward approach to help all employees, especially problem employees, significantly improve their work performance. Primarily, we offer guidelines for conducting a performance improvement interview—a process that we've found to be effective in handling on-the-job people problems and in maximizing the performance potential of most employees. Here's what *Problem Employees* features:

1. A course between covers. This book closely parallels a workshop that we conduct for managers and supervisors. It's designed so that as you read through and complete the practice exercises, you will, in effect, go through the process once, before you actually sit down with one of your employees.

2. A ten-step process. The book breaks down the process of conducting a performance improvement interview into ten steps that are very easy to follow. In the beginning, while learning how to conduct performance improvement interviews, the steps will act as a supportive guide through what can otherwise be a difficult and anxiety-producing task. After you've become more practiced and confident, you'll carry out the steps without thinking much about them.

3. Listening and presentation skills. The book covers, in depth, two essential managerial skills—active listening and effective presentation skills. If you learn nothing else but how to be a better listener and how to better present your ideas, you'll have bought more than your money's worth. These skills will not only make you a better manager, but also will help you in some of your other private roles, such as parent, spouse, intimate partner, or friend.

4. Alternative strategies. Throughout the book we've tried to offer alternative strategies and techniques you can use when you run into problems. We haven't covered all of the contingencies, but at least you'll have a backup strategy if things don't go according to plan. When you're dealing with human beings, that's almost as much the rule as it is the exception.

We strongly believe that learning should be enjoyable, so we've tried to make our book as interesting as possible. It's written in the same language and tone that we use in our workshops with managers and supervisors. It's very light on theory and very heavy on the application of specific techniques and skills. There are lots of examples and anecdotes, and we've really tried to share a little of ourselves with you. You can think of our book as a firsthand account—we've made all the mistakes we've written about!

We've read a lot of self-help books ourselves, and we've had many long discussions with others who've read them. We've concluded that a book's helpfulness is as much a function of how it's read as how it's written. This book in particular calls for a lot of active and thoughtful participation on your part. Therefore, we'd like you to get actively involved as a reader, complete the practice exercises, and try out the techniques we suggest with an employee *before* judging their validity. Make the book an enjoyable experience for yourself.

THE PERFORMANCE IMPROVEMENT PROCESS

STEP ONE: Analyze Your Employee's Performance

STEP TWO: Ask Your Employee to Meet with You

STEP THREE: Begin the Performance Improvement Interview

STEP FOUR: Find Out How Things Are Going

STEP FIVE: Get Your Employee to Do a Self-Analysis

STEP SIX: Present Your Analysis of Your Employee's Performance

STEP SEVEN: Negotiate the Performance Agreement

STEP EIGHT: Close the Interview

STEP NINE: Follow Up

STEP TEN: "What Do I Do if None of This Stuff Works?"

CHAPTER 1
WHO ARE PROBLEM EMPLOYEES?

This is a book about problem employees and how to deal with them. So, let's get right down to business.

Think of a problem employee—someone who has caused you trouble, gives you some supervisory headaches, or, in general, does not perform well on the job. If you're like most managers or supervisors, you'll have no trouble thinking of someone right away. More likely, several people will come quickly to mind. But, for now, focus on just one person. Fix the individual clearly in your mind.

What makes this person a problem employee? How does he create problems for you? What does she* do or fail to do in her job that creates problems for you? How often, and under what circumstances, is he a problem? What negative effects does she have on other coworkers, on the organization or work unit as a whole, and on you as her supervisor?

As you think about the answers to these questions, record your thoughts below in as much detail as you can:

Name of employee: _____

What makes this person a problem employee?

_____

_____

_____

_____

_____

EVERYBODY HAS PROBLEM EMPLOYEES

Over the past several years, we've talked with many different types of managers about their experiences with problem employees. We asked all of them to do the same thing we asked you to do — to think of a problem employee. Each one had little trouble thinking of somebody who fit that description. So, meet some of your colleagues' problem employees:

Sheila Ricks is a dentist in her mid-thirties. Having just taken over the practice of an older dentist she worked with for the last five years, Sheila also inherited a problem employee: Lyla Franks, her secretary and receptionist. As Sheila put it, "Lyla's so unpredictable. One day she's friendly and outgoing, and the next day she's sullen and grouchy. I don't know which Lyla is going to walk in the door in the morning." When asked about the negative effects of Lyla's behavior, Sheila responded, "This Jeckyll-and-Hyde routine of hers is beginning to alienate some of my old patients and turn off some of my new ones. My dental hygienist ignores her completely. And I end up feeling confused half the time about what to do. They don't have a course in dental school on how to deal with people like Lyla."

*We plan to use the pronouns *he* and *she* alternately to refer to problem employees and supervisors throughout this book. This style may be a little confusing at first, but you'll quickly get used to it.

Charles Bickford is a fifty-year-old vice-president of marketing for a large corporation. He recently promoted a promising, young regional sales manager, John Bailey, to assistant vice-president of sales for the eastern half of the country. "John's a real 'comer' in the organization, but I'm having trouble getting him to see the big picture," Charles said. "He's still behaving like a sales manager, not a vice-president. He's too concerned about meeting monthly quotas and not concerned enough with our long-range goals. He thinks, maybe, three months ahead. I need him to think five years ahead if we're going to have the kind of growth we've predicted for this part of the country. I've got to figure out some way to get him on my wavelength."

Barbara Stokes, twenty-nine years old, is a trained career counselor. Last year, she was promoted to a supervisory position at a downtown employment office in a large eastern city. Her problem employee is Walter Thompson, a fifty-three-year-old counselor who's worked in the same office for over twenty years. "I don't know whether it's an age issue, a sex issue, or a race issue," said Barbara, "but I just haven't been able to get this guy to come around. Often, he just seems to be going through the motions, not really caring about his job or the people we're trying to help. His lack of interest shows in lots of ways—careless mistakes on forms, perfunctory reports, and complaints from people about his lack of helpfulness. I don't know, his presence around here just seems to have a depressing effect on everybody. Especially me!"

Al Schmidt is a forty-three-year-old section supervisor for a medium-sized machine tool company. Al's been in this job for fifteen years and knows it inside and out. Four weeks ago he hired a promising apprentice-trainee, Brian Sullivan. "Brian's a hard worker, and he shows up every day," said Al, "but he's slow to catch on to things. I've tried to explain stuff carefully to him, and he seems to understand. But I can tell he doesn't by the work he turns out. Some of the journeymen are starting to complain that they don't want the responsibility of teaching him." Turning his hands upward, Al went on, "I don't know what to do. The guy really wants to work, and that's rare these days. On the other hand, maybe he doesn't have what it takes to make it in this trade. I don't know."

A PROFILE OF PROBLEM EMPLOYEES

Based on our discussions with scores of managers and supervisors, we've reached the following conclusion: Problem employees are everywhere! They can be found anywhere people work for a living. No manager or supervisor is immune from them. What else do we know about problem employees? We've devoted the rest of this chapter to profiling them for you.

PROBLEM EMPLOYEES COME IN ALL COLORS, SHAPES, AND SIZES

So far we haven't been able to detect any significant trends with respect to type of industry, level or status of job, race, sex, ethnicity, or any other of a host of variables that sociologists and psychologists often look at when they do research on organizations. For example, we've found that senior vice-presidents of large corporations are no less likely to have problem employees than first-line supervisors of small manufacturing firms. Professional workers are just as likely to be problems for their bosses as workers with less education who punch a time clock. In spite of widely held stereotypes, we haven't been able to identify differences between men and women, minorities and whites, or younger and older workers in their tendencies to be troublesome to their supervisors.

PROBLEM EMPLOYEES ARE NOT A CLEARLY IDENTIFIABLE GROUP

If given the task, census takers could probably get an accurate count on all Caucasian males in the country who are over twenty-one years of age and who have red hair and freckles. However, asking them to count all the problem employees in the country would be like asking them to count all the "wild and crazy" people in Las Vegas. We've learned that whether or not a worker is called a problem employee depends on a number of factors.

1. Who's the boss? Although it may seem obvious, supervisors differ greatly in their opinions and evaluations of workers. More than once, we've seen two managers in the same organization give us diametrically opposed assessments of the same employee.

2. What job is the person in? Many people can be tremendously effective in one job and incompetent in another. Just because someone's a good machinist doesn't mean he'll make a good shop foreman. Just because someone's a good accountant doesn't mean she'll make a good business manager. The right person can be in the wrong job.

    3. What's going on in the worker's personal life? Even the best workers become problem employees (at least temporarily) when they're contending with such personal crises as divorce, the death of a close friend or relative, or a child who gets into trouble. If you look at it from this standpoint, all of us can be problem employees, and probably have been, at one time or another.

BEING A PROBLEM EMPLOYEE OFTEN HAS LITTLE TO DO WITH ABILITY

Problem employees are often very talented, competent people with more than enough ability to perform well on the job. But they can *still* be problem employees. Their bosses often complain about bad attitude, poor motivation, or the inability to get along with others. Many managers seem more concerned about factors such as these than the employee's technical ability to do the job.

    Here's what supervisors have told us about their "unmotivated" employees:

"He does a great job when he's here, but he's often absent four or five times a month."

"She'll frequently come in twenty minutes late, and I don't think I've ever seen her stay after five."

"He doesn't take any initiative. He almost never starts a project on his own. He seems content to do only what I ask him to, no more."

"She always wants to study a problem to death. She doesn't seem to have any concept of deadlines."

"I know he has to catch a commuter train at 5:20, but sometimes we just have to work late around here to get proposals out. Sometimes I think he'd rather cut off his left hand than miss that train."

"When she's finished with her work, she's ready to sit down and read a novel. I don't think I've ever seen her go around to see if she could help somebody else out."

These are examples of what managers have told us about employees who have difficulty getting along with other people:

"The guy's always complaining to other people behind my back, but he'll never say anything directly to my face."

"She's really touchy about any criticism of her work. I feel I always have to handle her with kid gloves."

"He's very moody. One day he's all smiles and laughs, and the next day you can't get a word out of him. Nobody quite knows how to handle him."

"She's a put-down artist. She's always going around zinging and insulting people. I have a hell of a time getting anybody to work with her."

"He's really rough around the edges when it comes to dealing with customers. He never really listens to them. He's always telling them exactly what he thinks they need, without finding out what their problems are."

"I can't get her to speak up at staff meetings. I know she's got a lot of great ideas, but you'd never know it. She just sits there and doesn't say boo."

PROBLEM EMPLOYEES ARE A CONSTANT SOURCE OF CONCERN

Managers spend a lot of time worrying and thinking about their problem employees. They ruminate about them in the car or train going to and from work. They complain to their spouses, friends, and peers about the difficulties they experience with these workers. They begin to doubt their own competence as managers.

Supervisors also spend a lot of time cleaning up after their problem employees. This can mean redoing work that the employee has completed unsatisfactorily or defending the foul-ups of these workers to their own bosses.

Managers spend a lot of time figuring out ways to get around problem employees. They ask themselves questions like, "How can I tell him I don't want him to make the presentation without hurting his feelings?" or, "Who else can I give this project to because I know she's going to mess it up?" or, "How can I get somebody else in here to do all the things that he can't do?"

A QUICK SUMMARY

Problem employees come in all colors, shapes, and sizes. Depending upon certain factors and situations, anybody can be a problem employee at one time or another—including you and us. Problem employees are often as much of a problem in the areas of motivation and cooperation with other people as they are in their ability to do their work. Compared to other workers, problem employees are a constant source of concern to their supervisors.

CHAPTER 2
HOW DO YOU KNOW A PROBLEM EMPLOYEE WHEN YOU SEE ONE?

As we were writing the book, we'd occasionally mention the title to a manager or supervisor. Almost invariably we'd get a response like the one shown at the right.

"Oh yeah, I've got some of those. Like the older worker who's on active retirement. Or the young person just out of college who just wants to work from nine to five, forget weekends."

After a number of reactions like this, it became clear to us that most managers and supervisors feel they have a clear picture of who their problem employees are. Our experience has shown us a couple of other things:

- Sometimes managers and supervisors fail to recognize a problem employee when they see one.
- Sometimes managers and supervisors *think* they have a problem employee when they really don't.

In this chapter we'll try to give you some suggestions for identifying less obvious problem employees and for making certain that a person you assume is a problem employee really is one.

RECOGNIZING THE LESS OBVIOUS PROBLEM EMPLOYEE

As much as most bosses seem to feel they know who their problem employees are, why do they occasionally fail to recognize when a worker really is a problem employee? We see a number of reasons:

1. Sometimes managers and supervisors just don't want to admit that they have a problem worker. Admitting that somebody who works for you is a problem is like admitting that you're not as good a boss as you could be. Some people just have more difficulty owning up to their problems and mistakes than others do.

7

2. Some employees are so very effective in some aspects of their work that their strengths overshadow areas where they could stand to improve. For example, the cracker-jack computer programmer is brusque with people from other departments. The auto mechanic is very talented and thorough but always takes more than the estimated time to complete a repair.

3. Many supervisors accept the fact that some workers are weak in certain skills or habits. They don't view these areas needing improvement as problems that at least have a chance of being corrected. They simply see performance deficiencies as a fact of life.

4. The supervisor overlooks a lot of the employee's weaknesses because he or she is a particularly pleasant person to be around.

5. The employee is slick. Unfortunately, some workers are very good at forming a good impression with their bosses and still not turning out much work.

6. Managers get wrapped up in their own work. They simply ignore what their employees are doing.

7. Some managers are overly involved with their employees. Novelists are always writing about it, so we might as well mention it too. Occasionally a manager will form a romantic attachment with an employee that can completely obscure the manager's perception of the employee's effectiveness as a worker.

8. Bosses occasionally go through their own personal crises. Like all human beings, managers have personal problems that may divert their attention from work and from how effectively their employees are performing.

To help you decide if, and recognize when, a worker is a problem employee, we've come up with a series of questions that you can ask yourself. You'll find them on page 9.

We think that a yes answer to even one of these questions could mean that you have a problem employee, especially if the question touches on an area that's particularly important to you. If you can say yes to two or more questions, there's no doubt about it.

For a few of your employees, you may have a tendency to answer "Yes, but . . ." to some of the questions. If you do, that probably means you're having trouble accepting the fact that they're problem employees — especially if you feel they're valuable members of your team. *Go ahead and accept the fact.* Then you can get on with the important business of helping them improve their performance.

PROBLEM EMPLOYEE QUESTIONNAIRE

*Read each question below. If you find your-self thinking **yes** in response to a question, put a checkmark on the blank beside it. If the answer is **no**, leave the blank empty.*

_____ 1. Do you receive complaints from customers about his work or about his attitude toward customers?

_____ 2. Do her coworkers complain to you about her rudeness, about her trying to dump work on them, and so on?

_____ 3. Does your boss tell you about mistakes in his work?

_____ 4. Do your peers complain to you about how she has treated them or their workers?

_____ 5. If you don't check his work, will it often go out with major mistakes?

_____ 6. When you give her an assignment, does it rarely come back done the way you wanted it?

_____ 7. Do you often have to reschedule the work of your other employees at the last minute because he fails to show up?

_____ 8. Do you frequently spend time doing work that you should be able to delegate to her?

_____ 9. Does he rarely complete assignments on time?

_____ 10. As soon as she finishes a task, does she wait until you assign her another one?

_____ 11. After you give him an assignment, does he frequently return with a number of reasons why it can't be done?

_____ 12. Do you receive reports that she has been complaining about you to other people?

_____ 13. Are you always at least a little concerned that he will say something to embarrass you in front of other people?

_____ 14. Do you find it difficult to get your own work done because of the time you spend on her problems and mistakes?

_____ 15. When you decide to give an important assignment to someone, do you rarely pick him?

_____ 16. Do you assign work that she should be able to do to other employees because you know they'll do it better and faster?

_____ 17. When you point out mistakes he has made, does he almost always have an excuse or put the blame on someone else?

_____ 18. Do you occasionally learn that she has lied to you, or at least stretched the truth?

WHEN IS A PROBLEM EMPLOYEE NOT A PROBLEM EMPLOYEE?

While some managers fail to recognize their problem employees, we think it's just as common for some bosses to assume they have a problem employee when what they really have is somebody with a different operating style.

We've found that it's awfully easy for some managers to confuse *process* with *outcome.* That is, these managers make the mistake of focusing too much on how an employee works and not enough on what the employee produces in terms of quantity, quality, and timeliness.

These are some examples of the kinds of process concerns that managers often have. Remember, a process concern tends to have much more to do with the way employees get their work done than it does with the actual work they've produced.

1. Physical appearance. In spite of the relaxation in standards of dress for both men and women in business settings over the last ten years, many managers still object to long hair, unshaven legs, beards, blue jeans, and the like. They think that men should wear ties and sports jackets and that women should wear skirts and stockings. Clearly, there are some jobs that warrant or require someone to dress up. A maître d' in a swank restaurant, a receptionist, or a clothing salesperson ought to dress appropriately for work. But we know of no evidence that a bra, a tie, and a cleanshaven face or legs ever contributed much to a worker's productivity on a job that does not require a lot of public contact. If anything, the reverse is true.

2. Flexibility of work hours. There is certainly nothing sacred about the eight-hour day, especially when it's rigidly sandwiched between 9:00 A.M. and 5:00 P.M. More and more organizations are experimenting with flexible schedules, or flex time, which permits employees to start work early and finish early or to start late and finish late. If more managers and organizations adopted this approach to hours of work, we strongly suspect that the percentage of costly tardinesses and absences in American industry would drop significantly.

3. Extra hours and weekends. We've seen far too many managers equate long hours of work with high work productivity. Although there is some small correlation between the two, we find that managers who consistently spend ten to twelve hours a day on the job are not using their time effectively. We've also noticed that these same managers often get upset that their employees don't put in equally long hours, even when it's apparent that the employees are much more efficient users of their time than their bosses.

4. Participation in extracurricular activities. Almost all organizations have activities that are not directly related to day-to-day business functions. Christmas parties, bowling leagues, Friday afternoon "staff meetings" at the local pub, and office picnics are but a few examples. We happen to be pretty strong supporters of these kinds of activities because they can contribute significantly to worker morale. However, many employees steer clear of these functions; some workers even find them downright distasteful. As much as we personally enjoy them, we think it's a mistake for bosses to hold employees' lack of participation in these activities against them. After all, people are being paid to turn out the work, not to have a good time — even though it's great when the two can go together.

5. Differences in values, attitudes, and life-styles. People differ tremendously in their values, attitudes, and life-styles. Some people are staunchly religious; others are agnostic or atheistic. Some regularly smoke marijuana or consume alcohol; others strongly disapprove of these habits. Some people firmly believe that spouses should only have sex with one another; others approve of and regularly engage in extramarital affairs. Some are politically very liberal; others are quite conservative.

Occasionally managers will have employees who are so different from them that it's difficult to take an objective view of the employees' actual work performance. Some bosses can't seem to separate what employees do on the job from what they do off the job or from the views and opinions their employees occasionally voice on the job.

6. Demographic differences. In spite of the rapid social changes of the last twenty years, some supervisors are uncomfortable working with people who are different from them. Whites are often ill at ease working with minorities, and vice versa. Many males are convinced that women just don't belong in certain roles and certain jobs. Older workers often view younger workers as overzealous and inexperienced. Many younger workers see older workers as stodgy or as having retired on the job.

As with values, attitudes, and life-styles, it's difficult for some supervisors to look beyond the color of an employee's skin, religion, sex, and such to see the quality and quantity of work the individual actually produces.

To give you some practice in deciding whether a particular concern you have about an employee is a process or outcome concern, we've composed a list of ten sample concerns that bosses might have about their workers. Fill out the form on page 12, then check your answers with ours.

PROCESS AND OUTCOME CONCERNS

*In the blank next to each statement, write a **P** if you think it's a process concern and an **O** if you think it's an outcome concern. After you finish, compare your answers to ours.*

_____ 1. The employee has written a quarterly report that you feel is too long and disorganized. It needs to be rewritten.

_____ 2. You suspect that the employee has been dating another worker in your office. You're bothered by this, and you've been seriously considering confronting her with your suspicions.

_____ 3. The company vacation policy reads that "All employees shall take their vacations in segments of no less than five days." One of your people has objected strongly to this policy, and he's putting a lot of pressure on you to let him take his vacation days one at a time for a string of Mondays throughout the summer months.

_____ 4. You happen to overhear your receptionist speak rudely over the phone to someone who is obviously a customer. You are wondering whether you should speak to her about it.

_____ 5. The employee has made an arrangement with you to put his hours in on a flexible basis, some days working as few as three hours and others working as many as twelve or fourteen. You're beginning to find his schedule frustrating because you and several of your people are having difficulty reaching him when you need to have the answers to important questions.

_____ 6. The employee is an exceptional salesperson, but you know that she has a strong aversion to paperwork. She's failed to turn in three of the last five weekly progress reports, and you're beginning to get some pressure from your boss to get them in.

_____ 7. You strongly believe that neatness is an important part of high productivity. One of your account executives, who's been a consistently high producer, has an office that looks like it's been stirred with a stick. You're always teasing him about this, but he doesn't seem to take the hint. You're about ready to seriously suggest to him that he neaten the place up so he can be even more productive.

_____ 8. You have a younger person on your staff who frequently disagrees with positions you take. Her tendency to do this is especially strong at staff meetings. You're not bothered so much by what she says as you are by the tone in which she says it. You're about ready to speak to her about it.

_____ 9. Several months ago you instituted a policy in your office that calls for your employees to fill out forms indicating how they spent their time on an hourly basis for each week. One of your younger employees has said that he strongly objects to these forms and thinks they're a waste of his time. He's filled out the forms conscientiously for the first month, but now he refuses to do it. You're confused about how you should deal with his refusal.

_____ 10. One of the managers who works for you frequently conducts group working sessions with her staff. You have serious doubts about this approach to management and are seriously thinking of speaking to her about cutting down on the number of these work sessions.

LOOK AT THE NEXT PAGE AND COMPARE YOUR ANSWERS TO OURS.

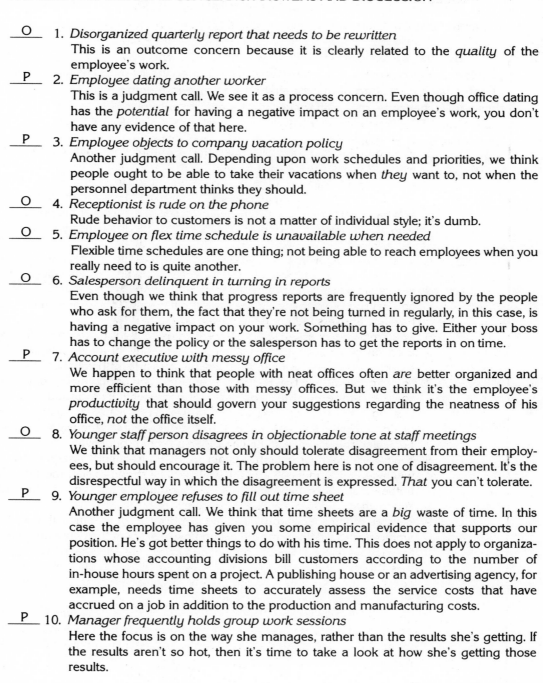

PROCESS AND OUTCOME CONCERNS: ANSWERS AND DISCUSSION

O 1. *Disorganized quarterly report that needs to be rewritten*
This is an outcome concern because it is clearly related to the *quality* of the employee's work.

P 2. *Employee dating another worker*
This is a judgment call. We see it as a process concern. Even though office dating has the *potential* for having a negative impact on an employee's work, you don't have any evidence of that here.

P 3. *Employee objects to company vacation policy*
Another judgment call. Depending upon work schedules and priorities, we think people ought to be able to take their vacations when *they* want to, not when the personnel department thinks they should.

O 4. *Receptionist is rude on the phone*
Rude behavior to customers is not a matter of individual style; it's dumb.

O 5. *Employee on flex time schedule is unavailable when needed*
Flexible time schedules are one thing; not being able to reach employees when you really need to is quite another.

O 6. *Salesperson delinquent in turning in reports*
Even though we think that progress reports are frequently ignored by the people who ask for them, the fact that they're not being turned in regularly, in this case, is having a negative impact on your work. Something has to give. Either your boss has to change the policy or the salesperson has to get the reports in on time.

P 7. *Account executive with messy office*
We happen to think that people with neat offices often *are* better organized and more efficient than those with messy offices. But we think it's the employee's *productivity* that should govern your suggestions regarding the neatness of his office, *not* the office itself.

O 8. *Younger staff person disagrees in objectionable tone at staff meetings*
We think that managers not only should tolerate disagreement from their employees, but should encourage it. The problem here is not one of disagreement. It's the disrespectful way in which the disagreement is expressed. *That* you can't tolerate.

P 9. *Younger employee refuses to fill out time sheet*
Another judgment call. We think that time sheets are a *big* waste of time. In this case the employee has given you some empirical evidence that supports our position. He's got better things to do with his time. This does not apply to organizations whose accounting divisions bill customers according to the number of in-house hours spent on a project. A publishing house or an advertising agency, for example, needs time sheets to accurately assess the service costs that have accrued on a job in addition to the production and manufacturing costs.

P 10. *Manager frequently holds group work sessions*
Here the focus is on the way she manages, rather than the results she's getting. If the results aren't so hot, then it's time to take a look at how she's getting those results.

Distinguishing between process and outcome concerns is a tough area for all managers, us included. Another question that we find helpful in making this distinction is:

"Am I really focusing on results, or am I really saying to the employee, 'Why can't you be a bit more like me?'"

By now, we hope you're getting a better fix on who your problem employees are, and who they aren't. After the next chapter, we'll be talking about the first step to take in helping these folks become more effective, productive members of your team. But first we'd like you to take a look at some ineffective ways of dealing with problem employees. Honestly compare your own managerial style with these ineffective tendencies.

CHAPTER 3
HOW NOT TO DEAL WITH A PROBLEM EMPLOYEE

For the next several minutes try to forget about the problem employees that you supervise. Instead, think about how some supervisors you've known have tried to deal with their problem employees.

Focus on two supervisors who you thought did a particularly bad job of handling their problem employees. Write down some of the things these bosses did that you thought were particularly ineffective. Be as specific as you can. For example, if you thought one of the bosses was too overbearing, you might want to write down such things as:

"He was always chewing the guy out in front of other people."

"She was always ordering this poor person around like a drill sergeant."

"He literally followed the guy around checking up on him just about every twenty minutes."

If you thought one of the bosses was not firm enough with the problem employee, you might write:

"She seemed to ignore the fact that the guy frequently came in twenty minutes late."

"He was always letting this person talk him into special privileges, like extra days off, that the rest of us really resented."

"I don't think that she ever told him that he wasn't doing a good job."

Ineffective Ways of Handling Problem Employees

Supervisor 1 _____

1. _____
2. _____
3. _____
4. _____
5. _____

Supervisor 2 _____

1. _____
2. _____
3. _____
4. _____
5. _____

In this chapter, we examine four ineffective tendencies we've observed on the part of managers and supervisors when it comes to dealing with problem employees. These ineffective tendencies are:

- Avoiding confrontation,
- Overreacting,
- Complaining, and
- Lecturing.

We'll describe each tendency, explain why managers behave this way when confronted with problem employees, and give reasons for why managers should behave differently if they want to improve employee performance.

As you read through the chapter, compare the ineffective tendencies we describe with what you wrote down earlier about the two supervisors. Then take an honest and hard look at yourself, and compare the ineffective tendencies to your own tendencies when it comes to dealing with problem employees.

AVOIDING CONFRONTATION

Avoiding confrontation means putting off, postponing, or deferring the act of sitting down with a problem employee to review the person's work performance and to set some goals for improved performance. Charlie Waters and Jane Sharp are good examples of managers who have this tendency.

> *Charlie Waters* is the owner of a medium-sized casualty insurance agency in the southwest suburbs of Chicago. For the past two months each of the agents who works for Charlie has come to him saying that something has to be done about the secretary who handles policy applications and claims. They say she just doesn't pay enough attention to detail and that the mistakes she makes on forms have been causing them all kinds of problems. Charlie's been meaning to sit down to talk with her for several weeks now, but he never seems to be able to find the time to do it.

> *Jane Sharp* is vice-president in charge of customer relations for a savings and loan association in Baltimore. One of the systems analysts who works for her is pretty abrasive with the representatives of the companies for which the bank prepares payrolls. Jane knows that she should be talking to the analyst, but for some reason she keeps putting it off. Recently she shared her reluctance with us:
>
> "I know I really need to sit down and talk with John. But at the same time I'm a little afraid he might quit. He's really good at the technical stuff he does, and systems analysts are hard to find these days. Besides, he's kind of touchy. Maybe I should wait a little longer; he may be just having some personal problems that he needs some time to work through."

WHY DO MANAGERS AVOID CONFRONTATION?

Why do managers avoid confronting their problem employees? There are a number of reasons.

1. Confrontation can be anxiety-producing. Sitting down and talking with an employee about the person's work performance makes managers and supervisors nervous, more so in the case of problem employees. Most people avoid things that make them nervous.

2. The employee may quit. Many supervisors and managers are afraid that giving negative feedback to employees will cause them to get very defensive and to overreact. Some managers fear that the employee will actually quit. This is especially true in the case of problem employees who have highly technical jobs in which the demand for skilled people often exceeds the pool of available job applicants.

3. It's not going to do any good. Many managers and supervisors frequently make protests like this:

"Look, what do you want me to do? I've spoken to this person on at least eight different occasions, and there hasn't been any change. Why do you think talking to the person one more time is going to do any good?"

It's frustrating when repeated efforts don't lead to change. Understandably, a lot of managers conclude, "The hell with it. I've got better things to do with my time."

4. I don't know how to do it. Most people, including us, avoid taking on a task that we don't think we're competent to perform. The same holds true for uncertain managers and supervisors when it comes to sitting down with a problem employee to go over that person's performance.

5. Things could end up worse off than they are now. This is a kind of catchall reason where the manager's logic seems to run something like this:

"Yes, the person is performing poorly now, but if I sit down with him to talk about his performance, I might have an even bigger problem on my hands. If the person is a member of a group protected by federal legislation, then the company, or even I, could get sued. Or it could backfire in another way. He could get all touchy and defensive and do an even worse job than he's doing now. And another thing that could go wrong is. . . ."

WHY AVOIDING CONFRONTATION IS BAD

As understandable as it is, we think that avoiding confrontation should be avoided. Here's why.

1. Avoiding the problem won't make it go away. The thought of confronting a problem employee may make you nervous, but the consequences of not confronting the person will usually make you a lot more nervous down the line. This argument really applies to most problems in life; procrastination rarely pays off. The idea of sitting down with Snidely to review his performance may be unpleasant, but nowhere near so unpleasant as the problems you'll face when your boss (and other important people in the organization) eventually feel the impact of his incompetence.

2. The problem is likely to get worse, not better. It's an unfortunate fact that adults find it very difficult to change their behavior. If you have any doubts about this, think back to when you tried to quit smoking, or to cut down on your intake of alcohol, or to diet, or to stop biting your nails, or to stop interjecting your speech with "You know." Changing behavior is plain hard work—work that a lot of us would just as soon duck. This holds true even more so for the problem employee. Problem employees are usually people who have had a history of avoiding positive change and of taking the easy way out. Without your help, the chances that a problem employee will change for the better are very small.

Moreover, the fact that the person doesn't change makes the situation worse. As the supervisor, you're becoming more frustrated. Other people who work with the problem employee are also becoming more frustrated and are beginning to feel resentful. The general pressure on you to take some decisive action keeps mounting.

3. Many problem employees must eventually be terminated; the termination process is much easier if the employee has had some advance warning. Many organizations cannot indefinitely sustain the burden of a problem employee. Something usually has to give, and in most cases it's the employee. However, an employee who has not been directly confronted about performance shortcomings prior to termination can be very difficult to handle. The first reaction is often shock, followed by disbelief, and then anger. Imagine for a minute how one of your problem employees would respond to a termination notice if the person had not received any prior notice of poor work performance.

We're not suggesting that termination of problem employees always goes smoothly if they've been confronted prior to receiving notice. Not at all. Getting fired is tough for anybody to take. But the chances are better that they'll respond rationally if they've been forewarned.

OVERREACTING

In the latter half of the 1960s it was fairly common to associate the term *overreacting* with a picture of a police officer about to strike a demonstrator over the head with a billy club. Well, it's pretty unusual to see a manager or supervisor physically strike an employee, but plenty of bosses verbally abuse their problem employees when they become frustrated and angry. Overreacting is the unnecessarily harsh manner in which a supervisor responds to an employee's performance problems. Tom Clark is a good example.

Tom Clark is a vice-president in charge of maintenance for a large railroad. Tom has an engineer working for him named Bob Driscoll. Tom thinks that Bob is actually very technically competent. But Bob tends to drive Tom up a wall because he doesn't give him direct answers to his questions. Last week at a staff meeting Tom asked Bob to give a brief report on the progress of some tests that the department was making on a new type of rail. That evening Tom told his wife what happened: "Well, right away he started off on some damn tangent like he always does. Well, we were running late, and I decided I just wasn't going to put up with it. I interrupted him mid-sentence and informed him that he was giving me everything *but* what I wanted to hear. Looking back on it, I wish I hadn't done it. There was this kind of embarrassed silence, and everybody at the table looked down, and Bob wouldn't even look at me for the rest of the day. I didn't mean to hurt his feelings, but you'd think he would have learned by now that all I want when I ask for a brief report are straightforward, *brief* answers to my questions."

WHY DO MANAGERS OVERREACT?

There are some major reasons that managers and supervisors overreact to their problem employees.

1. It offers a powerful outlet for frustration. There's something about losing your cool that has a very cleansing, purging effect for some people.

2. It seems so justified at times. Most of us feel that we have a right to get angry and frustrated when we repeatedly make reasonable requests of other people that never get fulfilled. It's not uncommon for managers and supervisors to say:

"Don't you think I have a right to chew her out after I politely ask her fifteen times to do something, and she still doesn't do it? Wouldn't you get frustrated with somebody like that?"

3. It gives some managers a sense of control and power. These are some of the things that employees do when managers make the mistake of losing their tempers:

☐ They look startled and frightened.
☐ They look down and remain very silent.
☐ After awhile, they apologize (even if they don't know what they are apologizing for).
☐ For at least a few hours, and sometimes several days, they treat their supervisors with kid gloves.

WHY OVERREACTING IS BAD

Because we're human and because anger is such a primary emotional response, it's very unrealistic to expect any manager or supervisor to call a complete halt to overreacting to problem employees. But we think there are some compelling reasons to keep it down to a bare minimum.

1. It can have bad physiological effects. When you get angry, a number of things happen simultaneously in your body. Your pulse rate increases, your blood pressure goes up, adrenalin starts pumping, your pupils dilate, your throat dries, and so on. In short, your body mobilizes itself for a fight. There is more and more evidence to confirm that if this mobilization process occurs too frequently, you end up giving yourself ulcers, high blood pressure, or any number of other physical ailments that are now associated with poor temper control.

2. Generally, its effect is temporary. It's a little hard to explain why, but overreacting doesn't have a lasting effect on employee behavior. As we observed earlier, people do tend to scurry around after they've been chewed out by a boss; but usually within a day or two, people go right back to their old behavior patterns.

3. It results in lowered respect for you. With some exceptions, we've noticed that managers and supervisors who frequently overreact eventually lose the credibility and respect of their employees. These are some examples:

☐ Employees start withholding more and more information from their supervisors and begin to tell them only the things they think the supervisors want to hear.
☐ Some people, especially problem employees, become passive-aggressive. They intentionally do things that will make a manager look bad. We know one employee who "accidentally" lets it slip whenever the boss leaves the office for a haircut, a dentist appointment, or other personal reason.

☐   Problem employees spend more time trying to shift the blame than they do on improving their performance. We find that most managers and supervisors who overreact really want their employees to take more responsibility and initiative. Unfortunately, the opposite usually happens. Their workers start coming up with ready-made excuses, alibis, and other ways of deflecting the boss's wrath onto somebody else.

4. It sometimes has destructive effects on employees. In every organization we've worked in there are people who are particularly sensitive to their bosses' overreactions. Unlike a lot of employees who can shrug it off and say, "It's just another one of Pat's temper tantrums," these people tend to take what a boss says to heart. They remain down in the dumps for long periods of time and, as a result, never even come close to fulfilling their potential.

COMPLAINING

Complaining means unloading your frustration over a problem employee on somebody other than the employee. This is a very common practice for managers and supervisors. Since we've been as guilty of it as most, we thought we might use ourselves as an example.

A number of years ago we were both in charge of a government-funded project to develop a series of instructional units on career development. The project had been underway for about three months, and we had finished hiring most of the staff. In reflecting on that experience, we now see that most of our staff members were problem employees of one form or another. Our secretaries either couldn't type or thought typing was beneath them; our instructional developers either couldn't write or were extremely defensive about any suggestions for improvement on their designs; our audiovisual people would often ignore our suggestions; and on and on. At times it seemed as if we were foundering in a sea of incompetence.

Even though we were completely responsible for the fix we were in, we didn't see it that way at the time. We would spend hours every week commiserating with each other about how nobody could do anything and how unfair it was for us to have to spend nights and weekends cleaning up after everybody else's mistakes.

Hindsight has given us a much clearer perspective on what was happening. We were doing what all managers and supervisors do when they complain to other people about their problem employees; we were simply talking to the wrong people. If we had spent only a fifth of the time sitting down with staff members to review their work performance as we did complaining to each other, we're convinced that we would have ended up with better results and more free time in the evenings and on weekends.

WHY DO MANAGERS COMPLAIN?

These are the main reasons we think we—and most other managers—complain:

1. Everybody complains once in a while. Unfortunately, complaining is a very common habit in our society. It's hard to be around other people for an hour, much less a day, and not hear somebody complain about something. There are lots of candidates to choose from: the weather, the crime rate, corrupt politicians, giant corporations, relatives, and on and on. One of our friends recently said:

"Complaining's a lot like overeating and smoking. We know it doesn't do us any good, but it's a damn tough habit to break."

2. It often creates the illusion that you're doing something about the problem. When you complain to another person about anything (assuming that the person gives you a sympathetic ear), you usually end up feeling better. Here's how it works: You express your frustration to another person; that person says that you have every right to feel the way you do; and you walk away feeling less upset. You haven't changed a thing, but you do feel better.

3. You usually get some support for your opinions. One of the things we've noticed that managers try to do when they complain about problem employees is get a little corroborative testimony. A lot of the things that problem employees do are frankly very puzzling. It's very hard to explain, for example, why employees continue to do something after you've asked them not to do it five or ten times. Oftentimes, when managers complain about problem employees, they're really asking the question, "Is it just me, or do you see the same things I do in Bob Johnson?" They're looking for confirmation of the fact that their perceptions of the employee's lack of effectiveness are accurate.

WHY COMPLAINING IS BAD

There are several reasons why complaining to other people about problem employees is ineffective. These are discussed on the following page.

1. You're talking to the wrong person, and your focus is on the wrong person. When you complain to another person about a problem employee, you're automatically talking to the wrong person. It may seem pretty obvious, but it's the problem employee that you should be talking to. However, we don't want to confuse complaining with seeking advice. If you go to another person to seek help on how you can do a better job in coping with a problem employee, that's not complaining because the focus of the conversation is on you, not the problem employee. In other words, when you complain about a problem employee, you're laying the responsibility for the problem on the employee. However, when you seek advice or help from another person on how to deal more effectively with a problem employee, you're accepting some of the responsibility for the problem, *and* you're taking some positive action to solve it. It's an important distinction.

2. It reduces your credibility as a manager. There are two important factors to think about:

☐   To whom are you complaining?
☐   How frequently are you complaining?

We think it's one thing to complain to a spouse or a trusted colleague about a problem. It's quite another thing, however, to complain to colleagues that you don't know all that well or especially to the problem employee's coworkers. Once you do either of these, your credibility as a manager begins to slide. Perhaps the most negative consequence is that people will stop being open with you for fear that you can't keep anything confidential.

The more you complain, the lower your credibility drops. The more you complain, the more people see you as someone who is only interested in talking about problems, not solving them.

3. Complaining is a big waste of time. We honestly believe that complaining doesn't move you even a fraction of a step closer to solving the problem. If anything, because complaining allows you to temporarily reduce your frustration, it fools you into thinking you're doing something constructive. It's a seductive habit that's hard to break but worth the effort.

LECTURING

We define *lecturing* as telling employees—in a condescending tone of voice—what they already know *or* aren't ready to hear. It's such a common practice for managers and supervisors that it's often a little difficult to recognize.

Consider this situation:

> ***Dave Richards*** has submitted a draft quarterly report to his boss Tom Pearson. The next day, as Dave and Tom are passing in the hall, Tom stops Dave and says, "Dave, you've got to remember to include an executive summary and cost figures with your quarterly reports. Those are the only things that the executive vice-president really looks at." Dave, looking a little puzzled and then slightly annoyed, replies, "Tom, give me a little credit, will you. I know that as well as you do. I just wanted to get your reactions to the draft before we sent the final up to the Executive V.P."

Here's another case:

> ***Judy Morris*** is an up-and-coming account executive for a large East Coast distributor of business machines. She's just finished making a presentation of the company's newest product line to the senior members of the purchasing department of a large potential customer. Her boss, Tom Jones, has come along to see her in action. From the customer's response after the presentation, Judy has the feeling that it went over pretty well, and she's obviously pleased. As they walk out of the customer's building, Judy and Tom have the following conversation.

JUDY: Gee, I think it went pretty well. I think we're going to get a big order from them.
TOM: Could be, but I think you've got some things to learn about making a presentation. . . .
JUDY: (*Frowning and looking down*)
TOM: For one thing, whenever you give a presentation, you've got to establish your credibility in the first five minutes, or you're never going to make a sale. Another thing, you always have to try to close as soon as you can. So you want to have order forms already filled out so all they have to do is sign.
JUDY: (*Still frowning and looking down*)
TOM: And another thing. . . .

Notice that in both situations the managers seemed to assume that their employees were ready to hear what they had to say, in spite of some pretty strong evidence to the contrary. This is one of the critical indicators of lecturing. Whenever you find yourself telling employees something that you really think they need to know and they start frowning, scowling, looking down, shaking their heads, or, especially, arguing, then you can be pretty sure you're doing what we call lecturing.

WHY DO MANAGERS LECTURE?

There are two major reasons why managers occasionally lecture their employees:

1. Lecturing is a very common way for managers to handle their anxiety when they see employees doing something that is obviously ineffective or counterproductive. For example, the head teller in a branch bank might observe a recently hired teller respond angrily to a rude customer. The manager tells herself that the employee is doing something that is definitely wrong, and consequently, the manager begins to feel nervous and anxious.

To bring down her level of anxiety, the manager immediately — or as soon as possible — informs the employee of what he has done wrong and why he shouldn't do it. In our example, the head teller might wait until the rude customer had left and then immediately say to the teller: "John, I know that customer was kind of a jerk, but he is a depositor, and we can't afford to alienate our depositors. We've got to try to be nice to everybody in here, even the jerks."

2. Managers lecture because they don't have the listening skills to behave differently. They don't know how to get other people to talk fully and freely about themselves. They tend to fill up the other person's silence with words of their own. When you're nervous and intent on telling employees what they've done wrong, it's easy to ignore the cues they may be giving you that they're not interested in what you have to say. Some managers don't notice when employees look down, appear embarrassed, start to get angry, or try to defend themselves. They continue to talk *at* employees, offending and frustrating them. The employees respond by drawing more and more into themselves.

WHY LECTURING IS BAD

We could list lots of reasons why lecturing is ineffective, but most of them boil down to one major reason: It's a big turnoff. Most workers resent being talked at. Most of us have been lectured to all our lives. It started with our parents, then our teachers and professors got into the act, our coaches and religious leaders piled it on, and by the time we started working for a living, we were pretty tired of it.

Most workers want to believe that their opinions and feelings are important to their supervisors. Even though they realize that the boss has the final say, they still want to be treated with respect.

HOW TO CONTROL INEFFECTIVE TENDENCIES

The best way to eliminate ineffective tendencies is to replace them with the effective strategies and techniques that you'll pick up throughout the rest of the book. In the meantime, there are a couple of things you can do to help yourself keep ineffective tendencies under control:

1. Learn to immediately recognize when you're avoiding confrontation, overreacting, complaining, or lecturing.
2. Tell yourself to stop these tendencies as soon as you recognize them.

RECOGNIZE YOUR INEFFECTIVE TENDENCIES

To recognize when you're behaving ineffectively will take some practice. To help get you started, we've listed thirteen short descriptions of things you might catch yourself doing over the next week or so. Read the form below and on page 28 and fill it in before you go on.

INEFFECTIVE TENDENCIES

In the blank space next to each description, write the letter:
  A if you think it describes avoiding confrontation,
  O if you think it describes overreacting,
  C if you think it describes complaining, or
  L if you think it describes lecturing.
Leave the space blank if you think the example describes some other behavior. Once you finish labeling each description, compare your answers to ours.

____ 1. You say to yourself, "I really have to speak to Terry about his tardiness. As soon as I get this report finished, I'm going to do it."

____ 2. You're sitting on a bus on the way to work and thinking about which one of your salespeople you're going to ask to make the presentation at Acme Tire. Your thoughts turn to Keith because there's a lull in his schedule right now. But you know that Keith makes lousy presentations, so you start thinking about assigning it to Rachel or even doing it yourself.

____ 3. You're driving home with the manager from another department. You say, "Do you want to hear what Celia did today? Remember how I told you that I had asked her at least five times to stop sending those purchase orders out? Well guess what. . . ."

____ 4. You're at a cocktail party talking to a friend whose judgment you really respect. You say, "Pat, I'm having a problem with one of my people at the office. I'm wondering if you could give me some advice on how to handle it because everything I've tried so far hasn't worked."

CONTINUED

_____ 5. You've just finished reading an evaluation that one of your employees has written on the market prospects for your product line in the southeast portion of the country. Although you think the evaluation has some merit, you see a lot of ways it could be improved. You take the evaluation into the employee's office, and after a little chit-chat, you say, "Bill, I'd like to give you some feedback on the evaluation you wrote. (*You pause as Bill nods and leans forward.*) Okay, let me start off by talking about what I see as some of the really positive aspects of what you wrote. . . ."

_____ 6. You've just been chewed out by your boss for something that one of your workers has done. You're about to get up to do the same thing with your employee, but you catch yourself. You stick your head inside your secretary's office and say, "Terry, I have to go outside for a while; I'll be back by a quarter after."

_____ 7. You've made a commitment to yourself to arrange a time to meet with one of your minority employees who has not been performing very effectively. The next day you read in the newspaper that a large corporation has had to pay large damages to a group of minority workers who claimed that they had been discriminated against by the company. As you read the article, your anxiety starts to rise and you begin to have second thoughts about speaking to the employee.

_____ 8. You've just tried to reach one of your salespeople on the intercom, but there's no answer. You need to see him right away, so you try buzzing him five minutes later. Still no answer. Annoyed, you call your secretary in and say, "Sally, do you know where the hell Jack is? I can never find him when I need him."

_____ 9. You're the foreman in a precision machine building company. You're having a conversation with one of your toolmakers about one of his coworkers. You say, "Pat, what do you think is wrong with Bill, anyway? He's got a good head on his shoulders, and he's a damn good mechanic, but he just doesn't listen to anything I tell him. Like just last week, he did the exact opposite of what I. . . ."

_____ 10. You're the chief resident at a university teaching hospital. One of the interns on your staff neglected to give you an update on a patient who's recovering from a complicated appendectomy. You're very upset about this. As soon as you see the intern in the hall, you stop her and say, "What the hell were you thinking about last night? Forgetting to bring me up to date on Mrs. Thompson's condition is inexcusable! I don't ever want that sort of thing to happen again."

_____ 11. You supervise fifteen customer account representatives for an air freight company. One of your representatives is sitting in your office telling you about how upset he is over an argument he had this morning with a fellow representative. As soon as he finishes describing the argument, you say, "Tom, the first thing you've got to realize is that there are many different kinds of people in the world. Why, I remember years ago when I first started working in this business. . . ."

_____ 12. You get a report from a fellow manager that one of your workers has been complaining about you behind your back to a number of other people in the company. As soon as you hear this, you call the employee into your office, and before he even sits down, you say, "Murphy, what's this I hear about you complaining to other people about me? Goddammit, if you've got something to say about me, I want you to say it to my face, not go bellyaching to everybody else in the plant."

_____ 13. In a staff meeting, one of your up-and-coming managers has said something that you feel upset and threatened one of your senior managers. The next time you see the younger manager you say to her, "Karen, I think you came on a little strong with Bob Wilson the other day. Let me tell you some things about him that you may not be aware of. For one thing, he's a lot older than you, even though he doesn't have your raw talent. Another thing is, even if you don't feel a lot of respect for him, you've got to. . . ."

NOW LOOK AT THE NEXT PAGE AND COMPARE YOUR ANSWERS TO OURS.

INEFFECTIVE TENDENCIES: ANSWERS AND DISCUSSION

A 1. *You decide you'll speak to Terry after you've finished your report.*

Even though you appear to be making a commitment to deal with Terry, you're avoiding confrontation by not setting an immediate date.

A 2. *Although Keith has the time, you decide to give the assignment to someone who makes better presentations.*

You've identified a major area that Keith needs to work on—making better presentations. By focusing your attention on Rachel or yourself as replacements, you're avoiding the problem of how to help Keith improve his presentation skills.

C 3. *You complain to a colleague in another department about your employee, Celia.*

Your colleague is probably getting pretty tired of hearing about Celia, especially since *he* can't do anything to help Celia change.

___ 4. *You ask a friend whose judgment you respect for advice on how you can handle a problem with an employee.*

This might sound like complaining, but it's not. You're asking Pat for some thoughts on what *you* can do about the problem. When you complain, your focus is almost always on the other person.

___ 5. *You want to give your employee some suggestions on how to improve a report he wrote. When he nods, you begin noting some of the positive aspects.*

This might sound like lecturing, but we don't think it is. In this case, you got a clear signal from Bill that he was interested in hearing your feedback.

___ 6. *Your boss has just blamed you for an employee's mistake. You take a 15-minute break before dealing with the problem.*

You almost overreacted, but you stopped yourself and took some time to get your thoughts together before speaking to the employee.

A 7. *You have second thoughts about speaking to a minority worker about the person's ineffective performance after reading about a discrimination lawsuit.*

This is a clear example of avoiding confrontation. You're allowing some possible (but not very probable) negative consequences to stop you from facing a problem that has to be dealt with.

C 8. *When you are unable to reach an employee, you express your exasperation to your secretary.*

If you wrote an *O*, we probably wouldn't argue with you. However, we think this is a better example of complaining. Your secretary can't change Jack's behavior. You only lose respect in her eyes by running down Jack in that way.

C 9. *You criticize one of your toolmakers in a conversation with his coworker.*

This is a clear example of complaining. It's especially bad because you're complaining to Pat, Bill's coworker, who's very likely to relay your comments back to Bill.

O 10. *You bawl out an intern who forgot to bring you up to date on a patient's condition.*

You sure told her off, didn't you?

L 11. *You offer some "words to the wise" to one of your representatives who is still upset over an argument with a coworker.*

Even though your advice to Tom may be very good, he's not going to listen to what you have to say right now. There's no sense giving him any suggestions until he's shown you that he's ready to listen to them.

O 12. *You tell off an employee who has been talking behind your back about you.*

Same as 10!

L 13. *You chide one of your younger workers for intimidating a senior manager, then offer her some advice.*

Again, your advice here may be very sound. But Karen has given you no evidence that she's ready to hear it. Unless you're sure that she's receptive to what you have to say, you're probably lecturing.

STOP YOUR INEFFECTIVE TENDENCIES

As soon as you recognize yourself starting to engage in one of the ineffective tendencies, you have to tell yourself to stop before you actually "commit the crime."

We think a good way to do this is to imagine a huge hand appearing before your face that says:

Using the *Hold It!* cue will buy you some time to:

☐ Think about a more effective strategy if you're about to lecture an employee or to complain to somebody else about an employee.

☐ Go outside to cool off if you're about to overreact to an employee.

☐ Make a commitment to do something about the problem right away if you're in the process of avoiding confrontation.

In this chapter we've given you a pretty hard look at some ineffective ways of dealing with a problem employee.

Now we're going to tell you how we think you should deal with a problem employee.

We'll do this by carefully taking you through the ten-step performance improvement process:

STEP ONE: Analyze Your Employee's Performance
STEP TWO: Ask Your Employee to Meet with You
STEP THREE: Begin the Performance Improvement Interview
STEP FOUR: Find Out How Things Are Going
STEP FIVE: Get Your Employee to Do a Self-Analysis
STEP SIX: Present Your Analysis of Your Employee's Performance
STEP SEVEN: Negotiate the Performance Agreement
STEP EIGHT: Close the Interview
STEP NINE: Follow Up
STEP TEN: "What Do I Do if None of This Stuff Works?"

Let's get started.

CHAPTER 4 • STEP ONE: ANALYZE YOUR EMPLOYEE'S PERFORMANCE

The purpose of this chapter is to get you started on the first step in the performance improvement process—analyzing your employee's performance. By the time you finish the chapter, you'll have learned:

☐   A valuable technique for shifting your concern from your employee's problem behavior to a behavior change goal;
☐   A method for helping you to specify the behavior change goals you have in mind for your employee; and
☐   A procedure for identifying and capitalizing on the work-related strengths of your employee.

Before getting into Step One, let's take a look at some mistakes managers and supervisors can make in getting ready to meet with an employee.

COMMON MISTAKES IN PREPARING FOR THE PERFORMANCE IMPROVEMENT INTERVIEW

Managers and supervisors often make at least one of several mistakes when preparing for a performance improvement interview with an employee:

☐   They don't see an obvious need to analyze the employee's performance.

☐   They spend too much time speculating on the reasons for the employee's ineffective performance and not enough time focusing on the performance problem itself.

☐   They think about the employee's performance in abstract rather than concrete terms.

☐   They focus only on what the employee is doing wrong.

NO OBVIOUS NEED
TO ANALYZE PERFORMANCE

When we talk to managers about Step One in the performance improvement process, they often respond, "Why should I analyze the performance of my problem employees when I already know what they're doing wrong?" Here's an example we looked at before.

> **Sheila Ricks** is a dentist with a small but growing practice in a middle-class, suburban town. She identified her problem employee as Lyla Franks, her secretary and receptionist. As Sheila put it, "Lyla's so unpredictable. One day she's friendly and outgoing, and the next day she's sullen and grouchy. I don't know which Lyla is going to walk in the door in the morning. This Jeckyll-and-Hyde routine of hers is beginning to alienate some of my old patients and turn off some of my new ones." In our interview with Sheila we asked her what further information she needed about Lyla's work performance. Her answer? "I know all I need to know about her work performance. She's unpredictable. I know what she's doing wrong. What I don't know is why she behaves this way or how I can change it."

SPECULATING ON THE REASONS
FOR INEFFECTIVE PERFORMANCE

Even though they think they know what the employee is doing wrong, many managers are confused and bewildered by an employee's poor performance. Because they feel puzzled, they tend to speculate about why the employee is behaving ineffectively:

"I don't know what it is, but something sure is bothering her these days."

"He must be having problems at home."

"She's been under so much pressure lately that it's beginning to show."

"I don't know; maybe it's because he didn't get that promotion he was expecting."

In focusing on the reasons the employee is performing poorly, these managers lose sight of the real problem—the poor performance itself.

THINKING TOO ABSTRACTLY

When thinking about any employee's performance, it's very common for managers to use language like:

- ☐ Poorly motivated,
- ☐ Not enough confidence,
- ☐ Lack of credibility with other employees,
- ☐ Uncooperative with other departments,
- ☐ Bad attitude,
- ☐ Not poised enough in making presentations,
- ☐ Poor written communication skills, and
- ☐ Not dependable.

Abstract concepts like attitude, motivation, dependability, and cooperativeness are useful for categorizing different aspects of an employee's performance. They don't, however, convey much meaning to an employee; they're too vague. Later in the chapter we'll talk about how you can translate these concepts (or "fuzzies") into concrete descriptions of observable behavior that will be much more meaningful to an employee.

EMPHASIZING WHAT AN EMPLOYEE IS DOING WRONG

Another strong tendency that we've noticed in managers when it comes to analyzing employee performance is focusing on the negative. They're much more likely to think about what employees do wrong than what they do effectively.

Regardless of why employers tend to zoom in on the negative, we're convinced that emphasizing what employees do ineffectively has a demotivating effect on them. Even employees who ask for criticism of their performance want to hear about what they're doing right as well as in what areas they could improve.

HOW TO PREPARE FOR THE INTERVIEW

We don't think preparing for the interview has to be a complicated, time-consuming process. If you break down the process into these three tasks, it should go pretty smoothly:

1. Formulate positive behavior change goals for your employee;
2. Identify specific behavior changes you want your employee to make for each goal; and
3. Identify the areas where the employee is performing effectively and give specific examples of effective performance in each area.

FORMULATE POSITIVE BEHAVIOR CHANGE GOALS

Supervisors often frame their concerns about problem employees in the negative. We suggest a slight but important shift in perspective. Rather than thinking in terms of what they're doing wrong, think in terms of what they need to do to improve their performance. Instead of saying, "What is he doing wrong?" try asking the question, "In what ways does he need to improve to function more effectively?" Let's see how this works with a couple of examples:

RATHER THAN SAYING:	*TRY SAYING:*
She's got a poor attitude.	She needs a better attitude.
He's got a very short fuse.	He needs better temper control.
She's not motivated.	She needs to be more motivated.
He's rigid.	He needs to be more flexible.
She's careless.	She needs to be more careful.

Now try it a couple of times yourself.

RATHER THAN SAYING:	*TRY SAYING:*
1. She's never on time.	1. _____
	_____
2. He's much too fussy.	2. _____
	_____

If for the first one you said, "She needs to be more punctual" or "She needs to come to work on time," then you answered as we did. If for the second one you said, "He needs to be better at telling the difference between important and unimportant matters on his job," then you understand the process.

Here's a rule of thumb that may help: In general, it's better to ask for more of something rather than less of something. For example, it's better to ask a person to be more flexible rather than less rigid. It's better to ask for more of a positive attitude than less of a poor attitude.

If you run into some difficulty answering the question, "What does the person need to do in order to improve?" try asking yourself, "What is the person going to have to do more of to improve?" This additional question should do the trick.

IDENTIFY SPECIFIC BEHAVIOR CHANGES FOR EACH GOAL

Just stating the behavior change goal is not enough. Imagine, for example, that your supervisor set the following goals for you: "You need to establish more credibility with your subordinates," or "You need to be more confident when you express yourself at staff meetings."

Let's examine these two goal statements. They're certainly much better than negative statements like "You don't have the trust of your staff," or "You're a Casper Milquetoast at staff meetings." And they ask for more rather than less. But do they clearly communicate the supervisor's intentions? We don't think so. You'd probably find yourself wondering what your supervisor really means by "more credibility" or "more confident." You might even question whether managers *know* what they mean when they use words like that.

The reason that phrases like these don't convey much meaning is that they don't describe observable behavior. For example:

(A) YOU CAN'T SEE SOMEONE:
☐   Establish more credibility with her subordinates.

BUT YOU CAN SEE SOMEONE:
☐   Look her subordinates in the eye when she talks to them.
☐   Speak to her subordinates in a soft, casual manner.
☐   Ask her subordinates for *their* ideas on how something ought to be done.
☐   Openly praise her subordinates for a job well done.

(B) YOU CAN'T SEE SOMEONE:
☐   Be more confident expressing himself at staff meetings.

BUT YOU CAN SEE SOMEONE:
☐   Sit up straight when he talks.
☐   Speak in an audible tone of voice.
☐   Make suggestions that are different from those already proposed.
☐   Disagree with the ideas and suggestions of other staff members.
☐   Give specific reasons why the department ought to take a specific course of action.

Once you've established a positively stated behavior change goal for an employee, the next step is to identify the specific behavior changes the employee would have to make to convince you the goal had been achieved. That's how you can ensure the employee will know what you mean by the goal. To do this we recommend that you:

1. State the original problem,
2. State the goal, and
3. Answer the question: What will my employee have to do to convince me that the goal has been achieved?

Here's an example:

ORIGINAL PROBLEM: He never listens to me; he usually misunderstands what I want him to do.
THE GOAL: He needs to be better at listening to me and following my instructions.

What will my employee have to do to convince me that the goal has been achieved?

1. When I ask him to do something in a certain way, he'll do it in the way that I ask him (unless he checks with me in advance about doing it differently).
2. He'll look me in the eye when I'm talking to him (instead of looking down at the floor or all about the room).
3. He'll repeat, or read back, to me his understanding of an assignment before he actually begins it.
4. He'll often ask for clarification of my instructions (saying things like "How do you mean that?" or "Can you give me an example of what you mean by that?").

Having seen how we've done it, why don't you give it a try? Imagine that you're Sheila Ricks, the dentist we mentioned at the beginning of the chapter. Your problem employee is Lyla Franks, who can often be sullen and grouchy with your patients. After you've finished, compare your list to Sheila's.

ORIGINAL PROBLEM: She's unpredictable! One day she's nice and friendly to patients, and the next day she's sullen and grouchy.

THE GOAL: Lyla needs to be consistently more courteous and friendly with all of the patients, both old and new.

What will my employee have to do to convince me that the goal has been achieved?

1. _____

_____

2. _____

_____

3. _____

_____

4. _____

_____

Here's the list that Sheila came up with:

1. Whenever a patient comes in, Lyla will look at the person directly, smile, and give the person an appropriate greeting (like, "Hi! How are you today?").
2. When talking to patients, she will actually use their first names or their formal names (like, "How are you today, Mrs. Salvucci?").
3. Instead of arguing with patients who are angry or upset about something, she will acknowledge the person's feelings and refer them to me (for example, "I can see that

you're very upset by this, and I'll have Dr. Ricks speak with you as soon as she's finished with the patient she's working with right now.").

4. She will stop using bad body language in all dealings with patients (like rolling her eyes to the ceiling or shaking her head back and forth when disagreeing with someone).

How did your list compare with Sheila's? What did you think Lyla would have to do to become a more courteous and friendly person? Were all of the items on your list concrete behaviors, something that you could actually see Lyla do? Or were some of the items a little fuzzy and imprecise? (You'll notice that Sheila handled this problem by giving actual examples of the behavior she wanted Lyla to exhibit.)

Your list may have been quite different from Sheila's. That's fairly common. We've noticed that when two people apply this process to the same goal statement, they invariably come up with different lists. People often mean different things when they're thinking of the same behavior change goal. But if you follow the procedure outlined above, you'll make certain that your employee clearly knows what you mean when you sit down to talk about performance improvement.

Now that you've seen how the process works, try it on one of your problem employees. Using the same format as before, translate the original statement of the problem into a behavior change goal. Then identify the specific behaviors that would convince you that the goal had been achieved.

ORIGINAL PROBLEM: _____

_____

_____

THE GOAL: _____

_____

_____

What will my employee have to do to convince me that the goal has been achieved?

1. _____

_____

2. _____

_____

3. _____

_____

4. _____

_____

IDENTIFY THE AREAS WHERE YOUR EMPLOYEE IS PERFORMING EFFECTIVELY AND GIVE SPECIFIC EXAMPLES

Earlier in the chapter we said that in a performance interview it's a mistake for managers and supervisors to concentrate only on what an employee is doing wrong. Employees like to hear about what they're doing effectively on their jobs. It helps keep them much more interested and involved than they would be if all the emphasis were placed on the areas where they need to improve.

When you give employees feedback on the effective aspects of their performance, we think it's just as important to be precise and specific as it is when you talk about how they can improve their performance. To do this, we recommend that you answer two basic questions:

1. What is the employee doing well?
2. What are some specific examples of this?

Here's an illustration:

What is your employee doing well? _He's pretty creative._

What are some specific examples of this? _1. He's come up with three good ideas this year for improving shop efficiency. These ideas have saved the company thousands of dollars. 2. He always has a couple of suggestions for different ways of doing a job._

What is your employee doing well? _She edits copy very well._

What are some specific examples of this? _1. She turned water into wine out of the material we gave her for the company's annual report. 2. She was invaluable in cleaning up the mess that our so-called public relations consultant left us with for the company brochure._

Now try it with one of your employees. Think of two things the person is doing well and come up with two examples of each:

What is your employee doing well? _____

_____

What are some specific examples of this? _____

_____

_____

_____

_____

What is your employee doing well? _____

_____

What are some specific examples of this? _____

_____

_____

_____

_____

_____

On page 41, we've included a Performance Analysis Form that you can use when preparing for performance improvement interviews with your employees. The form integrates all the suggestions and concepts presented in this chapter. The first column is concerned with employee strengths. For each employee strong point, the form asks you to come up with two specific examples. The second column is concerned with those areas where the employee needs to improve. For each of the areas of needed improvement, the form asks you to identify the specific things the employee will have to do to convince you that performance has improved. This particular performance analysis form has been filled in to show you how it works. But an identical form appears on page 42 that you can duplicate and fill out yourself.

Fill out a form such as this for all your employees before you meet with them. It's the best way to adequately prepare yourself for the meeting. It will also help you feel prepared; this is especially important if you've had a tendency to avoid confronting the employee or if you've had some misgivings about sitting down to talk with the person. By being prepared, you're on a solid foundation to move to the next step of the process—asking the employee to meet with you.

PERFORMANCE ANALYSIS FORM

WHAT IS YOUR EMPLOYEE DOING WELL?	IN WHAT WAYS SHOULD HE/SHE IMPROVE?

1. HE DOES HIGH-QUALITY WORK.

Example: _He almost always checks his work before turning it in._

Example: _I hardly ever have to ask him to do a job over._

1. BETTER ATTENDANCE

Specifically, the person will have to:

a. Show up every day for six weeks.

b. Always call in if he's going to be late.

---

2. HE'S PRETTY CREATIVE.

Example: _He's come up with three good ideas this year for improving shop efficiency_

Example: _He always has a couple of suggestions for different ways of doing a job._

2. INCREASE PRODUCTIVITY

Specifically, the person will have to:

a. meet all deadlines that we both agree on for the next six weeks.
b. Let me know at least 5 days ahead of time if a deadline can't be met so that we can set a new target date.

---

3. HE GETS ALONG WELL WITH OTHER WORKERS (AND CUSTOMERS).

Example: _People say nice things to me about him all the time._

Example: _I don't know of anyone who really dislikes him._

3. LISTEN AND FOLLOW INSTRUCTIONS

Specifically, the person will have to:

a. When I ask him to do something in a certain way, he'll do it the way I ask him (unless he checks with me first). b. Look me in the eye when I talk to him. c. Read back to me his understanding of an assignment before he begins it. d. Ask for clarification of my instructions(like "How do you mean that?")

---

4. HE'S VERY SAFETY CONSCIOUS.

Example: _He's always cleaning up his work area._

Example: _He tactfully reminds others in the shop of safety procedures._

4. NOT TALK TO EMPLOYEES WHO ARE WORKING

Specifically, the person will have to:

Confine his conversations with other workers to scheduled breaks for the next six weeks.

PERFORMANCE ANALYSIS FORM

WHAT IS YOUR EMPLOYEE DOING WELL?	IN WHAT WAYS SHOULD HE/SHE IMPROVE?
1. _____ Example: _____ _____ _____ Example: _____ _____ _____ _____	1. _____ Specifically, the person will have to: _____ _____ _____ _____ _____ _____
2. _____ Example: _____ Example: _____ _____ _____ _____	2. _____ Specifically, the person will have to: _____ _____ _____ _____
3. _____ Example: _____ _____ _____ Example: _____ _____ _____ _____	3. _____ Specifically, the person will have to: _____ _____ _____ _____ _____
4. _____ Example: _____ _____ _____ Example: _____ _____ _____ _____	4. _____ Specifically, the person will have to: _____ _____ _____ _____ _____

CHAPTER 5 • STEP TWO: ASK YOUR EMPLOYEE TO MEET WITH YOU

You've done a careful job of preparing for the performance improvement interview by analyzing the employee's strong points and areas needing improvement. Now you're ready to ask the employee to meet with you.

To most managers and supervisors we've worked with, this step seems pretty simple and straightforward. It is simple and straightforward. But, like a lot of simple tasks, it's easy to do it ineffectively the first time you try it.

This chapter is written to show you an effective, easy-to-follow method for arranging to meet with your employee. It starts out with a discussion of some typical mistakes that managers make when they ask their employees to meet with them. Then it goes on to describe a way to do it that lots of managers have found works very smoothly. It ends up with a description of some things that can go wrong when you speak to your employee about meeting with you, and what to do about them.

Let's start off by talking about some ways of asking your employee to meet with you that don't work very well.

HOW NOT TO ASK YOUR EMPLOYEE TO MEET WITH YOU

Here are some common mistakes that managers make when asking employees to meet with them to discuss their work performance:

☐   They don't do it themselves; they ask their secretaries to ask the employee to meet with them.

☐   They don't speak to the employee face-to-face; they send a note or memo about the meeting.

☐   They say too little about the meeting to the employee.

☐   They say too much about the meeting to the employee.

☐   They make light of the performance improvement interview when asking the employee to meet.

☐   They wait until they're angry or upset to ask the employee to meet.

DON'T HAVE YOUR SECRETARY DO IT

Here's the kind of thing that can happen when you have your secretary ask an employee to meet with you:

EMPLOYEE: (*Answering telephone*) Shipping and receiving. Hank Lennox.

SECRETARY: Hi Hank. This is Stella. How're things going?

EMPLOYEE: Fine, Stella, how're things goin' with you?

SECRETARY: Great! Busy, but just great. Listen, the reason I'm calling is because Sally wants to meet with you sometime next week. Can you get yourself free on Wednesday around 3:30?

EMPLOYEE: Sure, I'll be there. How long will the meeting last? Is there anything I should bring with me? And, by the way, what's the purpose of the meeting?

SECRETARY: Gee, I'm not sure for how long. I don't know if you need to bring anything either. I'll have to get back to you on that. I'm also not completely sure about the purpose, Hank, but I think it's employee review time again. She scheduled a formal meeting with me for next week, too.

EMPLOYEE: You're kidding! Why couldn't she ask me directly, on a man-to-man basis? Oh, you know what I mean!

SECRETARY: Hank, you know she's been very busy lately, with the new merger and all.

EMPLOYEE: I don't know. Frank always seemed to find the time. . . .

SECRETARY: (*Interrupting*) I'll be the first to admit that she has a different style from Frank's. But she is new to the job and she's really trying hard. Why just yesterday. . . .

Although having your secretary do the asking won't always turn out as badly as this, it's generally not a good idea for several reasons:

☐   You can never be sure what hidden messages your secretary will send to the employee. All you can be sure of is that he or she will say it differently (at least a little) from the way you would have.

☐   Your secretary will probably feel resentful at having to handle some of the predictable questions that the employee is likely to ask.

☐   The employee is probably going to feel confused and resentful at not having been asked directly.

DON'T SEND A NOTE OR MEMO
Imagine that you came back from lunch and found a note on your desk that went something like this:

"Next Thursday, at 2:30 P.M., I'd like to meet with you in my office. The purpose of this meeting is to review your performance over the past six months and to set some goals for the future. Please let me know if the time and date are convenient for you."

Notes and memos such as this almost never work. They arouse anxiety because they sound so ominous, and they cause resentment because they sound so impersonal.

If you're even tempted to ask an employee to meet with you via a note or memo, you might ask yourself, "How would I feel if my supervisor did this to me?"

DON'T SAY TOO LITTLE
Even when supervisors directly ask employees to meet with them, things can still go wrong. Some supervisors make the mistake of saying too little to the employee:

"Tom, let's get together next week at 2:30 to have your annual performance review, okay?"

"Ruth, could I see you in my office at 11:30 tomorrow morning?"

"George, it's time for your annual review again. How about next Wednesday at 3:00?"

When you keep your request to meet with the employee this brief, the employee is likely to feel a little bowled over. Once the mild shock wears off, the person will probably begin to speculate about the purpose of the meeting, what's going to happen, and so on. In the absence of more information, there's a good chance that the employee will think things like:

"Let's see. What have I done wrong?"
"I wonder why he wants to meet with me. I don't know of anybody else who's getting reviewed."
"It can't be good news. She'd have said more if it were."

The point is this: When you don't say enough, your message is ambiguous. And ambiguity often leads to anxiety.

DON'T SAY TOO MUCH

In anticipating their employee's concern about the meeting, some supervisors err by saying too much. They try to reassure the employee that nothing bad is going to happen in the interview. This often backfires, leading the employee to expect the worst. Here's an example:

SUPERVISOR: Hi, Jay. I'd like to meet with you on Friday to review your work over the last few months, okay?
EMPLOYEE: Okay, that sounds all right with me.
SUPERVISOR: Great! Now, listen, there's nothing to worry about. Things look pretty good this time around. I'm looking forward to talking to you about that Smith deal and how you could have done even a better job than you did. And that's not meant to take anything away from a job well done.
EMPLOYEE: Thanks. I was pretty pleased with how that went.
SUPERVISOR: You have a right to be. And I think I can offer you some suggestions for doing even better in the future. . . .

Sometimes supervisors talk too much because they let themselves get dragged into answering questions and comments about the interview from the employee before they meet. Later on in the chapter we'll show you how to respond to such questions and comments without entering into a prolonged discussion.

DON'T MAKE LIGHT OF THE PERFORMANCE IMPROVEMENT PROCESS

Some managers tend to make light of meetings where employee performance is discussed. They do things like walk up to an employee in the hall, slap him on the back, and say:

"Hey, Pete, next week we're gonna have to sit down and do the old, semiannual performance review. Waddaya say, tiger? Feeling up to it?"

Managers who do this are usually a little uncomfortable in their supervisory roles. In approaching the meeting in a lighthearted way, they attempt to send the message:

"Just because I'm your boss, I'm not trying to be any better than you. I just want to be one of the troops."

Unfortunately, this kind of message has the effect of making the employee fail to take the meeting very seriously and lose respect for you as a supervisor.

DON'T ASK TO MEET WHEN YOU'RE UPSET WITH THE EMPLOYEE

While some supervisors tend to gloss things over when asking an employee to meet with them, others tend to be too blunt. This is especially true of managers who overreact to their problem employees. They'll often ask an employee to meet with them when they're feeling angry or upset about the employee's performance, sometimes even when other employees are around.

A participant in one of our workshops described this type of supervisor quite accurately when he told us about his first boss:

"He'd always want to talk with me after I'd done something wrong and never after I'd done well. For him, a performance review meant that he'd want to review my foul-ups. And he had this way of humiliating me in front of the others by saying things like, 'I want to see you in my office tomorrow at 8:00 A.M. sharp!' "

As tempting as it may be to call an employee in to read the riot act, it's no way to improve employee performance. The employee will feel resentful or intimidated, or both. And you'll end up having to undo a lot of unnecessary damage before getting down to the business of trying to help improve the employee's work performance.

HOW TO ASK YOUR EMPLOYEE TO MEET WITH YOU

Asking the employee to meet with you is easy to do ineffectively, but it's not that tough to do effectively. Here are some important points to keep in mind:

☐ Approach the person when there are not a lot of other people around.

☐   Briefly and calmly explain that you want to meet with the employee to review his or her work performance. And mention that you'll also be doing this with other people that you supervise.

☐   Tell your employee how you plan to prepare for your meeting together.

☐   Suggest how your employee can prepare for the meeting.

☐   Arrange a specific date, time, and place to meet.

☐   End on a positive note.

Before explaining these points in more detail, here's an example of a supervisor putting them into action:

SUPERVISOR: (*To employee, out of earshot of others*) Pat, I'd like to arrange a time to meet with you to review your work performance. It's something I'm planning to do with everybody in the office.

EMPLOYEE: Oh . . . okay.

SUPERVISOR: I'm going to prepare for our meeting by writing down some of the things that you've been doing really well, and also some of the areas where I think you could stand to improve some (*Pause*) . . . .

EMPLOYEE: Uhm-humm.

SUPERVISOR: I'd like you to prepare for the meeting by doing the same thing. First, think about what you do well, your strengths. Second, think about some of the ways you could improve on the job (*Pause*).

EMPLOYEE: Okay . . . I think I got it.

SUPERVISOR: I'd also like you to be thinking about some things I could do to make your job a little less frustrating and more satisfying. Okay?

EMPLOYEE: Uh . . . yeah, sure. I'll do that.

SUPERVISOR: Great! How about next Wednesday at 2:00 in my office?

EMPLOYEE: Okay . . . sounds fine.

SUPERVISOR: Good. I'll look forward to seeing you then.

Now let's take a closer look at each of the six points.

APPROACH THE PERSON PRIVATELY

Approach the person when there are not a lot of people around. This is very important. If there are others around, the employee is likely to feel apprehensive. Further, if there are people within earshot, they begin to speculate about what's going on, a situation you definitely want to avoid.

EXPLAIN WHY YOU WANT TO MEET

As briefly, calmly, and as firmly as you can, explain why you want to meet with the employee and the other people you supervise. Since the purpose of the meeting is to review job performance, it's best to say it simply and directly. Don't gloss it over or beat around the bush. Saying you plan to review the performance of everyone you supervise will help reduce any anxiety the employee may feel about being singled out.

SUGGEST HOW TO PREPARE FOR THE MEETING

Don't assume that the employee knows what you mean when you mention that the purpose of the meeting is to review work performance. To make certain that the person has a clear idea of what you mean, mention how you plan to prepare for the meeting and suggest how the employee can get ready for the session. Say that you're going to identify some things that the person is doing well as well as some ways the person can improve. Then suggest that the employee do the same thing—identify performance areas where the employee feels personally effective, and some areas that could stand improvement. Also suggest that the employee identify some ways that you can make the job less frustrating and more satisfying.

In this way, you will have made it clear what's going to happen during the interview and the employee's role in the process. There are a couple of other benefits. First, you show that you know what you're doing and that you've thought this whole process through rather carefully. Second, you show that you expect the employee's active involvement in the process and that you think the performance improvement interview will work best when both of you put your heads together.

In our workshops we've noticed that some supervisors get a little uneasy about asking their employees to think of ways they could make their jobs less frustrating and more satisfying. As one of them put it, "It seems like that's only going to open Pandora's box, with the employee making all kinds of outrageous or ridiculous suggestions, like two-hour lunch breaks and six-week vacations." We've found that this happens so rarely that it's not worth worrying about. When it does happen, it's often just an attempt to inject a bit of humor into the process, usually followed by real suggestions.

It's natural to feel a little vulnerable when you ask somebody, especially an employee, to give you feedback on your own performance. But if you expect the people who work for you to accept your feedback, it's a good idea to accept a little from them.

ARRANGE THE TIME AND PLACE TO MEET

After telling the employee how to prepare for the meeting, agree on a specific time and place to meet. This may seem like a minor point, but it's an important one. It's no fun getting yourself prepared for a performance improvement interview only to learn that your employee is at the dentist on Thursday afternoon because she thought you meant Friday afternoon!

END ON A POSITIVE NOTE

When asking the employee to meet with you, it's important to end the interaction on a positive note. This simply means smiling, possibly shaking hands, and saying something like, "Good. I'll look forward to seeing you then."

PRACTICE ASKING YOUR EMPLOYEE
TO MEET WITH YOU

Here are some suggestions on how to practice asking the employee to meet with you. Don't say to yourself, "This sounds so easy that I can just skip the practice and go on." If you don't practice, you won't learn how to do it. That, we guarantee.

1. Review the six main points and script on pages 47–48.
2. Mentally rehearse asking an employee to meet with you. Just sit back, close your eyes, and imagine yourself walking up to the employee and doing it.
3. After you've rehearsed it a couple of times silently, engage in more active practice. Try saying it out loud as you look at yourself in a mirror. Or tape record your practice attempts and listen to how well you do it.
4. Find someone with whom you can role play this step of the process. It might be another supervisor in your company, your spouse, a close friend, or somebody from the company's training department. As long as it's somebody you trust and feel comfortable with, it doesn't make any difference who it is. Simply ask the person to play the part of the employee.

After you've silently rehearsed, then role played Step Two in the performance improvement process, check yourself on the following points:

☐ Did you imagine speaking to your employee in a place where there were not a lot of other people around?

☐ Did you explain the purpose of the meeting, mentioning specifically that it was to review the person's work performance?

☐ Did you mention that this was something that you plan to do with all of the people that you supervise?

☐ Did you tell your employee how you plan to prepare for the meeting, mentioning specifically that you will identify a number of things that the person is doing well and also some areas where the person could stand to improve?

☐ Did you suggest how your employee could prepare for the meeting, mentioning specifically that he or she should: (a) identify those things he is currently doing well on the job, (b) identify some areas where she could stand some improvement, and (c) suggest some ways in which you could make the job less frustrating and more satisfying?

☐ Did you agree to meet at a specific date, time, and place?

☐ Did you end the meeting on a positive note, perhaps by saying "I'll look forward to seeing you then," or an equivalent phrase?

If you answered no to any one of these questions or feel that you could improve your approach, don't hesitate to practice as many times as you need to.

POSSIBLE SETBACKS

There are any number of things that could go wrong when you ask the employee to meet with you, but most have to do with some fairly predictable questions or remarks the employee might ask or make.

It's fairly common for employees to probe for more specific information about what you plan to cover in the meeting. Look at these two examples.

> **Janet**, a problem employee who can be very abrupt and caustic, might respond this way after you've asked to meet with her: "Well, just what do you plan to cover in this meeting, anyway? No one has ever done this sort of thing around here before, you know."

> **Richard**, who is somewhat emotional and lacks self-confidence, might say, "What's the matter? Have I done something wrong? If I've done something wrong, why can't you tell me about it now?"

In situations like these, we think the best strategy is to:

1. Acknowledge the employee's feelings (whether the employee is concerned, upset, or angry).
2. Repeat the purpose of the meeting and how you and the employee can best prepare for it.

3. State calmly but firmly that you will go into more detail in the meeting, not right now.
4. Repeat these steps as many times as necessary until the employee gets the message that you will not be dragged into an extended discussion of the nature, purpose, or worthwhileness of the meeting.

Here's how this strategy would work with Janet's question and remark:

"Janet, I realize that this sort of thing hasn't been done here before and that this probably comes as a bit of a surprise to you. As I mentioned before, the purpose of the meeting is to review your work performance, and the best way for both of us to get ready for that meeting is to begin thinking about some of the things you do well and some of the ways you could improve. I'd also like you to be thinking of some of the ways I could make your job less frustrating and more satisfying. I'd like to save the details for when we actually meet, okay?"

In response to Richard, the supervisor might say:

"Richard, you seem concerned that I want to meet with you to discuss what you're doing wrong. That's not why I want to meet with you. I'm talking about a meeting to review your work performance. As I mentioned, it's a meeting in which the two of us should come prepared to talk about what you're doing well on the job—and you are doing some things very well—as well as ways you can improve—and there are some areas of needed improvement. I'd also like you to come to the meeting prepared to tell me how I can make your job less frustrating and more satisfying. We'll have plenty of time to talk things out when we meet. How does that sound?"

If Janet and Richard persisted in asking for more details, we'd recommend saying the same thing over and over (changing the words, but keeping the message the same) until they accepted the fact that you're not going to elaborate until you meet.

A QUICK SUMMARY
Let's briefly review the points we made in this chapter.

☐ Avoid some common mistakes in asking your employee to meet with you—having your secretary do it, sending a note or memo, saying too little or too much, making light of the interview, and asking when you're angry.

☐   Begin by approaching your employee when there are not a lot of people around.

☐   State clearly and directly why you want to meet: to review your employee's performance.

☐   Tell your employee that you plan to prepare for the meeting by identifying what the person is already doing well and some areas where improvement is needed.

☐   Ask your employee to prepare for the meeting by analyzing his own performance and by thinking about some ways you can make her job less frustrating and more satisfying.

☐   Arrange for a specific time and place to meet.

☐   End on a positive note.

☐   Respond to some of your employee's predictable questions and concerns, but don't get dragged into an extended discussion.

Now you're ready to meet with your employee.

CHAPTER 6 • STEP THREE: BEGIN THE INTERVIEW

Up to this point you've analyzed your employee's performance and you've asked the person to meet with you. Now comes what many supervisors consider to be the tough part— actually sitting down with the employee to discuss the person's performance.

We think you've already completed the toughest part. You've made a commitment to deal with the employee, and you've acted on that commitment by asking the person to meet with you. Now your job is to begin the interview so that you maximize the employee's involvement and cooperation. The purpose of this chapter is to show you how to do that.

HOW NOT TO BEGIN THE INTERVIEW

At many of the workshops we run, we ask supervisors to reflect on performance reviews they've had with their own higher-ups—especially meetings in which they felt uncomfortable right from the start. Then we ask them, "What did the person do (or not do) that caused you to feel ill at ease?"

Great to see you Bob, come on in.

These are typical answers:

"When I walked into his office, he said 'C'mon in.' But he didn't even look up from his desk when he said it. He just kept reading this report. I wasn't quite sure what to do."

"She was talking on the phone when I arrived. She waved me into the room with her hand and kept talking for what seemed like an eternity. When she finally stopped talking, she didn't apologize or anything. I guess she didn't realize the effect it had on me."

"When I got there, he was busy talking to another person. He said something like, 'I'll be with you in a couple of minutes.' Well, I was just left standing there in the doorway while the two of them were talking. I could tell that the other person was a little uncomfortable. And I just felt foolish."

"She was cordial enough when I arrived, but as soon as I sat down, she said, 'Let's get started,' and she proceeded to get right down to business. I hardly had a chance to catch my breath from walking up three flights of stairs, and here we were off to the races!"

"I walked in and he asked me to sit down on this spindly little chair right in front of his desk. He was sitting in this very expensive-looking executive chair behind this massive desk. There were pictures of his wife and kids, some kind of award he'd won, and a gold pen and pencil set. We were definitely on his turf! He was surrounded by things that made him feel comfortable. All I had was my ball-point pen!"

"I remember a meeting where, after about three minutes, there were people knocking at the door, telephones ringing, you name it. Not one of the interruptions lasted more than a minute, but each one threw us completely off track."

HOW TO GET OFF TO A GOOD START

To avoid having the kind of impact on an employee that the preceding examples demonstrate, there are three basic points to keep in mind:

1. Set the stage for the interview by minimizing distractions and potential interruptions.
2. Make the person feel comfortable and welcome.
3. Orient the employee to the purposes and procedures of the interview.

Let's look at each of these points in more detail.

SET THE STAGE

Before the interview begins, arrange for a private meeting between you and the employee. This means doing all you can to minimize potential distractions and interruptions. They have a negative impact on people, especially when they're feeling nervous or when sensitive subjects like performance are being discussed.

Unfortunately, too many supervisors think they can divide their attention between the employee and other matters that compete for their attention. But doing this just causes the employee to feel irritated and resentful.

Here are some suggestions for minimizing distractions and interruptions:

☐   If you have a secretary, ask that all telephone calls be held until after the meeting.

☐   If your office has a door, close it (your open door policy doesn't extend to private meetings with employees).

☐   If you share an office with others, ask them to leave while you're meeting with the employee. Find a private office, if necessary.

☐   Clear your desk (and your mind) of the other pressing matters that are competing for your attention.

☐   Don't plan to refer to notes or performance rating forms (including our own Performance Analysis Form). Nothing is more distracting, or disconcerting, than a meeting that seems to revolve around a piece of paper.

MAKE THE PERSON FEEL COMFORTABLE AND WELCOME

When your employee arrives at your office (or whatever private place you've chosen to meet), give the person a warm and friendly greeting. You can do this by standing, walking out from behind your desk, smiling, and saying something like, "Hi, _____. Thanks for coming. Please come in and have a seat." It's important to do this as naturally as you can. If you're by nature a bubbly, effusive person, you'll do this reflexively. If you're more reserved, push yourself a little, but don't come on too gooey. That just puts people off.

Try to sit down face-to-face with the employee, not across a desk or table. Desks and tables are nice things to hide behind when you're feeling anxious, but they create a psychological distance between people. If your office is designed so that you have to sit at your desk, have the person sit at the side of your desk rather than across it, as the diagram on the opposite page indicates.

Bad   **Better**   **Best**

It's a good idea to put the person at ease with a little casual conversation or chitchat to break the ice and to get the conversational juices flowing. Make certain that you select a subject that's interesting or relevant to the employee. Here are some examples:

"Your new baby must be about a year old now. How's she doing?"

"I hear you went to Disney World on your vacation. How did you like it?"

"Your son's at Notre Dame, isn't he? How's he enjoying school life?"

"Helen tells me you're a jogger. How long have you been at it?"

"I hear your team won the city bowling championship."

This kind of talk, especially about a subject of interest to the employee, can help to relieve some anxiety at the beginning of the session. It also communicates that you're interested in more than just the employee's work performance.

Sometimes an attempt at casual conversation can backfire. Here are several additional points to keep in mind:

1. Make certain that the subject is of interest to the employee. If you bring up a subject that you are intensely interested in (like football, jogging, or classical music), only to discover that the employee hates it, you're worse off than when you started.

2. When the employee starts talking, pay attention! Look the person directly in the eye, nod your head, say "uhm-humm," and communicate that you're listening. The worst thing you can do is ask a perfunctory question and then let your attention trail off during the person's answer.

3. Don't let things drag on for too long. That will only send the message that you want to avoid talking about the real purpose of the interview—improved performance.

ORIENT YOUR EMPLOYEE TO THE PURPOSES
AND PROCEDURES OF THE MEETING

When you orient employees at the beginning of an interview, you answer two important questions that are almost certain to be on their minds: What am I doing here? and What is going to happen? Not answering these questions early in the interview can have some negative consequences:

☐ If people don't know what's going to happen in an interview, they may get anxious or angry, or they may just tune out.

☐ If employees are preoccupied with wondering why they're meeting with you or what's about to happen, chances are they won't hear much of what you're saying.

☐ If these questions aren't answered early in the interview, employees have the irritating habit of asking them later on, often at the most inopportune time.

To answer these two questions for the employee, you need to explain the purposes of the meeting, and the procedures of the meeting (what's going to happen during the interview).

When you explain the purposes of the meeting, you should say that:

☐ The two of you are getting together to review the employee's work performance;

☐ Periodically sitting down with employees to discuss their work performance is an integral part of your job as a supervisor; and

☐ You're planning to meet with everyone you supervise (to keep the employee from getting the impression of being singled out).

When you explain the procedures of the interview, you should say that you want to:

☐ Find out, in general, how the employee thinks things are going on the job, and especially about any problems that the person is having;

☐ Get the employee's ideas and suggestions on how you can make his job less frustrating and more satisfying;

☐ Hear what the employee thinks she does well on the job and also the ways in which she thinks she can improve;

☐ Tell the employee what you think he does well and also the areas in which you think improvement can be made; and

☐ Mutually agree on some specific goals to improve the employee's performance in the future and to make her job less frustrating and more satisfying. You'll also want to identify some things that the both of you will have to do to help the employee achieve these goals.

WALKING THROUGH AN EXAMPLE

The following script is an example of how a supervisor might begin the interview by: (1) setting the stage, (2) making the person feel comfortable and welcome, and (3) orienting the employee.

SUPERVISOR: (*Sitting at her desk and hearing a knock on her office door*) Come in! (*Seeing that it's Janet, gets up from her desk and smiles warmly*) Hi, Janet. Thanks for coming. Please come in and have a seat.

EMPLOYEE: (*Looking a little apprehensive*) Hi. Thanks. (*Sitting down*)

SUPERVISOR: Are you still jogging as much as you used to, Janet?

EMPLOYEE: (*Smiling*) You'll never believe this, Mrs. Curtis, but I'm actually running three miles a day . . . and enjoying it. And to think that a year ago I was smoking and in such terrible shape. (*Leaning forward slightly*) Don't say anything just yet, but I'm even thinking seriously of preparing for the Bonnie Belle marathon next year. (*Looking proud but a little squeamish*)

SUPERVISOR: (*Smiling broadly*) That's great, Janet! I won't tell a soul! I'm so impressed with the tremendous positive changes you've made in your life. You should be very proud of your accomplishments!

EMPLOYEE: (*Looking down slightly*) Thank you.

SUPERVISOR: You deserve all of the credit. (*Leaning forward slightly*) Janet, let me explain why I asked you to meet with me. As I mentioned the other day when we set up this meeting, the purpose of our getting together is to review your work performance. I feel that it's a very good idea to periodically sit down with all of the people I supervise to discuss how they're doing on the job. As I said, I plan to do this with everyone in the office. (*Pause*)

EMPLOYEE: (*Nodding*)

SUPERVISOR: Janet, there are a number of areas I'd like to cover in our talk today. Let me describe them briefly so you'll know what's coming. First, I'd like you to tell me how things are going on the job in general, and especially about any problems you may be having. Then I'd like to hear your ideas and suggestions about how I can make your job less frustrating and more satisfying.

EMPLOYEE: (*Nodding*) Uhm-humm.

SUPERVISOR: After that, I'd like you to tell me what things you do particularly well on the job and what areas could stand some improvement. I'll build on that by offering some of my own ideas about what you do well and where you could improve. Finally, I'd like the two of us to set some goals for improving your work performance and making your job more rewarding and satisfying. To do that, we'll identify some specific things that both of us will have to do to achieve the goals that we've set. Well, before we get started on all that, I'd like to answer any questions you may have about why we're here or what we're going to do today. (*Pause*)

PRACTICE BEGINNING THE INTERVIEW

Now for a little practice. Since this step is more complicated than asking the employee to meet with you, try to get somebody (another supervisor, a close friend, your spouse) to help you go through it before doing it with an employee. When you do role play it, use a tape recorder so that you can hear how well you did. It's a good idea to mentally rehearse this step a few times before finding somebody to practice with.

When you're ready, imagine that you're sitting in your office and your problem employee is knocking on the door. Close the book and begin the interview. If you make a few false starts, don't let it bother you. Just start over. Try to run all the way through until you get to the point of asking if the employee has any questions. When you've finished, reopen the book.

Whether you practiced alone or with somebody else, check yourself on the following points:

☐ Did you give your employee a warm, friendly greeting? Specifically, did you stand up, walk out from behind your desk, and say, "Hi, _____. Thanks for coming. Please have a seat." If you used a tape recorder, listen to how you sounded. How would you feel sitting down and talking to someone who sounds like you?

☐ Did you sit down face-to-face with your employee, not across a desk or a table? How did this make you feel? You can expect a little discomfort at first if you're not used to doing this.

☐ Did you engage in some appropriate chitchat to put your employee at ease? What subject did you select? Were you able to keep it brief? Were you really listening?

☐ When you explained the purpose of the meeting did you: 1) Say that the purpose was to review the person's work performance? 2) Mention that you felt that sitting down periodically with employees was a good thing and something you plan to do with all the people you supervise?

☐ When you gave the person a preview of what was going to happen in the meeting, did you: 1) Say you wanted to begin by learning, in general, how things are going on the job and especially about any problems the person might be experiencing? 2) Add that you especially wanted to hear about suggestions for how you could make the person's job more satisfying? 3) Mention that you wanted to learn what the employee thinks he does well on the job, as well as those areas where he thinks he could stand to improve? 4) Add that you wanted to discuss what you think your employee is doing well and also the things that could be done to improve the person's work performance? 5) Say that you wanted to end by setting some goals for improving your employee's work performance and making the job less frustrating and more satisfying? Did you also mention that you'd be identifying some specific things both of you could do to help your employee achieve these goals?

☐ After you explained the procedures of the interview, did you find out if the person had any questions before you got started by saying, "Okay, before we go any further, I'd like to answer any questions that you have." (*Pause*)

If you left out any of the points on the list, don't hesitate to practice until you're satisfied that you've mastered this step.

If you find yourself getting a little discouraged when it doesn't come as smoothly or as easily as you'd like, think back to the times when you tried to learn some other complex task, such as driving a standard transmission car, or hitting a backhand in tennis. Although interpersonal skills don't require the finely honed motor coordination of most physical skills, they're often just as difficult to master. And the only secret to learning both kinds of skills is consistent, determined practice.

RESPOND TO YOUR EMPLOYEE'S QUESTIONS AND CONCERNS

After explaining the purposes and procedures of the interview, invite the employee to ask questions about the meeting before you continue. Most of these questions are likely to fall into one of these categories:

1. Neutral questions,
2. Questions expressing concern, and
3. Hostile questions.

NEUTRAL QUESTIONS

Neutral questions are simply requests for clarification about the purpose or procedures of the interview. Look at the examples on the following page.

"I do have one question. What do you mean by *goals*?"

"How long do you think we'll be meeting today?"

"Will we also be discussing salary issues today?"

"Do you mind if I refer to some notes that I've brought with me?"

If the employee asks you a neutral question, you shouldn't have much difficulty. Simply answer these questions as honestly and directly as you can, and then move to the main part of the interview. Here's how we'd answer the question about whether the interview would include a discussion of salary:

"That's a good question, Sheila. No, we won't be talking about salary today. I'd like to save our discussion about salary until a future meeting, when we can talk about that, and only that. Today, I want to concentrate fully, and solely, on the things we can do to improve your work performance and make your job less frustrating and more satisfying."

QUESTIONS EXPRESSING CONCERN

Questions that express some concern on the part of the employee often have to do with the possible negative consequences of the interview. Although they're phrased as questions, they are really statements that indicate some reservation the employee feels. Some examples include:

"Well, what effect is this going to have on my salary and chances for advancement in the company?"

"Is everything we talk about going to be placed in my personnel folder?"

"If I talk about other employees, will any of it get back to them?"

"Does all of this just mean that you're not happy with my performance?"

When the employee asks you a question that expresses some concern:

1. Say something that reflects your understanding of the employee's feelings of concern, pausing to give the person a chance to talk more about the nature of the concern. (We go into more detail on the technique of reflecting feeling in the next chapter.)
2. Say something that speaks directly to the person's question. As you would with neutral questions, answer as honestly and as directly as you can, and then move on to the main part of the interview.

Here's how this approach works with a relatively common employee question:

EMPLOYEE: Well, what effect is this going to have on my salary and my chances for advancement?
SUPERVISOR: You sound a little concerned that I'm going to evaluate you, Joe, give you a report card that might be used against you when it comes time for a promotion or a raise.
EMPLOYEE: Exactly! That kind of thing has happened around here in the past, you know. I guess that's what's making me wonder about it now.
SUPERVISOR: Yes, I'm sure that it has happened before, and I appreciate your concern. That's not what I intend to do here at all. As I said before, my only purpose is for the two of us to find some ways to help you improve your work performance and make your job more satisfying. I stopped giving people grades and report cards when I left teaching five years ago.
EMPLOYEE: Thanks, I feel better now. . . .

With the help of your role-play partner, respond to this question. If you don't have a partner, write in below how you would respond, using the strategy outlined earlier.

Employee: Yes, I do have a question. Is everything we talk about going to be placed in my personnel folder?

You: _____

_____

Employee: Yes, that's exactly how I feel.

You: _____

_____

Did you begin by reflecting feeling — saying something that showed that you understood the employee's underlying feeling? Did you do this so that the person had a chance to talk further about the concern? After acknowledging the person's feeling, did you say something that addressed the concern directly? Did you do this briefly and directly? Here's how we would have handled it:

EMPLOYEE: Yes, I do have a question. Is everything we talk about going to be placed in my personnel folder?
SUPERVISOR: Sounds like you're a bit worried that what goes on here will be recorded permanently in your files, possibly even to come back to haunt you, is that it?

EMPLOYEE: Yeah, that's it exactly! I don't want to feel as if everything I say is going to be available to other people in the company, too.

SUPERVISOR: I'm glad you raised that question, Clara. The only things that are going to find their way into your personnel folder are the goals that we eventually set for improving your work performance and the things that the both of us will be doing to achieve those goals. Everything else is between you and me.

HOSTILE QUESTIONS

Hostile questions or remarks often indicate the the person is feeling threatened or angry about having to talk with you. Often these questions have a smoke screen effect since they divert attention from the employee and the real purposes of the interview. Here are several examples:

"Well, if you're going to talk to everybody, why are you seeing me first? Do you think I'm the worst of the lot?"

"I'm glad we're going to talk about how you can improve too, because there are a lot of things you can do to improve!"

"Do you really think this is going to do any good?"

"Look, I've been through five supervisors in this company. They all start out gung ho, just like you. Then they begin to relax."

When employees ask hostile questions or make remarks that have a hostile or angry tone, we recommend the following:

1. Do not respond directly to the question. Ignore the content of the person's remark.
2. Reflect the person's feelings and attempt to draw him out with questions like, "Tell me a little more about that." Continue to reflect feeling and ask similar questions until the employee vents his feelings.
3. Reassure the employee that your only purpose is, as you said earlier, to find some ways for the both of you to help improve the employee's performance and make her job less frustrating and more satisfying.

Here's an example:

EMPLOYEE: Well, if you're going to talk to everybody, why are you seeing me first? Do you think I'm the worst of the lot?

SUPERVISOR: You sound kind of angry, James. I'd like to hear more about how you're feeling.

EMPLOYEE: Ah . . . well, I just have this feeling that you called me in here to pick on me, and I don't think that's fair. There are plenty of other people out there who you should be talking to instead of me.

SUPERVISOR: So you feel I'm singling you out to find fault with your work, to kind of give you the business, is that it?

EMPLOYEE: Right. (*Voice a little softer now*)

SUPERVISOR: James, I'm sorry you have that impression. I asked you to meet with me exactly for the reasons I described earlier, so that both of us could put our heads together to find some ways to improve your work performance and make your job less frustrating and more satisfying. I'm glad you told me what was on your mind. I'd like to hear about any other feelings you have before we go on. (*Leaning forward slightly*)

EMPLOYEE: (*Softer now*) No, I feel better now.

SUPERVISOR: Good. Okay, let's move on. . . .

The technique for dealing with hostile questions is very similar to the one for dealing with questions that express concern. In both cases, it's important to give the employee a chance to express the feeling that's being experienced.

A QUICK SUMMARY

Let's recap what's been covered in this chapter. First, you set the stage for a private interview by minimizing distractions and potential interruptions. Second, you do a number of things to make your employee feel comfortable and welcome, including greeting the person in a warm and friendly manner, engaging in a bit of casual conversation before getting down to business, and sitting down face-to-face with the employee. Third, you orient the employee to the purpose and procedures of the interview. And, finally, you respond appropriately to the employee's questions and concerns before moving on to the main body of the interview.

In the next chapter, you'll learn some new listening skills for getting the employee to talk openly and freely.

CHAPTER 7
GET YOUR EMPLOYEE TO TALK: LISTENING SKILLFULLY

Let's review for a moment where you are now in the overall performance improvement process. In Step One, you analyzed your employee's performance. You moved on to Step Two and asked the person to meet with you. In Step Three, you learned how to get the interview off to the best possible start.

Now we're going to take a time-out from this step-by-step process to introduce you to some skills that will help you to get the employee to talk fully and freely.

These skills are called listening skills. They're simple to learn but hard to get into the habit of using. They'll require a lot of practice until you feel comfortable and natural using them. But the rewards are worth it: Making a habit of using listening skills will greatly improve your effectiveness as a supervisor.

WHY LISTENING SKILLS ARE SO IMPORTANT

Think for a moment about a supervisor you've had who wasn't a very good listener. Fix the person clearly in your mind and think back to a time when the two of you sat down to talk about your job performance. What made your supervisor a poor listener? What did the person say or do that communicated the message, "I'm not listening to you," or "I don't really care about your ideas or feelings."

Now think about how you felt. What effect did your supervisor's poor listening behavior have on you? Record your thoughts below:

What did the supervisor say or do? _____

_____

_____

How did you feel as a result? _____

_____

_____

Here's a sample of responses that we've heard from other supervisors to these same questions:

"I could never tell if he was listening to me or not, because he was always doing something else when we were talking, like checking over last month's sales figures or going over invoices. It just seemed to me that my ideas weren't very important to him. I guess it made me feel kind of . . . trivial."

"The person I'm thinking of was a nonstop talker. I mean how can you listen when you talk all the time? Even though *we* were supposed to be talking, I could hardly get a word in edgewise. We used to call her 'motor mouth' behind her back. How'd it make me feel? Totally uninvolved, as if I weren't there at all. I'd just tune her right out!"

"I had this supervisor who would interrupt me whenever he disagreed with me. Not only would he butt right in, he'd also put me down by saying things like, 'That's a stupid idea' or 'I can't believe you could say such a thing!' He turned me off completely. I could never produce for a person like that!"

"I had a supervisor once who would always misinterpret— or even distort—what I said. After we'd agree on something, he'd go out and do just the opposite. Then when I'd call him on it, he'd look real innocent and say something like, 'Well, isn't that what we agreed on?' This happened so often that I got to the point where I almost tape recorded our meetings just to prove to myself I wasn't going wacky. I felt completely confused and bewildered by his behavior. And I lost complete faith in him as a supervisor."

Clearly, a supervisor with poor listening skills can have a negative impact on an employee. But what benefits can you expect from good listening skills? Here are several:

1. You'll show employees that you're interested and concerned about their problems, not just yours. When you communicate the message "I care about you and how you're doing," you meet your employee's basic need for respect as a human being.

2. You'll give employees the opportunity to express their feelings about their jobs in a way they've never done before. People want to talk, but only if they feel they're being heard. Listening to people's ideas is a way of getting them involved and keeping them involved.

3. You'll often find out why employees haven't been performing well. There's often a good reason behind a person's poor work performance. If you listen carefully, you might find out why. And that puts you in a much better position to begin the process of improving your employee's performance.

4. You'll find out things that will help make you a better manager. Because of the nature of their position, supervisors don't see things in the same way (or even the same things) as employees. A wise supervisor pays attention to the perspectives of employees, who are often quite good at identifying areas of inefficiency, irritation, or concern—areas you may not be aware of.

5. You'll greatly increase the chances that employees will listen to you. People's levels of receptivity—their willingness to listen to you—varies from very high to very low and depends in large part on what you do as a supervisor. If you have good listening skills, you'll raise an employee's level of receptivity; if you don't, you'll drive it down. It's that simple.

In the remainder of this chapter we'll show you three different types of listening skills* that will help you achieve these benefits:

- Attending behavior
- Requests for information
- Expressions of understanding

Attending behavior is the term used for nonverbal signals, such as the way you make eye contact and posture yourself, that communicate to other people that you're paying attention to them and are interested in what they have to say.

*While our approach to listening skills has been influenced by many people, we'd like to especially acknowledge the contribution that has been made by Carl R. Rogers and Allen E. Ivey.

Requests for information are verbal techniques designed to get people talking and to keep them talking.

Expressions of understanding are techniques you can use to make sure you've heard the other person correctly. These expressions have the effect of making the other person feel understood.

ATTENDING BEHAVIOR

Psychologists have long recognized the tremendous importance that attention from others plays in our lives. Infants need almost constant attention, thriving on the tender touching and close physical presence of their mothers and fathers. Children, spouses, and close friends require our undivided attention when they're troubled or upset. No one likes to talk to people who just don't pay attention.

Even though much has been made of the importance of attention, until recently relatively little mention was made of the specific things that people do—or don't do—when they're attending to one another. Attending, which is just a fancy way to refer to the process of paying attention to or showing interest in another person, is composed of these three simple elements:

1. Making eye contact,
2. Using good body language, and
3. Minimizing distractions.

MAKING EYE CONTACT

How often have you tried to talk to someone who wasn't looking directly at you? If not actually impossible, it's awfully disconcerting to try to communicate with someone who's not looking you in the eye. Yet, as important as it is, many people don't do it when they're listening.

Think of the times when you've been at a party and somebody says, "Oh, so that's what you do for a living. Tell me more about that." Then, just as you're getting warmed up, you notice that the person begins looking about the room, nodding at other people, and waving at new arrivals. If you're like most people, this behavior will stop you dead in your tracks. Making eye contact sends the message, "I'm listening." Not making eye contact says, "I'm not listening."

Here are some important things to remember about making eye contact:

☐ Instead of rigidly looking into the other person's eyes, break contact periodically.

☐   Try to maintain direct eye contact about 70 to 80 percent of the time. Much more than this makes people feel uncomfortable.

☐   When breaking eye contact, don't look all about the room or dart your eyes from side to side. Rapid eye movement suggests tension or anxiety and will make people less willing to tell you what's on their minds.

☐   Don't let your eyes give away or telegraph negative reactions. This can work against you. For example, a good interview can be wrecked when you unconsciously roll your eyes to the sky after a comment you find hard to believe.

USING GOOD BODY LANGUAGE

It's hard to read a popular magazine these days without finding some space devoted to the subject of body language. Some writers say our body language reveals our hidden personalities so that a shrewd observer can learn all kinds of things about our conflicts and secret desires. That's carrying things a bit too far. To us, body language simply means the way you use your face, arms, and upper torso to let people know you're interested in what they have to say.

There are four important aspects of body language:

1. Body positioning,
2. Nodding,
3. Using facial muscles, and
4. Using arms and upper body.

1. Body positioning. When listening, position your body so that your head and upper torso are directly facing the other person. "Aim" your body at the person. If you have to look over your shoulder or off to the side to see the person, then you're probably not doing it right.

2. Nodding. In addition to maintaining good eye contact, nod your head periodically to send the nonverbal message, "I hear what you're saying." If you're not a natural nodder, it's pretty easy to learn. Just stand in front of a mirror and start talking to yourself. (Do this in the privacy of your home; otherwise your coworkers may begin to suspect that the pressure of the job is finally getting to you!)

As you look at yourself in the mirror, nod your head a couple of times every few seconds. It'll appear even more natural if you say something like "Uhm-humm," or "I see," as you nod. When you feel comfortable, practice with a coworker or a friend. As they talk to you, experiment with nodding and not nodding for short periods of time. See if you can notice any difference in their involvement.

3. Using facial muscles. Learning how to use your facial muscles when listening is important. People with stone faces or poker faces communicate boredom or disinterest, even when they're really listening. People with expressive faces are much easier to talk to. Their faces come alive with interest in what the other person has to say.

There are a couple of things you can do to cultivate the use of your facial muscles:

☐ Pay attention to other expressive people. Turn down the volume on your television set and watch the variety of facial expressions used on talk shows, soap operas, or situation comedies. With the soaps you often don't even have to hear the action to know what's going on. Body language, especially facial expressions, tells it all.

☐ Once again, stand in front of a mirror. Begin by simply exercising your facial muscles. Wrinkle your forehead. Purse your lips. Drop your jaw. Furrow and then raise your eyebrows. Wrinkle your nose. Widen your eyes. Clench your teeth. Now try to express the following emotions just by changing your facial expression: confusion, surprise, shock, agreement, enthusiasm, anger, deep interest. It's easy once you get used to it.

Bad Listening Posture

4. Using arms and upper body. In general, it's best to assume a relaxed (not slouched) posture in which your torso is tilted slightly toward the speaker. For the most part, a body that is leaning backward communicates less interest and involvement than one that is leaning forward slightly.

It's also a good idea to avoid sitting with your arms folded. This is the classic closed posture. It's no accident that baseball umpires stand firmly planted with their arms folded tightly across their chests when they're being verbally assaulted by an irate manager.

Instead of folding your arms, place them comfortably on the armrests of your chair or rest them naturally in your lap. When combined with direct eye contact and a slight tilting forward of the upper body, this is a very good listening posture.

Good Listening Posture

Sometimes you'll want to really communicate that you're listening to the other person. They may be having trouble getting something out or you may just want to vary your listening posture. A simple movement on your part will do the trick. Just lean forward even further and rest your elbows on your knees as you look directly at the other person.

In the illustration, compare the bad listening posture to the more effective ones.

Intensive Listening Posture

Take a few minutes to practice these postures and imagine the effect each would have on an imaginary speaker. Better yet, try them out on a coworker, spouse, or close friend. Get their reactions. Remember, the key is to be relaxed and comfortable but still attentive.

MINIMIZING DISTRACTIONS

In Chapter 6 we talked about minimizing distractions of an external nature in setting the stage for the interview. But it's also important to minimize the distracting effects of personal habits and mannerisms.

While some distractions are unavoidable, most of them are under your control. To give you an idea, examine this list of guaranteed distractions:

☐ Maintaining an open door policy at all times.
☐ Failing to tell your secretary to hold incoming telephone calls.
☐ Using the time that you're meeting with people to get other things done, such as cutting and filing your fingernails, cleaning your desk, or balancing your checkbook.
☐ Keeping your eye on the clock to make certain that you won't be late for your next appointment.
☐ Relaxing and making yourself comfortable by sitting back, putting your feet up on the desk, or twiddling your thumbs.
☐ Making sure you're on top of everything by always keeping one ear tuned to the intercom, the PA system, your CB radio, or that FM station you like so much.

If you want people to feel heard, you've got to concentrate on them. Close your door, ask that incoming calls be held, and focus your attention on your employee. Before the interview clear your desk and your mind of things that will distract you from your purpose at this stage of the process — getting people to talk about themselves and their work.

To get some practice with these three aspects of attending behavior — making eye contact, using good body language, and minimizing distractions — try the following exercise:

1. Select a person to talk with. Tell the person that you'd like some help with a little experiment where all he or she has to do is talk for a few minutes.
2. To begin, ask a good comprehensive question to get the person talking. For example, "Tell me a little bit about your school experience. You know, your best and worst

subjects, extracurricular activities you took part in, your social life, the kinds of friends you had, and that sort of thing."

3. Once the person begins talking, really pay attention. Make direct eye contact, lean forward slightly, nod your head, and say "Uhm-humm" every so often.

4. After about a minute, gradually begin to attend poorly. Lean back, glance around the room, fold your arms across your chest, look at your watch, and that sort of thing. While you do this, notice the effect on the other person. Some will look confused and perplexed. Some will stop talking to ask what's going on. Some may even get angry.

5. After about a minute, start attending well again. After another minute or two, stop the experiment and get the other person's reaction to what happened. Then fill the person in on the details. A nice way to express your thanks is to teach the person all you know about attending behavior.

REQUESTS FOR INFORMATION

Good attending behavior is an essential tool of the good listener, but it's not sufficient to get another person talking fully and freely. An effective listener must also direct and guide the interview by suggesting different topics for the other person to talk about. The methods for doing this are called requests for information. There are six different types of requests for information:

1. The invitation to talk,
2. Open-ended questions,
3. Fact-seeking questions,
4. The comprehensive question,
5. Probing for specificity, and
6. Encouragers.

THE INVITATION TO TALK

Sometimes the best way to get people talking is not by asking a question at all, but simply by inviting them to talk about a given subject. For example, you could say, "I'd like to hear about the people you most admire in life." Notice that this is a statement, not a question.

The invitation to talk does exactly what it suggests: It invites people to talk openly and freely about a given subject.

"I'd like to hear about how things went for you while I was on vacation last week."

"Tell me what you think of the new computer we had installed in the financial department."

"I'd be interested in hearing your reactions to the school committee's meeting last night."

"Tell me about your working relationship with Terry."

The invitation to talk has several nice features:

☐ It focuses attention on a specific topic but gives people plenty of latitude for their response.
☐ If you periodically use an invitation to talk in your interviews, your employees will feel less like they're being grilled or interrogated than if you only asked questions.
☐ A good invitation to talk is an excellent way to get information without tipping your hand and having the employee's response colored by your views on the subject.

Here's some practice. In the space below, write an invitation to talk that you might use with one of your employees.

_____

_____

_____

_____

_____

_____

_____

_____

_____

_____

If you had a little difficulty, refer to the examples provided earlier. This time try to formulate an invitation to talk by beginning with phrases such as "I'd like to hear . . ." or "Tell me. . . ." They'll make it a little easier.

OPEN-ENDED QUESTIONS

The easiest way to understand open-ended questions is to compare them to closed-ended questions, which usually call for a Yes/No answer.

CLOSED-ENDED QUESTIONS	OPEN-ENDED QUESTIONS
"Did things go okay while I was away last week?"	"How did things go while I was away last week?"
"Has Lee been getting along with the other workers lately?"	"How has Lee been getting along with the other workers lately?"
"Do you like your job?"	"What do you like most and least about your job?"
"Have you learned anything from this experience?"	"What have you learned from this experience?"
"Do you think that book is appropriate for this course?"	"What are your thoughts about the appropriateness of that book for this course?"

As you can see, closed-ended questions don't give people much opportunity to respond. They're especially ineffective with employees who are reluctant to talk openly with their supervisors. Here's an example:

SUPERVISOR: Well, Chris, you've been working here for two months now. Are you pleased with your decision to transfer here from the fiscal department?

EMPLOYEE: Oh yes, Mr. Clayborn. I'm very pleased.

SUPERVISOR: When you started, you said that you were looking for a job with a lot more responsibility. Do you think we're providing you with that here?

EMPLOYEE: Yes, indeed! I have a lot more responsibility here than in my job with the fiscal department. A lot more.

SUPERVISOR: That's good, Chris. I'm happy to hear that. Have I been as helpful as I could be to you as you've made the transition to this new position?

EMPLOYEE: Oh, you've been very helpful, Mr. Clayborn. And I really do appreciate all you've done.

SUPERVISOR: Well, thanks for saying that, Chris. That's very nice. Is there anything I can do to make your job here less frustrating and more satisfying?

EMPLOYEE: (*A little startled*) More satisfying? Uh . . . gee, I can't think of anything right now.

SUPERVISOR: Okay, but if you think of anything, just tell me. Is that a deal?

EMPLOYEE: Sure, Mr. Clayborn. That's a deal.

In this illustration, Chris didn't give Mr. Clayborn much information. If anything, Chris was telling Mr. Clayborn what he wanted to hear. It might have gone very differently if the supervisor had asked open-ended questions such as these:

"You've been here two months now, Chris. How would you compare this job to the previous one you had in the fiscal department?"

"Chris, how would you assess this job in terms of your original goal of wanting a position with more responsibility?"

"What are some things I could have done to help you make the transition to this new job?"

"As you think about it, Chris, what suggestions do you have for how I could make your job less frustrating and more satisfying?"

It would be possible for Chris to answer these questions with very short answers, but he's less likely to do this because they're being asked in an open-ended fashion. In addition, these open-ended questions make it much more difficult for Chris to feed back to Mr. Clayborn what he thinks his boss wants to hear.

In general, open-ended questions are good ways to start a flow of conversation because they call for an extended answer. They communicate to employees that you're interested in what they have to say.

Here's a little practice. In the left column below there are a series of closed-ended questions. Turn each one into an open-ended question, writing your response in the right column. After you've finished, compare your answers to ours.

CLOSED-ENDED QUESTIONS	*OPEN-ENDED QUESTIONS*
Did you enjoy your summer vacation?	_____
Are you planning to take any night courses next semester?	_____
Do you have any recommendations for improving our personnel policies?	_____

Open-ended questions can differ widely in the amount of thinking that they ask of people. For example, look at the following transformations of the first question above:

"How did you enjoy your summer vacation?"

"What did you do on your summer vacation?"

"What did you like most and least about your summer vacation?"

"How did this summer's vacation compare to the one you took last year?"

The first open-ended question doesn't really challenge the employee to do much thinking. A simple "I really enjoyed it" would suffice. The other three questions call for progressively more thinking on the part of the employee. How do the rest of your open-ended questions compare with ours, especially in terms of how much they challenge the employee to do some thinking:

"What are your educational plans for next semester?"

"What changes would we have to make in our personnel policies to improve them?"

FACT-SEEKING QUESTIONS

When you want to get highly specific or factual information from employees, you can ask fact-seeking questions. Although they're often asked in an open-ended fashion, the focus of fact-seeking questions is narrow and precise. Here are some examples:

"How many minority applicants did we get for that position?"

"What's the percentage of nylon in that new swim-suit line?"

"What were our gross sales for the third quarter?"

"What's the name of the person who wrote that book on goal analysis?"

"When is the deadline for submitting that proposal?"

"What's the square footage of our property on Emory Street?"

"Where can we get an order of 5,000 filled on a twenty-four hour basis?"

We see two basic reasons for supervisors to ask their employees fact-seeking questions:

1. To obtain information they don't have that employees can provide, and
2. To learn whether employees possess certain kinds of information that they should have at their command. For

example, an auto mechanic should be able to describe the principles of electronic ignition. A life insurance agent should be able to answer specific questions about the difference between whole life and term policies. A biology teacher should know about the latest research on recombinant DNA.

If employees don't have the answers to fact-seeking questions, it doesn't mean they should be punished. It simply means that some corrective action is needed.

Fact-seeking questions can be asked at any time, in casual encounters or in formally scheduled interviews. When used in formal interviews, it's better to ask them later in the interview, after the employee has had a chance to loosen up. Used too early or too frequently, they give the employee the feeling of being quizzed or interrogated.

Imagine that you're about to sit down with one of your employees. What are some things you don't know but would like to learn? What are some things the employee should know, but may not? In the space below, write a couple of fact-seeking questions you might use in an interview. Compare them to the fact-seeking questions presented earlier.

_____

_____

_____

_____

_____

_____

THE COMPREHENSIVE QUESTION

One of the best ways to introduce a topic of conversation and to get somebody talking about it is to ask a comprehensive question.* When you ask a comprehensive question, you do two things:

1. You mention the broad area you'd like to discuss, either with an invitation to talk or an open-ended question; and
2. You identify some of the specific things the person can mention when answering the question, always leaving the person the opportunity to add anything else.

*Special thanks to Richard Fear, whose "comprehensive introductory question" in the context of selection interviews has stood us in good stead in many other situations.

Here are two examples of comprehensive questions:

"Gerry, I'd like you to tell me, in general, how things are going on the job for you. You might want to talk about the kinds of things you've been doing lately, the things you get excited about or bored by, some of the special projects you've been working on, and anything else you'd like to mention."

"How did things go on your vacation, Sandy? I'd like to hear about where you went, the kinds of things you did, some of the high and low points, and anything else you'd like to add."

One of the nicest features of the comprehensive question is that it gives people some helpful hints about what to include in their answer. Comprehensive questions are especially useful with people who don't tend to talk very much or who have a little trouble getting started, especially if they're feeling a bit nervous or uncomfortable.

Now try to formulate a comprehensive question. Remember the basic format:

Tell me about _____.

You might want to mention _____,

_____, _____

_____, and anything else you think is important.

Write your comprehensive question below.

_____

_____

_____

_____

You may have had a little trouble coming up with a good comprehensive question. That's natural; they feel a little uncomfortable until you get used to them. One way to practice using them is with kids. As every parent knows, the classic answer to the question, "How'd things go in school today?" is "Okay." or "Pretty good." Try a comprehensive question instead:

"Jordan, I'd like to hear about what happened at school today. You know, the new things that you learned, the stories you read, the games you played, the most interesting and most boring things that happened, and that sort of thing."

You may be surprised at the results.

PROBING FOR SPECIFICITY

It would be nice if people always communicated their ideas clearly and fully, but often they don't. Sometimes they say things that are unclear or confusing. Sometimes they use too few words or a word or a phrase that you don't understand. When this happens, it's a good idea to probe for specificity.

For example, imagine that an employee says, "Well, you know Jim. He can be a little difficult at times!" Rather than assume you know what the person means, you can probe for specificity by asking one of the following questions:

"Difficult?"
"I'm not sure what you mean by difficult. Could you expand a little on that?"
"How do you mean that?"
"Can you give me an example of how he can be difficult?"

Each of these examples conveys the message, "You've said something I don't quite understand. It would help if you'd clarify it for me."

Sometimes you don't have to say anything to probe for more information. Just pause for a moment or wrinkle your forehead with a puzzled expression (not a disapproving one).

There are two important points to remember in getting an employee to clarify something you don't understand:

1. Don't do it at the expense of cutting off the flow of conversation. Especially in the beginning of the interview, it's better to let the employee get warmed up by talking for a while than to interrupt to clarify something. You can always come back to it later.
2. Be careful to probe in a neutral, nonthreatening tone of voice. The last thing you want to convey is impatience or annoyance at the employee's use of vague or fuzzy language.

Below are three employee remarks that need clarification. For each one write in how you might probe for specificity. After you've finished, compare your probes to the ones we would have used.

Employee: I think I could use a little more support around here.

You: _____

_____

_____

Employee: She's a hard worker, but she doesn't show very good judgment.

You: _____

_____

_____

Employee: Seems to me that you've got a lot to learn about supervising people.

You: _____

_____

_____

Here's how we would have responded to these remarks:

"How do you mean that, Max? I'm not quite sure what you mean by more support."

"What are some things she's done that have shown poor judgment?"

"Tell me, how could I improve the way I supervise people?"

A good way to practice probes for specificity is to use them in your everyday conversations with people. You'll get much more detailed and specific information than you used to.

ENCOURAGERS

Encouragers are short signals that show you're interested in what people have to say. They encourage a person to talk freely. They're especially helpful after an open-ended question when an employee is having trouble getting started.

Encouragers fall into two categories, verbal and non-verbal. For example, assume that you've asked an open-ended question of an employee: "Well, Clara, how have things been going on your job?" Clara responds, "Uh . . . pretty good."

These are some examples of verbal encouragers you could use to get Clara to expand on her answer:

"Pretty good?"

"Uhm-humm."

"Tell me more, I'm really interested in how things are going for you."

"When you say 'pretty good'? . . ."

"That's a hard question to answer in a sentence or two. Take some time to think about it."

These are some examples of nonverbal encouragers you could use with Clara:

☐ Nod,
☐ Lean forward in your chair, and
☐ Raise your eyebrows a little.

Verbal and nonverbal encouragers are most effective when used together—for example, say "Pretty good?" while leaning forward a little and raising your eyebrows.

Encouragers gently prod employees to tell you in more depth what they're thinking and feeling. Encouragers are so much more effective than what most people do when someone either hesitates or gives a brief answer to a question—they start talking! Because silent periods make many people uncomfortable, it's very tempting to start talking to reduce the discomfort. Once you start talking, you don't feel uncomfortable anymore. However, when you're doing the talking, you can't expect to find out much about the employee. And the employee will be even less likely to talk when you finally finish.

So far we've covered two major listening skill areas, attending behavior and requests for information. Now let's move on to the third and final listening skill area.

EXPRESSIONS OF UNDERSTANDING

Whenever two human beings sit down to talk, misunderstandings and disagreements occur. This is most likely to happen when the two parties have very different perspectives or opinions—a situation often referred to as a communication gap. How people achieve understanding, despite their differences, is the focus of this third major listening skill area.

The primary purpose of expressions of understanding is to make certain that you really do understand what the employee is saying or feeling, that the communication channels are clear and open. Three techniques you can use to do this are:

1. Reflecting feeling,
2. Paraphrasing, and
3. Summarizing.

REFLECTING FEELING

Often it's not what people say but how they say it that counts. The emotion behind the message becomes much more important than the remark itself. When you want to respond to the emotion rather than the content of an employee's remark, use the technique of reflecting feeling. We touched upon it briefly in Chapter 6.

Reflecting feeling is a simple, two-part process:

1. You identify the feeling behind the other person's remark: confusion, anger, frustration, excitement, determination, or whatever.
2. You reflect the feeling back to the employee, beginning your response with words such as: "You're feeling . . ." or "Sounds like you're feeling. . . ."

When you respond to an employee's feelings in this way, you send an important message: "I'm as interested in your feelings as I am in your thoughts and ideas." Here are some other examples of reflecting feeling:

SUPERVISOR: Sally, I'd like to hear about any problems that you've been having on the job over the last several months.
EMPLOYEE: Don't you think they ought to do something about the air conditioning where our desks are? It gets like an oven over there during the afternoon!
SUPERVISOR: Sounds like you're pretty angry about that situation, Sally.
EMPLOYEE: I sure am! It's just terrible. . . .

SUPERVISOR: How's your work going with the new terminal manager, John?
EMPLOYEE: Pretty well, but he's kind of stiff and formal. I'm never really sure of what he thinks of my work.
SUPERVISOR: You feel a little uneasy and unsure of yourself because he doesn't give you much feedback, good or bad.
EMPLOYEE: Yes, I never quite put it in those words, but that's exactly how I feel, and. . . .

SUPERVISOR: How are you and Cheryl doing with the filing backlog?
EMPLOYEE: Well, we work on it at least an hour every day. But a lot of the time it seems like we're shoveling sand against the tide.
SUPERVISOR: So it's kind of frustrating and discouraging?
EMPLOYEE: Amen! And while we're on the subject. . . .

Notice that in these examples the employees were expressing some distinct feelings even though they did not come right out and say so. In each example, the supervisor reflected these feelings back to the employee but did not respond to the content of the employee's remarks. The reasons for doing this are to get employees to talk further about things that are bothering them and to demonstrate your concern about their feelings. Solutions to problems (and that's where content comes into play) can be dealt with later in the interview.

Practice reflecting the employee's feelings in the following examples. Write your answers in the space below each remark, comparing your responses to ours after you've finished.

Employee: (Raising his voice) How come you're always asking me to be the flexible one, the one with all the sensitivity? What about her?

You: _____

_____

_____

_____

_____

_____

_____

_____

_____

Employee: My biggest problem is dealing with criticism. When people start telling me how to do my job, especially those turkeys from upstairs, I get bent all out of shape. I know that exploding like a volcano is bad, and I've got to learn how to change that if I'm ever going to advance around here. I've got to stop being so damned thin-skinned!

You: _____

_____

_____

_____

Here's how we would have responded:

"You're feeling kind of angry at me because it seems like I'm being unfair, is that it?"

"Sounds like you feel really determined to bring your temper under control."

As practice, try using this technique in as many different situations as you can. For example, when your child enthusiastically tells you about the last-second home team victory, try saying "Sounds really exciting" or "You're really feeling thrilled." Or when your spouse says "How could you do that when I specifically asked you not to," acknowledge the anger by saying "You're really angry at me for not listening to you."

When you reflect people's feelings like this, especially when they're upset, be prepared for a continued outpouring of emotion. If you continue to listen sensitively by drawing them out further and by responding to their feelings, they'll invariably wind down and begin to feel more understood.

It's a waste of time to try to talk to people who are upset, angry, or experiencing some other strong emotion; they just aren't in a receptive mood. It's much better to listen to them, often by reflecting their feelings. Remember, if you want people to listen to what you've got to say, you've got to be prepared to listen to them first.

PARAPHRASING

Paraphrasing is a skill similar to reflecting feeling because it involves reading back to the employee what was said. However, reflecting feeling concentrates on emotion; paraphrasing focuses primarily on content. When you paraphrase, you simply repeat in your own words the gist of what you understood the employee to say:

EMPLOYEE: It's really hard to get things done in this place. The telephones ring, typewriters rattle, radios blare! Half the things I do I have to do over again just to make sure there are no mistakes.
SUPERVISOR: So the distractions are really affecting your productivity, is that it?

Paraphrasing has several purposes:

☐ It clearly demonstrates to employees that you've been listening.
☐ It gives employees an opportunity to correct any misunderstanding you may have had about what was said.
☐ It encourages employees to build on what they've already said.

Often a good paraphrase will tie together an employee's remark concisely through the use of a word or phrase that seems to fit perfectly. When this happens, employees often brighten up and say things like "Exactly!" or "That's it!"

Try to paraphrase the following remarks, comparing your responses to ours after you've finished.

Employee: The trouble with Tom is that everything has to be done *exactly* his way. He doesn't realize that we all have our own ideas and feelings about how things could be done. And it doesn't make any difference if the final product is perfect or not. If you don't do it exactly his way, it's not done right.

You: _____

_____

_____

_____

_____

_____

_____

_____

_____

Employee: I'm just not sure what to make of those trainee ratings. Whenever they complete those rating forms, they always say "very satisfied, very satisfied." But when they talk among themselves, they're always complaining about how bad things are. Listening to them then, you'd think they hated the program. I just don't know what to make of it.

You: _____

_____

_____

_____

_____

_____

_____

_____

_____

This is how we would have responded:

"So the 'right' way to do things is his way, and his way only, even though you see other ways to go about it."

"It's hard to know what to believe when they say such different things in different situations."

SUMMARIZING

Summarizing is similar to paraphrasing because it reads back to the employee the content of what was said. It differs in the amount of information that is restated. A paraphrase is a rephrasing or restatement of the central message contained in one or two employee remarks; it basically says the same thing but in different words. A summary highlights or recapitulates only the main points made in a more lengthy exchange between supervisor and employee. It is a *condensation* of a good deal of information into several major points or themes. Its purposes are similar to paraphrasing:

☐   It shows that you've heard what the employee has been saying.

☐   It gives the employee an opportunity to correct any misperceptions you may have.

☐   It helps the employee add anything else of importance that wasn't mentioned previously.

Here's an example of how a supervisor might summarize a rather long series of statements by an employee:

SUPERVISOR: Chris, I'd like you to take a few minutes to describe the things you do particularly well on your job.

EMPLOYEE: The things I do well. Okay. Of course, there are a lot of things I don't do so well, but here goes. A number of people have told me that I type accurately and rapidly. And I guess I'd have to agree with them. I picked up typing real fast and it does come easy for me. (*Pause*) Let's see, I think I'm also pretty good on the telephone. You know, being polite and cheerful, taking good messages, that sort of thing. Bob Peters and Penny Marshall have complimented me on more than one occasion about my being good on the telephone. Let's see . . . oh yeah, my shorthand's pretty good even though I don't use it much on this job. I remember I got the highest grade in shorthand class. But that was ages ago. (*Laughing*) Hmm . . . one more thing. I almost always get my work done on time. I know that's true because you've mentioned that yourself . . . and also because nobody ever has to bug me to get things done. I guess that about does it.

SUPERVISOR: Okay, so there are a number of things you do well. You mentioned that you thought you were a good typist, that you have very good telephone answering skills, that your shorthand is good, and that you can usually be counted on to get your work done on time.

EMPLOYEE: Yes, that's right. Oh, I just thought of another thing. . . .

In addition to the purposes mentioned before, summarizing can be helpful in several other ways.

☐   A good summary often sharpens a rambling, disconnected series of remarks by highlighting the main points in a clear, concise manner.

☐   Just knowing that you're going to summarize a lengthy series of remarks provides excellent motivation to listen carefully to what's being said.

☐   Summarizing is especially helpful in winding up one major segment of the interview and making the transition to a new one. All you have to do is conclude your summary with something like, "Unless you've got something else to add, I'd like to move on to a new topic."

A QUICK SUMMARY

Listening can be broken down into three areas:

- Attending behavior,
- Requests for information, and
- Expressions of understanding.

Attending behavior includes three techniques that show you're paying attention and showing an interest in what employees are saying:

1. Making eye contact,
2. Using good body language, and
3. Minimizing distractions.

Requests for information include six techniques for getting people to talk and for keeping them talking:

1. The invitation to talk,   4. The comprehensive question,
2. Open-ended questions,   5. Probing for specificity, and
3. Fact-seeking questions,   6. Encouragers.

Expressions of understanding include three techniques for clearly demonstrating that you've correctly heard what employees are saying or feeling:

1. Reflecting feeling,
2. Paraphrasing, and
3. Summarizing.

In the next chapter you'll see a detailed illustration of how a supervisor combines these listening skills in a meeting with an employee. You'll have an opportunity to practice these skills in that chapter. But to become a really proficient listener, you'll also need to practice these skills on your own.

CHAPTER 8 • STEP FOUR: FIND OUT HOW THINGS ARE GOING

So far in this book we've covered the first three steps in the performance improvement process:

STEP ONE: Analyze Your Employee's Performance
STEP TWO: Ask Your Employee to Meet with You
STEP THREE: Begin the Performance Improvement Interview

In the last chapter we introduced you to a series of listening skills to help you get employees to open up and to talk freely. These skills will come in very handy in finding out how things are going. Here's what this chapter includes:

- The reasons why it's important to find out how things are going with an employee;
- A walk-through example of a supervisor using good listening skills to find out how things are going with an employee;
- The possible setbacks that can occur at this stage of the interview and the strategies for dealing with them; and
- Time out for practice and a self-evaluation on this part of the process.

WHY IT'S IMPORTANT TO FIND OUT HOW THINGS ARE GOING

Let's get back to where you left off in the ten-step process. In Step Three you got your interview off to a good start:

☐   You set the stage by minimizing potential distractions and interruptions.
☐   You made the employee feel comfortable and welcome.
☐   You oriented the employee to the purposes and procedures of the interview.
☐   You responded to any of the employee's questions and concerns.

Now you're ready to find out how things are going with the employee. This means asking the employee to talk to you about three basic things:

1. How things are going in general on the job,
2. Any problems the employee might be experiencing on the job, and
3. Suggestions for how you can make the employee's job less frustrating and more satisfying.

There are several reasons why it's important to cover these points at this stage of the interview:

1. You signal to employees that you really do want to listen to what they've got to say. And it gives employees a chance to say what's on their minds — something that doesn't happen as often as it should between supervisors and employees.

2. You allow employees to vent some of their frustrations. That's something we all need to do now and then. And it helps clear the air so that the interview can proceed more openly.

3. You give employees a chance to talk about problems that should be brought to your attention. While some of these problems will concern your relationship with a specific employee, others will concern the functions of your work unit as a whole.

4. You begin to get some feedback on your own performance as a manager or supervisor. This is especially helpful when you hear some common themes from different employees. Sometimes the feedback will be hard to take, but it's almost always useful to hear it.

5. By finding out how things are going with all of the people you supervise, you begin to get a perspective on your work unit that most managers and supervisors never have. You'll begin to see things from your employees' point of view as well as your own. If you have any doubts about the value of this, think back to supervisors you've had in the past. How many times did you wish they could see things the way you saw them?

WALKING THROUGH AN EXAMPLE

Here's an example of a supervisor finding out how things are going with an employee. Throughout the script there is commentary on the techniques the supervisor is using. Try to read through the script the first time ignoring these comments so that you get a feel for the interaction. Then reread the script paying close attention to the comments.

GERRY: Well, Chris, now that we've covered the reasons why I asked to meet with you and what's going to happen here today, I'd like to hear about how things are going on the job. •

CHRIS: Uh . . . how things are going?
GERRY: (*Leaning forward slightly*) Uhm-humm.
CHRIS: Well, I guess things are going pretty well. . . .
GERRY: (*Nodding head and smiling slightly, but saying nothing*) •

CHRIS: Uh, let's see. . . . That's kind of tough to answer all at once.
GERRY: (*Nodding and smiling*) Yes, it is. Take your time. I'm interested in what you have to say.
CHRIS: (*Loosening up a little*) Let's see. Well, things have been going pretty well. I like it here much more than my last job. The atmosphere's a lot more relaxed. The people are very nice. You'd be amazed how many of them have come up and introduced themselves to me and asked if they could help in any way. Uh. . . .
GERRY: (*Nodding*) Uhm-humm.
CHRIS: Well, I guess . . . oh, uh . . . the benefits! Thaaank goodness for the benefits! (*Smiling broadly*)
GERRY: (*Smiling back*) Sounds like you're pretty happy about the benefits package. •

CHRIS: Am I ever! My son broke his leg—pretty badly, too. He was in the hospital for almost two weeks. I won't even tell you what the bill was, but the medical plan covered all of it.

• How might the interview have gone differently if the supervisor had begun with a comprehensive question rather than an invitation to talk?

• Notice the good use of verbal and nonverbal encouragers.

• What technique is the supervisor using here?

GERRY: I'm glad to hear that. How's he doing now?

CHRIS: Fine, just fine. He's so back to normal that he's likely to break another one soon, with all his running around.

GERRY: Great! Well, Chris, it sounds like you're pretty pleased with things. You like the job much more than your previous one. You appreciate the relaxed atmosphere, the people are friendly and helpful, and the benefits have been a great help. •

> • A concise summary. Notice how it gets the employee to mention one more important item.

CHRIS: Absolutely! And one more thing. I also see an opportunity to advance here. My last job was strictly dead-end.

GERRY: Okay, so one more thing on the plus side of the column is the chance to advance to a better or more responsible job.

CHRIS: Exactly! That's very important to me.

GERRY: Great! I'm glad you feel that way. Well, Chris, you've talked about a number of things you like. But no situation is perfect. I'd like to hear about anything you don't like or any problems you've been having on the job. •

> • See how the supervisor smoothly makes the transition from one topic to the next.

CHRIS: Problems? (*Looking down and hesitating*) Ah . . . well, there are a couple of things that've been kind of bothering me. (*Pause*)

GERRY: (*Leaning forward slightly and nodding*) I'd like to hear about them.

   After some initial hesitation, the supervisor's use of an encourager (combined with good attending behavior) gets the employee talking.

CHRIS: Well, for one thing, the work load gets pretty heavy sometimes, and I have a little trouble keeping up. All the managers act like their work is the most important to do right now. And sometimes they get pretty upset if they don't get what they want right away.

GERRY: I imagine that can get pretty frustrating for you.

CHRIS: Well . . . I'm not so sure if it's frustrating so much as it is, well, a feeling of being really under pressure, especially when I'm behind schedule and they all start asking about their own pet projects. •

> • One of the nicest things about the skill of reflecting feeling is that employees will correct you if they think you're reading them wrong.

GERRY: So you really feel under the gun at those times.

CHRIS: Under the gun is right! Sometimes I feel so tense I just want to run away from the entire situation. I don't quite know how to handle it.

GERRY: Well, I'm glad you told me about it. And I think there are a number of things we might do about it. (*Pause*) But let's talk about solutions to that problem a little later. First, I'd like to hear about any other problems. •

CHRIS: Okay. Well. (*Pause*) There is (*Pause*) it's, uh (*Pause*) Terry (*Pause*)
GERRY: (*Wrinkling forehead with quizzical expression*) Terry?
CHRIS: I don't want to speak out of turn, but she can be difficult at times.
GERRY: When you say difficult, how do you mean it, Chris?

A probe for specificity that leads to some very good information. Imagine how little information the supervisor would have received if the following statement were made instead: "Yes, we do know how difficult Terry can be."

CHRIS: It's related to the work load problem. As you know we're supposed to help each other when the crunch is on. I mean I'll ask her for some help and she'll say that she's so busy doing her own work that she has no extra time to help with mine. But then she seems to find the time to gab for a half-hour on the telephone while I'm breaking my neck to keep the managers off of my back.
GERRY: So you get pretty annoyed when she does that. •

CHRIS: You bet! I guess I never realized how much I let it get to me. Even though it annoys me I've never said anything about it to her.
GERRY: Okay, Chris. Well, it sounds as if your main problems have to do with the work load, the pressure you feel when all the managers want things done at once, and Terry's unwillingness to help out when the crunch is on.
CHRIS: (*Nodding*) Right. And those really are problems! (*Smiling*) •

GERRY: Yes, they are, and a little later we'll talk about some ways to deal with them. But now I'd like to move on to another subject for a while. I'd like you to think about some ways I could make your job a little less frustrating and more satisfying. What ideas or suggestions do you have along those lines?
CHRIS: (*Smiling broadly*) I've never had a supervisor ask me anything like that before.
GERRY: You're kind of surprised at the question?
CHRIS: Yes, very. But pleasantly surprised. Let me see. Well, one thing is . . . uh, I'd really like to know more about what everybody does around here. I mean, I know Bill Sutton is the business manager and Fran Smith is the purchasing agent, but I don't know what they really do or why they do it.

• An inexperienced supervisor might have started talking about solutions now . . . and gone completely off track.

• Good reflection of feeling. This time the supervisor gets clear confirmation that Chris feels heard.

• Just having mentioned problems often makes employees feel better. It takes a load off their minds. Notice how the supervisor keeps to the game plan by once more deferring any talk about solutions.

GERRY: So you'd like to find out more about the nature of their jobs and how they fit into the company's big picture, is that it?

CHRIS: Right.

GERRY: What else can I do to make things less frustrating and more satisfying for you?

CHRIS: You know, I can't think of anything else! Here's the first time ever that a supervisor asks that question, and I can hardly think of a thing to say. But, in all honesty, I can't think of anything else. •

GERRY: (*Smiling*) Well, it's not like this is your last chance. If you think of something else later on, I'd like to hear about it.

CHRIS: Okay, I'll do that.

GERRY: Well, based on everything you've said so far, it sounds like I need to work on three things to make life more satisfying and enjoyable for you around here. First, I need to speak to the managers about the work load problem. Maybe I can help them set up some kind of priority system so you don't get hit all at once with everything. •

CHRIS: That'd be great.

GERRY: Okay, I'll do that. Now, second, I may have to speak with Terry about being more cooperative when the crunch is on.

CHRIS: (*Nervously*) Are you sure that's a good idea?

GERRY: The thought of my doing that makes you feel a bit uncomfortable? •

CHRIS: Yeah! I don't want her thinking I'm a squealer.

GERRY: I can appreciate that. But, believe me, I won't handle it that way. As I said when I asked you to meet with me, I'm going to be doing this sort of thing with everybody in the office.

CHRIS: Okay, then it shouldn't be a problem.

GERRY: Let's see. Oh yes, third, I think it would be a very good idea if I arranged for you to meet Bill Sutton and Fran Smith, and maybe several others I have in mind, so you can find out more about what they do and what roles they play in the overall operation.

CHRIS: I'd like that.

GERRY: I'm glad to hear that. Okay, I'd like to move on to another topic.

With receptivity as high as it is, the supervisor now feels comfortable about moving to a discussion of the employee's work performance.

• The employee appears to be very comfortable. Receptivity is going up and up.

• The supervisor begins to summarize the problem areas and some ideas about how each might be solved. The supervisor could have also asked Chris for any suggestions for solving them.

• Notice how the supervisor ignores the question and goes straight to the feeling that Chris is experiencing. Imagine how differently it might have gone if Gerry had said, "Yes, I do think it's a good idea."

PRACTICE FINDING OUT HOW THINGS ARE GOING
After reviewing the walk-through example at least once, practice handling this stage of the interview yourself. Find another supervisor or a close friend to help you, someone that you feel comfortable with. Give the person as much information as you can about a real employee, someone that you currently supervise. Tell your partner how you expect the employee would behave in an interview and ask the person to play the employee's role as accurately as possible. Then go ahead and give it a try. Tape record the interview if at all possible. After you've finished, review the tape or recall your conversation carefully. Use these questions as a guide for self-evaluation:

☐   How did you sound on the tape? Relaxed, tense, loose, tight? Did you sound like a person you'd feel comfortable talking to? If you sounded a little stiff or gruff, you might want to practice softening your tone. If you tended to speak too fast or too slow, practice varying your tempo by slowing down or speeding up. If you found yourself sounding a little bland, add a little enthusiasm to your voice by emphasizing certain words and using the upper and lower registers of your voice.

☐   Did you follow the overall format of this approach? Did you begin by asking how things were going in general and then asking about any problems the person was experiencing? Did you end by asking for suggestions on how you could make the employee's job less frustrating and more satisfying?

☐   How was your attending behavior, especially your body language? Did you make and maintain direct eye contact, lean forward slightly as the person was talking, and minimize any distractions that might have gotten in the way?

☐   How would you assess your question-asking technique or, as we called them in the last chapter, your requests for information? Did you use a whole variety of approaches—the invitation to talk, open-ended questions, comprehensive questions, and probes for specificity? We find that many people fall back into the bad habit of asking yes/no questions at this point. If this was true for you, practice asking questions that can't be answered with only a yes or no.

ASK QUESTIONS
LIKE THESE:

"How do you feel about. . . ."
"What are your thoughts
   about. . . ."
"I'd like to hear what you
   have to say about. . . ."
"What do you think of. . . ."

AVOID QUESTIONS
LIKE THESE:

"Do you. . . ."
"Is it. . . ."
"Can't you. . . ."
"Wouldn't you. . . ."

☐   What encouragement did you give the other person to continue talking? Did you use verbal encouragers such as "Uhm-humm," "I see," "Tell me more," and "Go on"? Did you use nonverbal encouragers such as nodding your head, wrinkling your forehead, and, in general, using your facial muscles?

☐   How effective were your expressions of understanding such as reflecting feeling, paraphrasing, and summarizing? For many managers and supervisors, it's common to conduct an entire interview and to use none of these valuable skills. If you didn't use them at all, or if you used them only once or twice, this is an area where you need more practice. If you did use these skills, how well did you use them? If you did reflect feelings, get your friend to tell you how accurate you were. Ask how effective you were in reading back or paraphrasing remarks. How clear and concise were your summaries as you ended one segment of the interview and made the transition to the next?

☐   How did you deal with silence? If you had a tendency to fill in your friend's silence with words, you may have to work on pausing in two-way communication. You might practice counting silently to five (or even ten) after each time that you ask an open-ended question. You may be surprised at some of the thoughtful answers you'll get before you finish counting.

☐   Did you probe for specificity? If your partner used words or phrases that weren't clear or that you didn't understand, did you ask the person to clarify them, elaborate on them, or give you examples?

☐   Overall, how involved and cooperative did the person become? Did your partner feel that you were really interested and really listening? Or did it seem as if you were just going through the motions? Were you successful in building the person's receptivity?

POSSIBLE SETBACKS

When things go wrong in this stage of the interview, they tend to fall into two categories:

1. Employees who make critical remarks about you or the performance review process to express feelings of anger, frustration, or general dissatisfaction, and
2. Employees who talk a lot and ramble on and on whenever someone gives them an opportunity to talk.

THE EMPLOYEE WHO MAKES CRITICAL REMARKS

Imagine that you asked your employee how things were going, in general, on the job and you heard one of these replies:

"I don't quite know whose fault it is, but we just don't have much leadership around here. And I'm not the only one who feels that way."

"Well, now that you mention it, we haven't been getting very good supervision around here."

"Well, things would go a lot better if you supervisors would do your jobs better. There are a lot of problems in this place that you don't know anything about."

"I tell you, some changes better get made around here pretty soon or a lot of people are going to quit. And I'm not the only one who'll tell you that."

"Well, I just don't think you've been a very good supervisor."

Although it would be very tempting, here are some things you should not do when an employee talks to you in this way:

☐ Don't get angry or respond in kind. That's playing right into the employee's hand and won't get you anywhere.
☐ Don't get defensive and start explaining your behavior or citing mitigating circumstances.
☐ Don't lecture the employee about behaving inappropriately or saying things that are out of line. The employee probably won't listen anyway.
☐ Don't avoid responsibility by blaming problems on somebody else or factors that are beyond your control.

So what *do* you do? Paradoxical as it may sound, drawing the people out and getting them to talk *more* is an effective way of dealing with angry, critical, and disparaging remarks. Bring all of your listening skills —especially reflecting feeling, probes for specificity, and encouragers—to bear on the particular problem area. Here's an example:

EMPLOYEE: I tell you, some changes better get made around here pretty soon or a lot of people are going to quit. And I'm not the only one who'll tell you that!
SUPERVISOR: I hear a lot of anger in your voice, Lee. (*Leaning forward slightly*) I'd like to hear more about how you're feeling. •

EMPLOYEE: (*Slightly startled*) Well . . . maybe I am a little angry. As a matter of fact, I guess I am pretty angry! I don't know whose fault it is, but we don't get much leadership around here. I'm not the only one who thinks that the quality of supervision in this place leaves a lot to be desired!

• Notice that the supervisor has ignored the content of the employee's remark and has focused on the feeling of anger. Notice also the invitation to talk even more.

SUPERVISOR: Sounds like your anger has a lot to do with the supervision you're getting . . . or maybe that you're not getting. I'm also wondering if a good deal of that anger isn't directed at me?

The supervisor continues to reflect feeling, but now confronts the employee with a suggestion that the critical comments are probably directed at *this* supervisor and not some undefined group of supervisors.

EMPLOYEE: Well, uh. . . . (*A little flustered*) I . . . uh . . . didn't mean anything about you personally. Well . . . uh, that's not true either. It does have something to do with you. (*Pause*)
SUPERVISOR: Lee, I really want to hear what's on your mind, even if it is critical of me. I'd like you to level with me and to speak to me as directly as you can. What suggestions do you have for how I could improve the way that I supervise you?

Once again, the supervisor encourages the employee to speak openly and frankly. Notice how the supervisor asks for constructive suggestions for improvement rather than gripes about what is being done wrong.

EMPLOYEE: Well . . . uh . . . sometimes you have the tendency to . . . uh . . . to give me a lot of work to do without telling me why I should do it. Sometimes it seems like I waste a lot of my time doing things for no purpose at all.
SUPERVISOR: So one of the things I could do is to explain the purpose of the work that I assign to you, to give you a better idea of why I want it done and why it's important.
EMPLOYEE: That would help a lot. A whole lot.
SUPERVISOR: What else could I do to be more helpful to you, Lee?
EMPLOYEE: (*Much more relaxed*) Well, there are a couple of other things . . . if you're sure you'd like to hear them. (*Smiling*)
SUPERVISOR: (*Smiling*) I would like to hear them. Go ahead.

In this example the supervisor made good use of reflecting feeling and probing for specificity to deal with the employee's critical remarks.

PRACTICE RESPONDING TO CRITICAL REMARKS
For some practice, fill in the form on page 99. Use the techniques of reflecting feeling and probing for specificity to respond to the critical remarks.

RESPONDING TO CRITICAL REMARKS

After you read each critical remark, write down how you would respond to the employee who made it.

1. "When you said we were going to have a meeting to review my work performance I didn't realize that it was just going to be another one of these little fireside chats we have every so often."

_____

_____

_____

_____

_____

2. "Why is it that the employees are always having their work performance evaluated and not the supervisors? Can you answer that question?"

_____

_____

_____

_____

_____

3. "Am I having any problems on the job? You're darn right I'm having problems. I'm having problems just having to sit down here to talk with you about my work peformance!"

_____

_____

_____

_____

_____

4. "I think there're a lot of things you could do to become a better supervisor. The most important is to be more sensitive to the needs of your employees!"

_____

_____

_____

_____

LOOK AT THE NEXT PAGE AND COMPARE YOUR ANSWERS TO OURS.

RESPONDING TO CRITICAL REMARKS

*Compare your responses to the ones we'd
have made in each of these situations:*

1. *"When you said we were going to have a meeting to review my work, I didn't realize that it was just going to be another one of these little fireside chats we have every so often."*

   We probably would have reflected feeling and probed for more information by saying, "Carol, you sound pretty annoyed at having to be here. I'd like to hear more about your feelings." If the employee denied this feeling and said, "No, really, I was just kidding," we'd probably persist and say, "Okay, but if you are feeling annoyed, I want to hear about it. We won't be able to get much out of a session like this unless we're open with one another."

2. *"Why is it that the employees are always having their work performance evaluated and not the supervisors? Can you answer that question?"*

   We would not have answered the question, at least not at this moment, when the employee's receptivity was so low. This is a classic example of a question really being a statement in disguise. We would've ignored the content of the remark and responded to the underlying emotion by saying, "Sounds like you're feeling kind of angry and resentful at what seems like an unfair situation." Then we'd have continued to draw the employee out until the person was ready to hear what we had to say.

3. *"Am I having any problems on the job? You're darn right I'm having problems. I'm having problems just having to sit down here to talk with you about my work performance!"*

   We would have reflected feeling first and probed for specificity, if necessary. We probably would have started off by saying, "So you really don't want to be here today." If that failed to move things forward, we might have probed for specificity by saying, "You said it was a real problem to have to sit down here to talk with me about your work performance. What is it that makes it a problem for you?"

4. *"I think there're a lot of things you could do to become a better supervisor. The most important is to be more sensitive to the needs of your employees!"*

   We would have probed for specificity, probably saying, "Tell me, Jack, how could I become more sensitive to the needs of the employees here?" We'd have continued to probe for specificity until the person was able to come up with some concrete and useful advice.

Although it happens rarely, sometimes employees can sabotage the interview by stubbornly refusing to go along with your game plan. When this happens, the interview is at a precarious stage. Here, we'd suggest that you use the *stop, look, and listen technique* to get the interview back on track. It's a simple three-part process in which you:

1. *Stop* the interaction as soon as you see that the discussion is becoming argumentative or unproductive.
2. *Look* squarely at the problem by describing it succinctly and objectively.
3. *Listen* for suggestions that you both can live with for resolving the problem.

Let's say that you've asked an employee to describe any problems that he might be experiencing on the job. After listening to a couple of problems, and actually drawing the employee out in some detail, you respond as follows:

SUPERVISOR: Okay, Jason, I think I've got a pretty good idea about some of the problems you're experiencing on the job. I'd like to defer talking about solutions to those problems until a bit later and move on to a new topic. What—

EMPLOYEE: (*Interrupting*) What do you mean "defer talking about solutions" until later? What's the sense of identifying problems if you don't want to talk about solutions to them?

SUPERVISOR: You're feeling kind of frustrated and irritated about changing the subject before talking about solutions, is that right?

EMPLOYEE: You're damn right I'm feeling frustrated. I mean, it just doesn't make sense to me. Do you understand what I'm saying?

SUPERVISOR: Yes, I think so. You're saying that you want to talk about solutions right now, not after we've discussed other topics.

EMPLOYEE: Exactly. That's exactly what I'm saying.

SUPERVISOR: I also think that talking about solutions is important. And I had planned to spend a lot of time later in the interview to do just that—after we'd talked about some other things, such as your suggestions for how I could make your job more satisfying and a thorough review of your work performance.

EMPLOYEE: Well, I still think it's important to talk about solutions while the problems are still fresh in our minds rather than when they've cooled off.

SUPERVISOR: (*Using stop, look, and listen*) Jason, let's step back from this just for a minute to get a fresh perspective.

It looks like we disagree about how to proceed. You'd like to discuss solutions to some of the problems you identified, while I'd like to talk about solutions after we've covered some other matters. I'd like to find a way out of this disagreement, preferably with a solution that we both can live with. What suggestions do you have for how we might proceed at this point?

EMPLOYEE: (*Thoughtfully*) Hmm . . . I don't really know. (*Smiling*) We can always do it my way. (*Both laugh*) Hmm . . . something we both can live with. Well, we can maybe spend a few minutes talking about solutions. Then, if it looks like we're not going to come up with any solutions quickly, we can talk about it later in the interview.

SUPERVISOR: Good suggestion. How about if we spend ten minutes now talking about some potential solutions. If, after that time, we don't. . . .

When using the stop, look, and listen technique, it's very important to come up with solutions that both people can live with—"win-win" solutions. So often in disagreements, people tend to see things in either-or terms, from a win-lose perspective. However, with a little resourcefulness and a willingness to compromise, it's often easy to identify solutions that will move things forward *and* will be acceptable to both parties. Some of the best "win-win" solutions come from employees.

To review, to deal more effectively with employees who make angry, critical, and disparaging remarks:

☐   Don't lose control of the interview by getting defensive, becoming angry, or biting back.

☐   Focus on the feelings of the employee rather than the content of the remarks. You'll generally get to the heart of the matter more quickly.

☐   Encourage the person to talk even *more*. Probe for specificity.

☐   If necessary, use the stop, look, and listen technique. Stop the unproductive interaction, look at the problem the two of you are facing, and listen for a "win-win" solution.

THE EMPLOYEE WHO TALKS TOO MUCH

Now let's look at the employee who talks a lot—the person who tends to go on and on, especially in the presence of a good listener. Here are some techniques that seem to work pretty well with these long-winded types:

1. Limit the number of open-ended questions or invitations to talk. These are usually quite effective with shy, reticent, or less verbal people, but the talker may see them as an opportunity to hold forth.

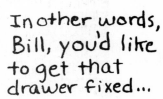

2. Hold down your use of verbal and nonverbal encouragers. Don't nod so much, reduce the number of "uhm-humms," and cut back on direct eye contact. You don't want to completely discourage the person; you just don't want to be too encouraging.

3. After a long-winded response, succinctly summarize what the person said and then move on to another topic quickly, before the person can build upon the summary. This will convey that you are listening but that the message could have been delivered more concisely. However, make certain that the person agrees with your summary before going on. The person will usually let you know with a nod or with some other nonverbal indicator.

4. If you don't get a reasonably direct answer to a question, ignore what the person has said and repeat the question.

5. Reflect the feeling you think the person is trying to express. Many times long-winded people will use a lot of words to avoid expressing their feelings more directly. Reflecting feeling usually helps to cut through a lot of the verbiage.

6. Set some time limits on the interview and remind the person of these time limitations during the course of the interview. This technique often communicates to the employee that long-winded answers will eat up some valuable time.

7. When the employee does give concise and succinct answers, make positive and rewarding comments. Remarks such as "Nicely put" or "That was a very clear and concise answer. Nice job!" help get an employee to reply briefly.

Here are a few examples of supervisors using some of these approaches:

EMPLOYEE: (*Responding to a question about how things are going*) Oh, pretty well, I guess. I guess I'd have to say that the thing I like most about working here is the convenient location. You know, the subway stop is less than a block from my house and only a block from here. (*Employee continues to talk about this subject, while supervisor maintains eye contact, but reduces frequency of nodding and facial expressions*) Uh . . . oh . . . things have really improved since Buff was hired. You have no idea the effect that it's had on lightening the work load and brightening up the morale around here. Why just the other day several of us were talking. . . .
SUPERVISOR: (*Listening for several more minutes, then breaking in when the employee stops for a second to catch*

a breath) Okay, so what I hear you saying is that things are going pretty well. You seem especially happy about how easy it is to get to and from work and you're pleased with how things have gone since we hired that additional person to lighten the work load.

EMPLOYEE: Oh yes. (*Looking as if he's ready to say something else*)

SUPERVISOR: (*Quickly interrupting*) Okay, good. Now, let me get your ideas on another subject. Tell me, what. . . .

SUPERVISOR: You mentioned that Bill wasn't very reliable. I'm not sure what you meant by *reliable*. Tell me a little more about that.

EMPLOYEE: Oh, Bill's all right. You know, he really does some things very well. Why, I've seen him take a whole stack of orders and. . . . (*Continuing for several minutes about Bill's good points*)

SUPERVISOR: (*Ignoring answer and repeating original question*) I see. Now earlier you said that he wasn't very reliable. How did you mean that?

SUPERVISOR: Pat, how do you feel about the new assignment you got last week?

EMPLOYEE: You know, that's gonna be a lot of work. For one thing. . . . (*Explaining for several minutes about how much work will be involved*) Now that's not to mention all of the other responsibilities I currently have. For example, . . . (*Enumerating current responsibilities in more detail than is necessary*)

SUPERVISOR: (*As employee pauses*) Sounds like you feel pretty frustrated with the assignment and also maybe a little annoyed that we didn't think about all your current responsibilities when we made the assignment?

EMPLOYEE: (*Slightly taken aback*) Uh . . . yes! That's exactly how I feel!

SUPERVISOR: (*Responding quickly*) I can understand that, Pat. And I want you to know that you don't have to beat around the bush with me. I want to know how you're feeling. The more direct you are with me the better.

PRACTICE RESPONDING TO A TALKATIVE EMPLOYEE

Ready for a little practice? Again, if you've got a tape recorder and someone to practice with, you'll get more out of this than if you just use your imagination.

Imagine that you ask the employee, "I'd like to hear your thoughts on the new quality control procedures," and you get the following response: "Well, I'm not really sure. But the thing is, I'm more concerned about the inventory problems we've got. Why, just yesterday. . . . (*Going off on a tangent that has nothing to do with your question*)

How would you respond? Write in your answer in the space below and compare your response to ours.

Employee: Why, just yesterday. . . .

You: _____

_____

_____

_____

_____

_____

_____

In a situation such as this, we'd suggest ignoring the answer the person gave and just repeating the original question. We'd wait until the person winds down a bit to break in with, "I see. And what's your opinion of the new quality control procedures we've instituted?"

A QUICK SUMMARY

Finding out how things are going means asking the employee to talk to you about three basic things:

1. How things are going in general on the job,
2. Any problems he or she might be experiencing on the job, and
3. Suggestions for how you can make the employee's job less frustrating and more satisfying.

After walking through an example of a supervisor conducting this part of the interview, you had an opportunity to practice it and to give yourself some feedback. Finally, you learned some useful techniques for dealing with two possible problems that may crop up at this stage of the process: the employee who makes critical remarks and the employee who talks a lot.

In the next chapter you'll learn how to get employees to do an analysis of their own performance before you present your analysis of their performance.

CHAPTER 9 • STEP FIVE: GET YOUR EMPLOYEE TO DO A SELF-ANALYSIS

Up to this point we've covered the first four steps of the ten-step performance improvement process:

STEP ONE: Analyze Your Employee's Performance
STEP TWO: Ask Your Employee to Meet with You
STEP THREE: Begin the Interview
STEP FOUR: Find Out How Things Are Going

Now we're ready to move into a more sensitive area: a discussion of the employee's actual work performance. Before your pulse rate goes up too high, however, remember that we're talking about a constructive discussion, a discussion that's designed to help the employee improve and grow in the job. This doesn't mean that you can always avoid a situation in which an employee will get defensive or touchy during the discussion. But the approach we recommend in this and the next step will help you keep these kinds of negative reactions to a minimum.

Well, I'd have to say I'm a pretty good nurse...

WHY YOUR EMPLOYEE'S SELF-ANALYSIS IS IMPORTANT

The best way to begin a discussion of an employee's work performance is to get the employee to talk about it before you, the supervisor, do. A little later in this chapter we'll get into the specifics of how to get employees to do a self-analysis. But first let's take a look at the several reasons why it makes good sense to have employees talk with you about how they see their own on-the-job performance:

1. Getting employees to talk freely and openly about how they view their work performance is one of the best strategies for getting them involved in improving their performance. It's rare for a person who plays a significant role in our lives—a boss, spouse, parent, or friend—to give us an open invitation to talk about the things we think we do well and the areas in which we'd like to improve. By going through this kind of analytical process, it's almost impossible for employees not to get more involved and invest more effort in improving their job performance. And the interest you have already shown in their viewpoints will act as a form of encouragement.

2. You get a much clearer picture of how your view of an employee's performance compares with the employee's view. This will be important later in the interview when you negotiate a performance agreement with the employee—that is, when the two of you try to reach an agreement on specific tasks that you'll both work on to help the employee improve job performance. The more initial agreement between the two of you on the specific areas where the employee needs to improve, the smoother this negotiation process will go. Even if the two of you initially disagree in your opinions of what needs to be worked on, a good understanding of how the employee views personal strengths and deficiencies will make you a much more effective negotiator than you'd be without this information.

3. You often get new information about what an employee is doing well on the job and about the areas where some improvement is needed. You may be surprised to learn that employees are able to document that they're performing very effectively in ways that you weren't even aware of. You may also be pleased to learn that an employee has identified some specific skills—for example, technical writing or public speaking—that the person would very much like to improve and may have already started to do so. This can be valuable information later in the interview when it comes to negotiating the performance agreement. By acknowledging improvement in these areas, you may make employees more willing to work on others.

HOW TO GET AN EMPLOYEE TO DO A SELF-ANALYSIS

Step Five in the performance improvement process is as simple and straightforward as the previous four. Its purpose is to help an employee:

☐ Identify several areas where he thinks he's performing effectively and cite at least one concrete example of how he's performing effectively in each of these areas; and
☐ Identify several areas where she thinks she could stand some improvement and discuss some specific things that she could do to actually show improvement in each of these areas.

What you're trying to do, then, is to help employees do some careful, analytical thinking about their job performance. To get an employee to do this kind of thinking out loud:

1. Make some kind of transition statement that lets your employee know you'd like to move on to a new topic.
2. Explain exactly what it is you'd like the employee to talk about.
3. Actively listen (with special emphasis on attending behavior, probing for specificity, summarizing, and paraphrasing) until you're satisfied that the person has given you the kind of detailed information you're looking for.

To show you how this is done, let's listen in on a performance improvement interview between Clara Boothby, a forty-two-year-old head nurse of the pediatric ward in a suburban hospital, and Maura Meskill, a pediatric nurse in her first job after nursing school:

CLARA: Maura, I think I have a pretty good idea of how things are going for you on the job and some of the problem areas I can help clear up. Now I'd like to change the subject a bit. Earlier I mentioned that I'd ask you to describe how you think you're doing on your job. . . .

Notice how the supervisor starts off with a transition statement that makes a nice link between the old and new subjects of conversation. Now notice how Clara explains to Maura what she would like her to talk about.

CLARA: I'd like you to start by telling me several things that you think you do particularly well on the job. And for each one of those things I'd like you to give me a specific example of how you do that particular thing well. (*Pause*)

MAURA: Okay. (*Looking a little puzzled*)

CLARA: For instance, let's say that my boss had just asked me to do this kind of self-analysis. And let's say that one of the things I thought I was pretty good at was written communication. To give her an example of how I think I'm good at written communication I might say, "I think I write clear memos that get right to the point, and a number of people in the department and throughout the hospital have actually told me that they never have any trouble understanding what I've written." See what I mean?

MAURA: Okay, I think I see what you mean.

CLARA: All right, Maura, why don't you give it a try.

Now that Clara has made a transition statement and has explained how she'd like Maura to do a self-analysis, let's see how she gets the kind of specific information she's looking for. Notice how Clara makes heavy use of the listening skills covered in Chapter 7. Also notice that she's very careful to avoid making judgments or evaluations of what Maura is saying, even though she may disagree. Doing this would make Maura's receptivity drop like a stone.

MAURA: Well, as you know, this is my first real nursing job, and I'm still learning a lot about what I'm good at and not so good at. (*Pause*) But even though it sounds like I'm tooting my own horn, I guess I'd have to say that there are some things I'm pretty good at.

CLARA: (*Nodding and leaning forward slightly*) What are some of them, Maura?

MAURA: Well, for one, I think I relate well to the children. (*Pause*) I also think I'm flexible. (*Pause*) Oh yeah, I also think I'm good at responding quickly in an emergency. (*Pause, looking thoughtful*) I guess that's about it.

CLARA: All right, Maura, I heard you mention three things. One, you're good at relating to the children. Two, you're flexible. And three, you respond quickly in emergency situations. (*Pause*)

MAURA: That's right. (*Tentatively*) And I think there's one more thing.

CLARA: Go ahead, Maura. I'd like to hear it.

MAURA: I guess it has to do with relating well to the parents of the children as well as to the children. You know, answering their questions, paying attention to their feelings, too. That sort of thing.

CLARA: Okay, so another thing you feel you're good at is responding to parents' questions and concerns, is that it?

MAURA: Right. Exactly.

CLARA: Maura, let's take the first thing you mentioned, relating well to children. In what ways are you good at relating to children? What are some of the things that you do that lead you to conclude that this is one of your strong points?

MAURA: Well, that's a hard question. (*Smiling*) But a good one! (*Pause*) Let's see. I think it's because I try to communicate with the children on their level.

CLARA: Uhm-humm.

MAURA: You know, I try to use the kinds of words they use. I try to explain medical terms in their language, in words they can understand. (*Pause*)

CLARA: Okay. Anything else?

MAURA: Another thing is . . . well, so many children are so fearful when they come here. They're sick or injured, away from home for the first time, and in a strange and scary place. I try to take the fear out of the situation by becoming their friend.

CLARA: How do you mean that, Maura?

MAURA: Oh, I guess by playing little games with them, telling them stories and jokes to make them laugh, by saying good-bye when I'm going off duty. (*Pause*) Also by getting them to tell me about their family lives, about their brothers and sisters, their parents, and their pets.

CLARA: (*Pausing to make sure Maura is finished*) I see. So some of the ways in which you're good at relating to the children is by communicating with them at their level and by helping to reduce the fearfulness of the situation by becoming their hospital friend, is that right?

MAURA: Right. I think things like that are so important.

CLARA: So do I. Very important. (*Pause*) Maura, let's move on now to a second thing you're good at — one that's probably similar to this first area — that of relating well to the parents of the children. Tell me what you do that makes you good at responding to the questions and concerns of parents.

Having covered the first area, Clara now moves on to the second area, where she'll also probe to find out what Maura actually does that makes her conclude that this is one of her strong points. After that, she'll move on to the third area that Maura identified — being flexible. Let's pick up their interview as they begin to discuss the fourth area Maura identified.

CLARA: I think I've got a pretty good idea of what you mean by being flexible, Maura. Let's move on to the last area, responding quickly in emergencies. How did you mean that?

MAURA: (*Pause*) Uh, I guess I mean that I'm good at keeping my head in a tense or critical situation. I guess I've always been that way. I don't get all discombobulated like some people do.

CLARA: Can you give me an example of what you mean?

MAURA: Sure. (*Pause*) Of course, you remember the Kalas child. How could we forget all the scares she gave everybody around here! (*Pause*) Anyway, I'll never forget that night when Katie discovered that she had stopped breathing. She yelled out for me and I dropped everything. When I got there, I could see that she was all plugged up with mucus, so I suctioned it out right away. Then I gave her a couple of seconds of oxygen to get her breathing normally again. I wasn't nervous or scared during the entire episode. But afterward. . . .

Once Clara was satisfied that she'd gotten enough information in the areas where Maura thinks she's performing effectively, she'd briefly summarize all of the main points that were covered. Then she'd make a transition statement and ask Maura to do an analysis of how she could improve her work performance.

CLARA: Okay, Maura, I think you did a nice job of explaining how you're performing effectively on the job. Now let's move to the other side of the coin. (*Pause*) I'd like you to identify several areas where you could stand to improve your work performance, those areas where you aren't performing as effectively as you might be. I'd also like you to think about some of the specific things you'd actually have to do to say that you had improved in each area. (*Pause*) For example, one of the areas where I'd like to improve is handling conflicts between nurses and other hospital staff. One thing I know I could do to improve in that area is to sit down with both parties together rather than one at a time, which is what I have a tendency to do. Okay?

Notice that Clara gives a complete explanation of what she wants the employee to do, in spite of the fact that Maura is probably catching on by now. At this point, Clara will shift back into an active listening mode, just as she was doing earlier.

MAURA: I think I see what you mean. But don't you think you're in a better position to tell me what areas I need to improve. I mean you're very familiar with my work now. (*Pause*)

CLARA: Yes, I do think I'm in a good position to talk about some ways you could improve. But for now, I'd like to get some of your thoughts. I'll add my suggestions later.

Notice how Clara puts the responsibility back on Maura's shoulders and how Maura accepts it. If she hadn't, Clara would have used her listening skills to resolve the problem.

MAURA: Okay. That sounds fair enough. (*Pause*) Let's see. (*Thinking out loud*) Areas where I could stand to improve. (*Pause*) Uh, the biggest thing—and I know you'll agree with this because you've reminded me of it often enough—has to do with the nursing care plans. I, uh, I definitely think I can improve by being more conscientious about writing up the nursing care plans when I finish my shift. (*Pause, looking thoughtful*) Oh yeah, another thing has to do with being better about getting here on time, especially when I'm working the day shift. (*Smiling*) Getting going in the morning has always been a bit of a problem . . . and it's starting to show up here, too.

CLARA: Uhm-humm. (*Pause*) So two areas where you could stand to improve are being more conscientious about writing up nursing care plans and getting to work on time.

MAURA: Yeah, and . . . and another thing I can think of has to do with being more interested in my professional growth and development.

CLARA: I'm not sure I understand how you mean that, Maura. . . .

MAURA: You know, attending workshops and seminars to improve my nursing skills. I haven't done anything in that area this past year. I guess I've been away from school long enough now that the idea of being back in a classroom doesn't sound too bad anymore. (*Smiling*)

CLARA: I think I know exactly what you mean there! (*Smiling*) Okay, the third area, then, has to do with improving your nursing skills through some kind of in-service training. Anything else?

MAURA: No, I can't think of anything right now.

Up to this point Clara has gotten Maura to identify three general areas where she'd like to improve her job performance. After summarizing the three major areas, Clara will help Maura think out what she'll have to do specifically to improve in each area.

CLARA: Maura, let's start with the first area you mentioned, being more conscientious about writing up nursing care plans. What are some of the things you'd have to do to satisfy yourself that you'd actually improved your performance in this area?

MAURA: Hmm . . . that's a toughie. (*Pause*) Well, for one thing, I'd just have to spend more time working on them. I put them off until the last minute, and I usually end up scribbling my notes so they're kind of hard for incoming nurses to read. (*Pause*) Uh, another thing is that, because I'm rushing, I sometimes forget to write in some important information, like medication that I gave or some kind of request that a patient made. (*Pause*)

CLARA: Okay, so to improve in this area you'd have to take the time to write notes that are legible and also complete?

MAURA: Right. If they were legible and complete I would definitely say I had improved in this area. And so would quite a few other people who have to read them. (*Smiling*)

CLARA: (*Smiling*) All right. A little later, we'll talk about what you might actually do to achieve that goal. But now let's turn to the second area where you thought you could stand some improvement—arriving at work on time. What do you think you would have to do to convince yourself that you had improved in that area?

MAURA: (*Smiling*) That's easy! Just get to work on time.

CLARA: Okay. But I wonder if you could be just a little more specific than that. For example, if you got to work on time every day for the next five days, would you say you had achieved your goal?

MAURA: Oh . . . I see what you mean. (*Pause*) Uh . . . I guess now I arrive just a few minutes late about twice a week. Hmm. I guess I'd say that if I cut that down to being late only once a month that I'd have achieved the goal.

A QUICK SECTION SUMMARY

When you want to get employees to do a self-analysis of the areas in which they think they're performing effectively and where they think they could stand some improvement, you do the following three things:

1. You make a transition statement to the new topic of discussion.
2. You explain precisely what it is you want the employee to talk about.
3. You actively listen to the employee, making heavy use of attending behavior, asking open-ended questions, probing for specificity, and summarizing and paraphrasing, until you think that the employee has thought through the self-analysis in enough detail.

POSSIBLE SETBACKS

It's unlikely that you're going to encounter much difficulty in getting your employees involved in this part of the interview. We've found that most people actually enjoy taking a thoughtful look at their own performance and that they often get very caught up in and stimulated by the process.

However, there are a couple of areas where you may run into a little difficulty. Both have to do with situations in which the employee's analysis is very different from the one you would make. More specifically:

1. An employee identifies as areas of strength precisely those areas where you think he needs a lot of improvement.
2. An employee identifies areas of needed improvement that are very different from the areas you think she needs to work on.

DISAGREEMENTS ABOUT AREAS OF STRENGTH

Let's take the first situation in which employees think they're very capable in precisely those areas where you think they need a lot of improvement.

Imagine that you're a manufacturing plant supervisor and you're conducting a performance improvement interview with one of your foremen. You've explained that you'd like him to describe some of the areas where he thinks he's performing particularly effectively on the job and also to give you some examples of his performance in each of these areas. You feel that the areas that need improvement include motivating his people, meeting production deadlines, and making judgment decisions. The employee starts his self-analysis by saying:

EMPLOYEE: Okay . . . let me think about that for a second.
YOU: (*Nodding*) Fine, take your time. I'm really interested in what you have to say.
EMPLOYEE: Well, I think I get along pretty well with my people and get a lot of production out of them. I think I'm a pretty good decision maker. And I think I'm pretty good at getting the work out on time.

At this point, you're very surprised. The employee has described himself as being pretty good in the three areas where you frankly think he needs a lot of improvement. In the space below, write down how you would respond to the employee at this point. Once you've filled in your response, compare it with ours.

Employee: Well, I think that I get along pretty well with my people and get a lot of production out of them. I think I'm a pretty good decision maker. And I think I'm pretty good at getting work out on time.

You: _____

_____

_____

_____

_____

If we were you, here's how we would have responded to the employee:

YOU: All right, so it sounds like you feel you're pretty good at motivating your people, meeting production deadlines, and making decisions.

EMPLOYEE: Yeah, I'd say those are the things I think I'm pretty good at.

YOU: (*Very calmly, without letting on that you disagree*) Okay. Let's take the area of motivating your people. Why don't you give me some examples of things that you've done that you feel were effective in motivating your people.

EMPLOYEE: Okay. Well one thing I can think of right away is the production records notebook I keep and how I review it every so often with my machinists.

YOU: (*Leaning forward slightly*) That sounds interesting. Tell me more about that.

EMPLOYEE: Well, it works like this. . . .

Notice what we were trying to show you here. It was very tempting for you to openly disagree with the employee and to say something like:

"Now wait a minute. I think we're pretty far apart in our thinking on what you do well on the job and what you don't. I think we have to find some way to clear up this difference of opinion."

However, saying something like this would have had a very negative effect on the employee's receptivity, and it almost certainly would have forced you into an argument. By using active listening skills instead, you gain several advantages:

1. You get a much more detailed picture of why an employee thinks he's good in these particular areas. It may be, in this example, that "motivating his people" means something very different to your foreman than it means to you. This is potentially important information about how he sees his job that you could only get by actively listening to him.

2. By asking for specific examples of effective per-formance in each area, you may well learn some things that you didn't know the employee was doing. For instance, in this example you weren't aware that your foreman was keeping a production notebook. Based on this kind of information, you might even want to revise your analysis of the employee's performance.

3. You'll keep the employee's receptivity high. At this point, it simply pays to keep the employee talking. Given that this kind of self-analysis is motivating to most employees, the last thing you want to do is interrupt a person, injecting your own opinions and noting how they differ from the employee's. It could seriously damage all the hard work you had done so far to build up the person's receptivity. You'll have a chance to present your analysis of the employee's performance in the next step of the process.

DISAGREEMENTS ABOUT AREAS IN NEED OF IMPROVEMENT

Now let's consider the second potential trouble spot—the situation in which the employee mentions areas in need of improvement that are very different from the areas of improvement that you had in mind. What do you do in a case like that?

Our advice is exactly the same as it was in the first situation—actively listen. At this stage of the interview your goal should be to learn as much as you can about:

☐   What areas the employee would like to improve in,
☐   The specific evidence that he would accept for improved performance in each of these areas, and
☐   Why she feels it is important to improve in these areas.

Active listening is the best way to get this kind of information. Even if you strongly disagree with an employee's self-analysis, this is not the place to share your opinions. You'll have your opportunity to do that in the next step when you present your analysis of the employee's performance.

CHAPTER 10
GET YOUR MESSAGE ACROSS: PRESENTING IDEAS EFFECTIVELY

Up to this point in the interview you've been primarily in a listening mode—asking questions, drawing your employee out, probing for further information, and making sure you heard things correctly. Except for the first few minutes of the interview, when you explained the purposes of the meeting and what was going to happen, the employee has done almost all of the talking.

Now it's time to shift gears. You're about to present your analysis of the employee's performance. Instead of listening to the employee's ideas, you'll be presenting your own. The purpose of this chapter is to help you do this as effectively as possible. It will show you how to:

- Hear yourself as others hear you (maybe for the first time),
- Attend to people when you talk to them by using your eyes, your arms, and the rest of your body as tools to get your messages across,
- Avoid the fuzzies by speaking clearly and not using confusing or ambiguous language,
- Avoid emotionally loaded expressions that lower an employee's receptivity,
- Stop talking and start listening when the employee's receptivity dips,
- Pay attention to pace and timing while you talk, and
- Preview, deliver, and summarize your messages.

WHY PRESENTATION SKILLS ARE SO IMPORTANT

Think about some supervisors you know who are pretty lousy at communicating their ideas to other people, particularly their employees. What makes them so bad? What do they do that confuses, distracts, or turns off other people? Try to be as descriptive as you can, recording your answers in the space below.

_____

_____

_____

_____

_____

_____

_____

_____

_____

Here's a sampling of complaints we've heard from employees about their supervisors' poor presentation skills:

"I had this supervisor who would never look at me when she was talking. She was kind of timid and would always look down or slightly away from me when she talked. Because she didn't look me straight in the eye, I never really gave her ideas much weight."

"The supervisor I'm thinking about was always trying to impress people with his knowledge and expertise. If there was ever a choice between a five-cent word and a twenty-five-cent word, you know which one he'd choose. Half the time we couldn't understand him and the other half we were so turned off we didn't pay any attention to what he said."

"I had this supervisor who had longish brown hair. Every time she started talking, she would run her fingers through her hair, starting close to her scalp and slowly going all the way to the end. At times it was very distracting. I'd just watch her do it and not even hear her words."

"I had a supervisor once who talked verrry slooowly and in a real monotone. He always talked the same way, too, whether he was excited or bored. He put me to sleep whenever he opened his mouth."

"I once worked for this young woman who was fresh out of college. She had this particularly irritating habit of saying 'ya know' after every two or three words. It was 'ya know this' and 'ya know that.' She was quite intelligent, but this made her sound almost inarticulate."

"I had this supervisor that we used to call 'garbage mouth' because he never said anything nice. He was often fairly abusive, calling people 'stupid,' 'bitchy,' or 'asinine.' You can imagine how much we listened to his suggestions."

Just as good listening skills have an important effect on employee receptivity, so do good presentation skills. Lack of skill in both areas will reduce a person's openness to what you've got to say. To get a person ready to listen, you have to listen skillfully yourself. To keep a person listening, you've got to present your ideas and thoughts effectively.

HEAR YOURSELF AS OTHERS HEAR YOU

Many people don't know how they sound to others, much less how well they present their ideas. When people do hear their voices for the first time, they're often surprised at the difference between how they sound to others and how they sound to themselves. This is true even for people who have heard themselves on audiotape many times. A participant in one of our workshops recently told us:

"I dictate all my correspondence, so I'm used to hearing my voice. But I always thought I sounded that way because I was using a cheap tape recorder!"

To get an idea of how you sound to others, tape record yourself talking naturally to someone else. Find a friend or coworker who'll listen attentively as you talk. If you can't find someone, go it alone. Just pretend you're talking to someone. The goal is to come up with a recording of your normal speaking style.

When you've finished, replay it quickly. Don't be too surprised if your initial reaction is a little negative. Many people don't like the way their voices sound the first time. Listen to the tape once more. This time try not to evaluate it; just become familiar with your voice and your speaking style. Use the following questions as a guide:

☐ Listen to the tempo of your voice. How quickly or slowly do you speak? Does your voice speed up and slow down or does it always travel at about the same speed? How does your voice reflect changes in your level of excitement or enthusiasm?

☐ What do you like most about your voice? What makes it an interesting or entertaining voice? In what ways would you change your voice to improve it? How could you become even more easy or pleasant to listen to?

☐ What distracting mannerisms do you have that get in the way? Do you have bad habits such as saying "Ya know" or "Okay" much too often?

☐ How well do you articulate your words? Are the words crisp and clear when you speak or do you tend to slur or run them together?

☐ How about your volume? Do you tend to speak so softly that people have to lean forward just to hear you speak? Or do you bowl them over with your loudness?

☐ What do other people have to say about your voice or your speaking style? Ask them for their reactions to the tape. What do they think you do well? What do they think you could change to improve?

☐ How much do you use the upper and lower registers of your voice? Is your voice high or low? Nasal or throaty? How does your voice change when you become sober or serious? When you become happy or friendly?

ATTEND TO PEOPLE WHEN YOU TALK TO THEM

In Chapter 7 we talked about listening skills and the importance of attending behavior when you're trying to get other people to talk. Attending is probably even more important when *you're* talking.

To review, *attending* means paying attention to and showing interest in another person. It has three components:

1. Making eye contact,
2. Using good body language, and
3. Minimizing distractions.

MAKING EYE CONTACT

We've noticed an interesting thing about eye contact. Some people are very good at looking people directly in the eye when they're listening. But when they start talking, they break direct eye contact. They look up, down, and all around. It's almost as if they're literally searching for the exact words to express their next thought. This is distracting for the listener, who usually assumes the talker is nervous, uncertain, or lacks confidence.

When you're talking to people, make a conscious effort to look them directly in the eye. Rather than stare at them, break eye contact periodically so that you're looking at them directly 70 to 80 percent of the time. You'll probably tend to break contact when you're making a transition from one topic to another or when you're thinking about what to say next.

That's fine. Those natural breaks are expected. But don't make them too frequent or too prolonged. Otherwise you'll lose your listener's attention.

USING GOOD BODY LANGUAGE

You don't just talk with your voice. You also use your body, particularly your face, arms, and hands. Too often, bad body language gets in the way. For example, no matter how eloquent you are or how much sense you make, you aren't likely to get your message across very well if you:

☐ Don't directly face the person you're talking to,
☐ Look down at the floor or up at the ceiling when speaking,
☐ Talk with an expressionless stone face,
☐ Slouch or lean way back in your chair, or
☐ Don't use any hand or arm gestures.

Here are some ideas on how you can use body language to improve your presentation style:

1. "Aim" your body and eyes directly at the listener. Try to position your head, shoulders, and torso directly toward your listener. There should also be a direct line between your eyes and the other person's eyes. Some people have the habit of tilting their heads upward when they speak so that they literally look down their noses at the listener. Others have a tendency to tilt their heads down and look up as they're talking, as if they were speaking over those old-fashioned, half-circle reading glasses. Remember to face the person directly.

2. Use your facial muscles. Your face, especially around your mouth and eyes, is filled with muscles. Take advantage of them when you speak:

☐ Smile,
☐ Wrinkle your forehead,
☐ Widen your eyes,
☐ Clench your teeth, and
☐ Raise your eyebrows.

Using these techniques will not only make you more interesting to listen to, but you'll seem more persuasive because you'll be expressing how you feel about your message.

3. Lean forward slightly. In addition to facing the listener and making direct eye contact, it's a good idea to tilt your upper torso slightly toward people when you're speaking to them. Don't slouch. Get into a comfortable position with your body directly facing the listener and leaning forward slightly.

4. Use gestures. Gesturing simply means using your arms, hands, and other body parts to help give the listener a clearer picture of what you're saying. It helps to emphasize certain points (hold up two fingers and say, "I want you to remember just two points"), and it brings life to scenes and situations that you're trying to describe.

Below is a brief anecdote. As you read through it, imagine how a stiff, uninteresting person would present it to an audience. Then imagine how one of your more animated friends might tell it. Then try it yourself. Stand in front of a mirror and describe the same scene out loud, first underplaying and then exaggerating the use of gestures.

"I was jogging along the other day, and I happened across these two interesting guys. One was built like a Sumo wrestler: very short, very round, with a protruding stomach. He was bald on top, but he had this very curly hair that stuck out all around his head. Just like Bozo, the Clown. The other guy was about six feet two and thin as a rail. They were both talking a mile a minute, laughing and talking and using a lot of arm and hand gestures. They were completely tuned in to each other and totally oblivious to anything or anybody around them. Then I just kept jogging right along."

To summarize, your presentation style will improve if you adopt these effective uses of body language:

☐ Directly face people you're talking to.
☐ Use your facial muscles.
☐ Lean your upper body forward slightly.
☐ Use gestures.

MINIMIZING DISTRACTIONS

Minimizing distractions is as important to good presenting as it is to good listening. In addition to the distractions covered in Chapter 7 in regard to listening skills, some others to avoid when you start talking to people include:

☐ The overuse of phrases such as "you know," "right," "okay," and "like,"
☐ The frequent repetition of stock phrases such as "to reiterate," "ipso facto," "albeit," and "if I might be so bold,"

☐   The use of the same example again and again,

☐   Mannerisms such as running your fingers through your hair, stroking your beard, using a toothpick, and twirling a strand of hair around a finger.

Listeners often pay so much attention to these repetitive behaviors that they completely tune out the person who's talking. We know a manager who had the habit of closing his eyes and placing his thumb and index finger on his temples when he was listening (bad enough) and when he was talking (even worse). One of his employees said, "Who could listen to him? It was like watching someone with a perpetual migraine headache."

If you have any distracting habits and mannerisms, you probably aren't aware of them. That's part of the problem; they're real blind spots. Periodically listening to yourself on audiotape (or, even better, seeing yourself on videotape) will help. It's also a good idea to ask for feedback from people you feel comfortable with and whose judgment you trust. In either case, you'll end up more aware of how you come across to people and the effect that your habits and mannerisms have on them.

To summarize, good attending behavior is as important when you're presenting as when you're listening. Maintain direct eye contact, use good body language, and minimize distractions.

AVOID THE FUZZIES

Here are some typical comments we've heard managers and supervisors make to their employees:

"You should take more pride in your work."
"I'd like you to improve the credibility of your sales pitch."
"I think you should adopt a more professional orientation."
"You need to work on being more decisive."
"You're going to have to improve your attitude."

What's wrong with them? If you examine them carefully, you'll see that they don't describe how supervisors want their employees to behave. They're a series of abstractions, or what Robert Mager, in his book *Goal Analysis* (Pitman Learning, 1972), calls "fuzzies."

Fuzzies are words that sound good but don't say very much. They aren't useful because they don't describe what employees need to *do* to show that they've lived up to their supervisor's expectations. And if employees aren't clear on what their supervisors want them to do, they're not very likely to do it.

The best way to avoid a case of the fuzzies is to use action words rather than abstractions. Action words clearly describe the specific behavior that you'd like to see an employee demonstrate.

Whenever you find yourself about to use an abstract word, ask yourself the question, "What are some of the things the person would have to do to convince me that the person has accomplished what I'm asking?" For example, say you're thinking about asking for improvement in an employee's attitude. When you ask the question, "What are the things the person will have to do to demonstrate an improvement in attitude?" you come up with the following list:

☐ He'll ask for additional work when he's completed tasks already assigned.
☐ She'll ask me to explain company policy when she disagrees with it.
☐ He'll speak to me directly about complaints instead of to coworkers.
☐ She'll speak more positively about her job, her coworkers, or the company.
☐ He'll discuss areas of disagreement with me without raising his voice.
☐ She'll greet me and coworkers with a smile in the morning when she arrives.

Here's a little practice. Imagine that you want the receptionist in your office to be more friendly and courteous to people when they walk into your office. This is another real fuzzy. Ask yourself the question, "What will the employee have to do to show more friendly and courteous behavior?" Answer the question in the space below and then compare your ideas to ours.

What will the receptionist have to do to show more friendly and courteous behavior?

The receptionist will have to: _____

_____

_____

_____

_____

_____

Here's how we would have answered the question:

The receptionist will:

☐ Make direct eye contact and smile at visitors when they enter,
☐ Use the names of people when addressing them,
☐ Ask "How can I help you?" when people approach the desk,
☐ Say "Please make yourself comfortable," or an equivalent, when asking people to wait in reception area,
☐ Engage in friendly conversation with people while they're waiting,
☐ Ask visitors if they have any questions the receptionist can answer while they're waiting, and
☐ Make positive comments about the dress or appearance of visitors.

Later in the book we'll show how points like these can be made by a supervisor in a performance improvement interview.

AVOID EMOTIONALLY LOADED EXPRESSIONS

Emotionally loaded expressions are words, phrases, or sentences that cause employees to feel resentful, hurt, or angry. They tend to fall into three categories:

1. Criticisms that include potentially insulting words:

   "Bill, you're just too fussy."
   "If you weren't such a hothead, we could resolve this dispute."
   "That was a stupid thing to say."

2. Questions that put employees on the defensive:

   "Is that the best you can do?"
   "Do you really think you can gain his cooperation by threatening him?"
   "Do you really expect me to believe a story like that?"

3. Absolute statements or exaggerations:

   "You always take ten minutes longer for lunch than anybody else."
   "That was the most ridiculous thing you could possibly have said."
   "You always blame your mistakes on everybody but yourself."

You should try to completely avoid using emotionally loaded expressions: They turn people off. Some employees don't respond openly to them but try to get back at you in subtle ways. Others are more direct. They remind you that you're not perfect, and they start pointing out some of the areas in which you need improvement. Or they get flustered and defensive by explaining all the mitigating circumstances that led them to act the way they did. Whatever their reactions, you can forget about getting much involvement or cooperation from them for a while.

Emotionally loaded expressions are tempting to use, especially when you're feeling angry, annoyed, or frustrated over what an employee has done. But try to avoid them. They'll only make things worse. On the opposite page you'll have a chance to practice analyzing emotionally-loaded expressions.

B E PREPARED TO STOP TALKING AND TO START LISTENING

Sometimes an employee's willingness to listen to you—his or her receptivity—drops very quickly. Maybe it's because you used an emotionally loaded expression. Perhaps you used a "fuzzy" that confused the person. Or maybe you said something that the employee flatly disagreed with. Whatever the reason, it's usually pretty easy to see a decline in receptivity. For example, your employee may:

☐ Look confused,
☐ Start to argue,
☐ Look away,
☐ Show an expression of disagreement,
☐ Shake his head back and forth,
☐ Look startled or astonished,
☐ Furrow her eyebrows,
☐ Raise his eyes to the ceiling,
☐ Begin to interrupt,
☐ Fold her arms firmly,
☐ Lean way back in the chair,
☐ Hold out his hands to signal "stop," or
☐ Look like she wants to say something.

Whenever you see an employee's level of receptivity drop, stop talking and start listening. If you keep on talking, the person won't listen. And talking to somebody who's not listening is a big waste of time.

Here's an example. The supervisor, an office manager, has sat down with the company's receptionist to discuss work performance. It's at the point in the interview where the office

EMOTIONALLY LOADED EXPRESSIONS

In the following list of phrases, there are five emotionally loaded expressions and five helpful comments. Put a check mark (√) next to the emotionally loaded expressions. Then compare your answers to ours.

_____ 1. "I'd like you to come and tell me when you have no more assigned work to do."

_____ 2. "I think you'd be a lot better off if you weren't so thin-skinned."

_____ 3. "That was kind of a silly remark, wasn't it?"

_____ 4. "I'd like you to spend more time on planning and less on double-checking the expense reports."

_____ 5. "Before you decide yours is the best way, I'd like you to listen to my idea."

_____ 6. "What were you trying to prove in there anyway?"

_____ 7. "What are some other ways you might be able to reach the same objective?"

_____ 8. "You're never at your work station when I need to talk to you."

_____ 9. "Why do you always do that when the boss comes around?"

_____ 10. "What did that buyer say or do that made you so angry?"

ANSWERS AND DISCUSSION

_____ 1. This is a specific, reasonable request.

__√__ 2. Most people don't like to be called thin-skinned.

__√__ 3. Being called silly is insulting.

_____ 4. Same as 1.

_____ 5. Same as 1.

__√__ 6. A hostile question.

_____ 7. A helpful, open-ended question.

__√__ 8. An absolute, unhelpful statement.

__√__ 9. A double whammy: an absolute statement combined with a question that puts the employee on the defensive.

_____ 10. Probing for specificity gives the employee an opportunity to explain things without becoming defensive.

manager is offering her analysis of the receptionist's performance:

SUPERVISOR: Well, I think one of the areas where you could stand to improve is the way you handle visitors when they walk in the door. I think you could be friendlier and more courteous to them. . . .
EMPLOYEE: (*Sitting up straight and interrupting*) What?!!

Now, it would be very easy for the supervisor to continue talking, perhaps to document clearly what she meant by friendlier and more courteous treatment. This temptation would be especially strong if she were well-prepared for the meeting. Notice how easily she shifts from presenting to listening.

SUPERVISOR: You seem pretty surprised by my comment, Tracy. I'd like to hear your reactions before I continue. (*Pause*)
EMPLOYEE: (*Very animated*) Surprised is right! I can't believe you could say that. I think getting along with people has always been one of my strong points. •

• Realizing that the employee's receptivity is low, the supervisor keeps listening.

SUPERVISOR: So it's especially surprising—and maybe even a little confusing—to hear that I'd like you to improve in an area that you see as one of your strengths? (*Pause*)
EMPLOYEE: (*More calmly*) Yes, it is surprising. I mean . . . well, I know that everybody has some room for improvement, no matter how good they are. And I suppose that applies to me, too. But I was pretty surprised when you mentioned it. (*Leaning forward*) I guess I'm wondering what you meant when you said I could stand to improve by being friendlier.
SUPERVISOR: First of all, I agree that getting along with people is one of your best points. For one, you've got a great smile. For another, you have a very warm and sensitive voice. But there are also some things I think you could do to improve how you deal with visitors. But before I mention them, I'd like to make certain that we've fully discussed your reaction when I raised the subject. (*Pause*)

Notice how the supervisor moves gradually back into a presenting mode, beginning by paying attention to some natural strengths of the employee. Notice also how the supervisor checks with the employee to make certain that there are no lingering thoughts or feelings that would lower receptivity.

EMPLOYEE: (*Smiling*) No, I think I got all that out of my system. I really would like to hear your suggestions.
SUPERVISOR: (*Smiling and leaning forward slightly*) Good. Okay, to begin. . . .

Even though employee receptivity can drop rapidly, it usually takes some time to build back up. Once it's been brought up by skillful listening, you can shift back to a presenting mode. However, you've always got to be ready to start listening again if receptivity goes back down.

PAY ATTENTION TO PACE AND TIMING

Public speakers and comedians pay very close attention to pace and timing when they talk. Managers should too. You'll have a much better chance of getting your message across to your employees if you:

- ☐ Pause after your main points,
- ☐ Vary your speaking style—avoid sameness, and
- ☐ Don't interrupt the other person when you want to talk.

PAUSE AFTER YOUR MAIN POINTS

Pausing when you're talking to another person is helpful for several reasons:

1. It gives your main points a chance to sink in. You give your employee a moment to digest what you've said before moving on to your next point.

2. You give people an opportunity to let you know that they're still with you or that you're losing them. It's during pauses that you can detect dips in employee receptivity.

3. It ensures that you don't monopolize the conversation. When you pause, you send a message: "If you've got an important reaction to what I'm saying, go ahead and jump right in."

Notice how this supervisor uses pauses effectively:

SUPERVISOR: After thinking a lot about your work performance, Gerry, I think there are two major areas where you could stand some improvement. (*Pause*)
EMPLOYEE: (*Looking attentively*) Uhm-humm.
SUPERVISOR: The first thing I'd like to do is offer my suggestions in both areas and get your reactions to them. (*Pause*)
EMPLOYEE: (*Nodding*) Okay, sounds fair enough to me.
SUPERVISOR: Good. After that, I'd like us to spend some time talking about the ideas you came up with as well as my own for how you could improve. The goal will be for us to reach some agreement on what makes the most sense for us to work on in the next four to six weeks. (*Pause*)

EMPLOYEE: (*Nodding*) All right.
SUPERVISOR: And, finally, I'd like the two of us to identify what I'm going to be doing in the next month or so to help you improve in those areas we agree on. (*Pause*)
EMPLOYEE: (*Smiling*) I can't wait to get to that part! (*Both laugh*)
SUPERVISOR: (*Leaning forward slightly*) I am looking forward to doing whatever I can to help you do your job better and get more out of working here. (*Pause*) Okay, Gerry, the first thing. . . .

VARY YOUR SPEAKING STYLE

There are at least two ways you can vary your speaking style to make it more interesting:

   1. Try to make the speed of your voice reflect what you're saying and feeling. When you're enthusiastic or excited, speed it up. When you're very serious or sober, slow it down. Make important points slowly. You can do this by pausing or by simply saying your words more slowly.

   2. Use the upper and lower registers of your voice. A person in one of our seminars called it hitting the high notes and the low notes. It's related to voice tempo. For example, when you're really serious and want people to remember what you're saying, speak with a deeper voice and more slowly. When you're excited or happy, bring your voice up a bit and speak more quickly.

DON'T INTERRUPT THE OTHER PERSON

The tendency to interrupt is understandable. People often say things you flatly disagree with and you want to let them know right away that you disagree. Sometimes people say things that stimulate your thinking, and you want to let them know what's on your mind before you forget. But when you get down to it, interrupting is just a plain old bad habit. Here are several reasons why it's worth a little effort on your part to give it up.

   1. It cuts people off before they've had a chance to finish what they have to say. You don't get as much information when you interrupt.

   2. It colors people's remarks. They learn what gets you excited or upset and start feeding you what they think you want to hear.

   3. It's annoying and irritating, and that leads to lowered receptivity. People who feel that you won't listen to them probably won't listen to you.

To review, you can make your presentation style more effective if you:

1. Pause after your main points,
2. Vary your speaking style, and
3. Don't interrupt.

TELL 'EM WHAT YOU'RE GONNA TELL 'EM (AND WHAT YOU TOLD 'EM)

Public speakers often begin their talks with a preview of what they're going to say and end their talks with a summary of what they've said. This is popularly known as:

☐ Tell 'em what you're gonna tell 'em.
☐ Tell 'em.
☐ Tell 'em what you told 'em.

This technique is a good one to use when you're meeting with employees. By giving a preview of what's coming you give them a chance to get on your wavelength before you get to the heart of your message. By summarizing briefly what you said, you reinforce the major points that you want remembered. It's a useful model for many types of speaking situations.

Here's an example of a supervisor using the technique:

SUPERVISOR: I've been thinking a lot about your work performance lately, Terry, and I've come to the conclusion that there are three major areas where you're really doing well.
EMPLOYEE: Only three? (*Both laugh*) Just kidding! Just kidding!
SUPERVISOR: (*Smiling*) Seriously, Terry, I'd like to begin by mentioning all three strong points and then cover each one in detail. (*Pause*)
EMPLOYEE: (*Nodding*) Okay. Sounds fine to me.
SUPERVISOR: The first thing that really jumps out when I think of your strong points is your skill in writing and editing copy. You're better at that than almost anybody I know. (*Pause*)
EMPLOYEE: (*Slightly embarrassed*) Thanks.
SUPERVISOR: A second major strength is your ability to spot younger talent. You've been the first person to identify some people who've become valuable assets to the organization. (*Pause*)
EMPLOYEE: Well, it's actually pretty easy to recognize real talent when it's staring you in the face.
SUPERVISOR: Easy for you, perhaps. But not so easy for me and a helluva lot of other people.

EMPLOYEE: (*Smiling*) Okay.

SUPERVISOR: The third major area where I think you're doing a really good job is bringing in new business. If all my people were as effective as you were in that area, I'd be a vice-president by now!

EMPLOYEE: (*Smiling broadly*) I was hoping you'd mention that. As you know, I've been pretty happy with myself in that area, too.

SUPERVISOR: I know you have, Terry. Now to get back to that first area. . . .

After the supervisor and employee fully discuss what the employee is doing well ("Tell 'em."), the supervisor closes this part of the interview by summarizing what they had talked about using the technique of "Tell 'em what you told 'em."

SUPERVISOR: Okay, Terry, before we move on, let's take a quick look at what we've just discussed. As I see it, there are three major areas where you're performing very effectively. The first is writing and editing copy. The second is identifying new talent in the company. And the third is bringing in new business. I'm really pleased with your performance in all of those areas.

EMPLOYEE: (*Beaming*) Thanks. It makes me feel good that you've noted my strong points.

"Telling 'em what you told 'em" is a valuable technique for several reasons:

1. It helps people remember major points covered in a conversation. Sometimes so much detail is discussed that people forget to see the forest for the trees. Summarizing brings things back into perspective.

2. Summarizing a segment of conversation is a nice bridge for making a transition to the next topic. For example, in the preceding illustration, it would have been very easy for the supervisor to make a transition by saying, "Now I'd like to move on to some areas where I think you could stand some improvement."

3. Summarizing is a good way to send the message, "These are some important points we've just covered and I'd like to repeat them for emphasis." It's a good way to give you and your employee credit for making valuable contributions.

A QUICK SUMMARY

In this chapter, we've suggested a number of ways you can improve the way you present your ideas to other people.

We've talked about the importance of hearing yourself as others do and argued that attending is as much a presenting skill as a listening skill. We've suggested some ways that you can speak more clearly to employees by using specifics instead of fuzzy language. We've talked about the dangers of using emotionally loaded expressions and stressed how important it is to stop talking and start listening whenever you notice a dip in receptivity. After discussing some aspects of pace and timing, we introduced you to a public speaking technique called "Tell 'em what you're gonna tell 'em (and tell 'em what you told 'em)." Now you're in a good position to move on to the next chapter where you'll finally get to present your analysis of the employee's performance.

CHAPTER 11 • STEP SIX: PRESENT YOUR ANALYSIS OF YOUR EMPLOYEE'S PERFORMANCE

Let's quickly review what we've covered in the ten-step performance improvement process:

☐ In Step One you *analyze your employee's job performance* by identifying several things that the employee does well along with some concrete examples. You also identify several areas where the employee could stand some improvement, along with a specific statement of what the employee would have to do to show that performance had been improved in each area.

☐ In Step Two you *ask your employee to meet with you* by briefly explaining the purpose of the interview, how you plan to prepare for it, and how you'd like the employee to prepare for it.

☐ Step Three is the point at which you actually *begin the performance improvement interview.* You help the employee to feel comfortable and welcome. Then you fully explain the purposes and procedures of the meeting.

☐ In Step Four you use a variety of active listening skills to *find out how things are going* in general on the job, any problems he's encountering that you ought to be aware of, and any suggestions he has on how you can make the job less frustrating and more satisfying.

☐ In Step Five you *ask your employee to make a self-analysis* of her own job performance in much the way you analyzed her performance in Step One.

Now you're at Step Six, the very heart of the interview that all your patient planning, explaining, and listening have been leading up to. You have an opportunity to present your ideas and suggestions at a time when the employee is likely to be most receptive to hearing them.

The procedure you follow in Step Six should sound familiar. You're going to present your analysis of the employee's work performance—the analysis you prepared in Step One—in the same manner you had the employee do it in Step Five. Specifically, you're going to:

1. Identify several areas where you think employees are performing effectively and provide a couple of concrete examples in each of these areas.

2. Identify several areas where you think employees could stand to improve their performance and suggest specific things they might do in each area to convince you that their performance had, in fact, improved.

Your ultimate goal, however, is to reach as much agreement as possible about the areas where both you and your employee see a need for improvement over the next several months. The two of you will try to agree on specific evidence that you'll accept as an indication that the employee has indeed improved in each area.

HOW TO PRESENT YOUR ANALYSIS

Before you begin this stage of the interview, it's a good idea to reread Chapter 10 to review the various tips that will help you to present your ideas effectively. In addition to these techniques, here are a few points to keep in mind when you get to this stage of the interview:

1. Use your performance analysis form as a guide. The form, if you fill it out conscientiously, represents your best thinking on what your employees are doing effectively on the job and the areas where you think they need to improve. It serves as an excellent outline for presenting your ideas and suggestions to an employee.

2. Start with the positive. Most managers and supervisors don't give their employees much, if any, positive feedback. If they do, it's often in the form, "I think you're doing a fine job, but . . ." followed by a fairly long list of specific things the employee needs to work on.

It's very important to point out to the employees the specific things that they're doing effectively. If you've tried your damnedest and simply can't come up with anything positive about an employee's performance, then you ought to seriously question whether it's worth your time and energy to try to help the employee improve.

3. Try to establish as much agreement as you can between your analysis and the employee's analysis. It may seem pretty obvious, but the more you and your employees can agree on the areas where they're performing effectively and the areas where they need to improve, the more receptive they're going to be to improving their performance. We're not suggesting that you pretend to agree with an employee's self-analysis as a way to con or manipulate the person into changing. On the other hand, it just makes good sense to emphasize, early in your presentation, the areas where the two of you agree.

4. Always be ready to shift from a presenting mode to a listening mode. We talked about the importance of being able to make this kind of shift in the last chapter, but it bears repeating. The critical thing to remember is this: Just because your employee's receptivity to your ideas and suggestions is very high at one point, there is no guarantee that it's going to stay high. Keeping your employee's receptivity up is a little like trying to walk on a balancing beam. You can be moving along just fine one moment and find yourself sitting on the ground the next. As soon as you sense that the employee's receptivity has dropped (the signals are pretty clear), go back into an active listening mode. That's the best and easiest way to get back on the beam.

5. Get your employee's reactions to your analysis after you've presented it. As you present your analysis, carefully monitor the employee's reactions for any drop in receptivity. In addition, get the employee's overall reactions to your analysis after you've gone all the way through it. This will give the employee an opportunity to express any strong reactions that may have been held back while you were talking. It will also give the employee a chance to think out loud and to digest what you said, and it will give you an opportunity to make certain your message got across.

WALKING THROUGH AN EXAMPLE

Each employee is unique, so we can't cover all the bases — all the different kinds of reactions and how to respond to them — with one example. However, we've tried to strike a balance by choosing a hypothetical employee who is far from being an all-around star performer but who definitely has some strengths. As you'll see, she also has some pretty typical reactions to certain portions of the analysis of her performance that she doesn't fully agree with. Let us introduce you then to Lisa, a salesperson, and her supervisor, Tom.

Tom Heyman and Lisa Straban both work for a large midwestern industrial furniture manufacturer. Tom, who's forty-seven years old, is a regional sales manager and supervises ten salespeople, including Lisa. Lisa is twenty-four years old, has had considerable sales experience for a person her age, and is the first female salesperson on Tom's sales team. They've been working together now for about nine months. Tom feels that Lisa has very strong potential as a salesperson, but, at this point, still has a lot to learn. Lisa seems to like and respect Tom, but she's the kind of person who's reluctant to accept anybody's advice until she sees the stuff really work out there where it counts. This performance review is a brand new experience for Lisa and a relatively new one for Tom.

When asked to do a self-analysis earlier in the interview, Lisa talked about three areas where she thought she was performing effectively and three areas where she thought she could stand some improvement. She said she thought her strong points included: (1) making sales presentations. (When asked to be more specific, she said she thought her sales presentations were well-prepared, that she made good use of graphics, and that her presentations were interesting because she used a lot of arm and hand gestures and occasionally told jokes to lighten things up.); (2) managing her time effectively; and (3) following up on prospects.

Concerning areas where she could stand to improve, Lisa said that she would like to: (1) close more sales. (Specifically, she said she'd like to improve her closing rate for large orders from 30 percent to 40 percent and that she would like to decrease the closing period from an average of six weeks to an average of thirty days.); (2) do a better job of getting interviews with prospects; and (3) do a better job of developing leads, especially leads to new markets.

Read over the performance analysis form on page 139 that Tom filled out in preparation for this session with Lisa. He'll use this form as a guide for this stage of the interview. Notice that there are some similarities between Lisa's self-analysis and Tom's analysis of her work performance. However, there are really more differences than similarities, especially in regard to what both Lisa and Tom think Lisa should be working on to improve her performance. It will be interesting to see how Tom handles what appear to be some pretty big differences of opinion between them.

Now let's listen in on the performance improvement interview. Periodically, we'll comment on how we think Tom is handling some of the issues and problems that inevitably crop up at this stage of the interview.

TOM: (*Nodding and then pausing for several seconds before speaking*) Anything else you want to add?

LISA: No, Tom. I really think that pretty much covers it.

TOM: Fine. Well, Lisa, I think that was a very complete and thoughtful analysis of your job performance. You really seemed to get into it.

LISA: (*Smiling and obviously pleased*) Yeah, I guess I did, didn't I?

TOM: Yep! Now, as I mentioned a little earlier, I'd like to take a crack at it.

LISA: Uh-oh. (*Smiling broadly*) Here it comes!

TOM: You're a little concerned about what I have to say? •

• Can you identify the listening skill Tom just used? Why did he use it?

LISA: Yeah . . . as well as this seems to be going, I guess I am. It just isn't always the easiest thing to have somebody give you honest and objective feedback on how you're doing on your job. Especially when it comes from your boss. (*Smiling and turning her palms upward*)

TOM: (*Nodding and smiling back, but saying nothing*)

LISA: That's all. (*Leaning forward slightly*)

TOM: (*Smiling and gesturing like an orchestra leader*) On with the show! I asked you to start with the areas where you feel you're performing effectively. I'd like to do the same thing.

LISA: (*Smiling*) Okay. Good place to start.

TOM: Lisa, one of the areas where you felt you were performing effectively was making sales presentations. I'm in full agreement with that. Two of our more demanding customers have told me independently that you make an excellent sales presentation. And they're pretty choosy about the way they hand out compliments.

LISA: (*Smiling and looking a little embarrassed*) That's nice to hear.

PERFORMANCE ANALYSIS FORM

| WHAT IS YOUR EMPLOYEE DOING WELL? | IN WHAT WAYS SHOULD HE/SHE IMPROVE? |

1. MAKING SALES PRESENTATIONS

Example: Two of our customers have told me (independently) that Lisa is one of the best presenters they've ever seen.

Example: Our training department has asked me several times if they could use Lisa as an instructor in the presentation portion of the training of salespeople new to the company.

1. HANDLING OBJECTIONS

Specifically, the person will have to:

Explore the prospect's objections to the product line with open-ended questions before countering the objection with a specific statement about the line.

2. FOLLOWING UP ON PROSPECTS

Example: At least 3 of our customers have told me they never would have chosen our line if it hadn't been for Lisa's persistence.

Example: I know we would never have gotten the Grayban account if it hadn't been for Lisa's persistence in following up on them.

2. MEETING REPORT DEADLINES

Specifically, the person will have to:

Get all her monthly reports in on time for the next six months.

3. DEVELOPING LEADS

Example: Lisa uses a lot of different sources to develop leads — everything from newspaper articles to other salespeople from other companies.

Example: Lisa has a card file on prospects— she keeps very good records on what happens to her leads — this is potentially very valuable information.

3. KNOWING THE COMPETITION

Specifically, the person will have to:

Meet with me every quarter to offer her analysis of new competitive product lines that she needs to be aware of and to compare her analysis with my own.

4. MORALE BOOSTER

Example: She's always trying to help out the salespeople in other departments— sharing techniques, leads, etc.

Example: Several of the newer salespeople in the department have told me how helpful Lisa was to them when they were first starting out.

4. TIME MANAGEMENT

Specifically, the person will have to:

Set both weekly and daily written goals for herself that reflect the major tasks she wants to accomplish for the week and for each day.

TOM: Yes, it is nice to hear. Another thing. I think you already know that our training department has asked me several times if they could use you as an instructor in the presentation portion of their training program for new salespeople.

LISA: (*A little surprised*) No, I didn't know that. Maybe we could talk about that sometime.

TOM: Good. Let's talk about it a little later in the interview.

LISA: Great.

TOM: Another area that you mentioned that you thought you were doing pretty well in is following up on prospects. Again, I'm in full agreement.

LISA: (*Nodding*)

TOM: At least three of our customers have told me that they never would have considered, much less chosen, our line if it hadn't been for your persistence in following up on them.

LISA: (*Smiling*) I hope they weren't saying I was a pain in the neck.

TOM: (*Chuckling*) No, not at all. Along those same lines, I know for a fact that we never would have gotten the Greybar account last year if you hadn't been so doggedly persistent in following up on them.

LISA: (*Laughing and holding up her thumb and forefinger about a centimeter apart*) Yeah, but I must say that I came about that far from giving up on them.

TOM: (*Chuckling*) But you didn't, and we got the account.

Notice that Tom, in discussing the areas where he thinks Lisa is performing effectively, has chosen to lead off with two areas that he and Lisa are in solid agreement on. So far, this has had the effect of keeping Lisa's level of receptivity very high. Now Tom is about to embark on some areas where there doesn't appear to be much agreement between them. Let's see how he handles this potential problem.

TOM: Lisa, now I'd like to talk about some areas where I think you're performing effectively that you didn't mention.

LISA: (*Smiling and leaning forward a little*) Okay.

Notice something that Tom does not do here. He doesn't mention the fact that he disagrees with Lisa about her time management skills. Since Tom sees time management as an area where Lisa needs to improve, he'll simply defer discussing it until he has finished talking about all the areas where he thinks that Lisa is performing effectively.

TOM: Well, Lisa, I think you're a pretty good morale booster around this place.

LISA: (*Looking genuinely surprised*) What? I don't believe you'd say such a thing about me!

TOM: Sounds like that one came out of left field for you?

What's happening here? Tom is in the process of telling Lisa that he thinks she's a good morale booster in the sales department. Tom expects Lisa to react very positively to this message. But her reaction appears to be much more one of confusion than pleasure. Now here's the key: Tom does not continue talking to clarify what he means. He stops and reflects feeling. This will give Lisa an opportunity to talk about what's confusing her. If, on the other hand, Tom continues to talk, Lisa may not be listening. Why? Because she's still trying to figure out what Tom meant by morale booster.

LISA: (*Both smiling and scowling at the same time*) Yeah. I'm not sure I like the sound of that.

TOM: (*Nodding and leaning forward slightly*) What is it you don't like about the sound of it, Lisa?

LISA: Well, I guess all I could think of when you said morale booster were those rah-rah cheerleaders that I always hated in high school. You know the type. All good looks and no brains. And always on the sidelines, cheering somebody else on!

TOM: (*Chuckling and smiling broadly*) Ah! I see what you mean.

LISA: (*Shaking her head*) Isn't that what you had in mind?

TOM: No, that's not what I had in mind.

LISA: (*Smiling*) Good. So what did you mean when you said I was a good morale booster?

Receptivity is back up.

TOM: (*Pausing and looking up at the ceiling for a few seconds before speaking*) What I meant by morale booster was that a lot of the things you do around here have a sort of motivating, almost inspirational, effect on the other people in the department.

LISA: (*Looking a little puzzled but really paying attention*)

TOM: Let me be a little more specific. Ever since we've been working together I've noticed that you're always trying to help out the salespeople in other territories. You share techniques with them that you've found successful and give them leads that you've gotten from your own customers and prospects. You know, that sort of thing.

LISA: (*Smiling and nodding*) Yeah, well I do try to do those things. But I wouldn't call that morale boosting. I just call that being helpful.

TOM: (*Smiling and nodding*) I agree. I think helpful is a much better way to characterize what you do. Another example. Several of the girls in the office have told me quite openly how helpful—

LISA: (*Interrupting*) Tom, I don't want you to misunderstand this, but don't you think it's a little inappropriate to refer to the adult women in the office as girls? •

• Another drop in Lisa's receptivity, this time as a result of using an emotionally loaded expression. Let's see how he handles this one.

TOM: (*Softly*) It sounds like you're feeling a little offended, or maybe irritated, by my use of that word, Lisa?

LISA: Yes, I am, Tom. That's exactly how I feel. I have to listen to customers talk that way all of the time. And I always bite my tongue when they do. But when you use that expression, I really feel that I've got to say something about it.

TOM: This sounds like something you really feel strongly about. (*Pause*)

LISA: Yes, I do. I'm a woman, not a girl. And that's also true for the women who work in the office. I know you don't mean any disrespect by it, Tom, but I would really prefer it if you wouldn't use that expression.

TOM: Lisa, thanks for telling me how you feel about that. As you may know, it's an old habit. But I'll try very hard to refer to the . . . *women* in the office as women from now on. . . .

Tom handles this drop in receptivity the same way he would handle any of them, by reflecting feeling. If he had chosen to discuss or, worse, debate the point, the entire interview might have been sidetracked or completely derailed. Whatever his personal view on this matter might be outside of this interview, he chooses here to reflect—and respect—Lisa's feelings.

TOM: Okay, let me talk about another area where I think you're performing effectively on the job. In fact, it's an area in which you. . . .

Tom will now talk about the final area where he sees Lisa performing effectively, developing leads. As before, he'll use concrete examples to make his points. When he's finished talking about this fourth area, he'll summarize briefly the four major areas where he sees Lisa doing well on the job and ask if she'd like to add anything to the summary. Then he'll make a transition statement and begin to identify some of the areas where he thinks Lisa could improve. Let's pick up the interview at that point.

TOM: Okay, let's move on now to some of the areas where I think you could stand to improve. (*Pause*)

LISA: (*Nodding*)

TOM: Based on observing your performance lately, Lisa, and thinking quite a bit about it, I'd say there are four areas where you could stand some improvement. (*Pause*)

LISA: (*Looking attentive*)

TOM: The first thing I'd like to do is explain my thinking in each area and get your reactions to what I've said.

LISA: (*Nodding*) Okay.

TOM: Then I'd like us to talk about how these areas tie into the areas you said you'd like to improve in. And finally, I'd like us to reach some agreement on what it makes most sense for you to be working on to improve your performance over the next couple of months. (*Pause*)

LISA: Okay.

TOM: And after that, I'd like us to agree on what I'm going to do to help you improve in these areas. (*Pause*)

LISA: Sounds good.

At the very beginning of the interview, Tom gave Lisa a preview of what was going to happen in the interview. But since this is such a critical and sensitive stage of the interview, Tom has chosen to repeat the preview, going into a little bit more depth than he did at the beginning. This should help to remind Lisa of the big picture — that is, the overall purpose of the interview is not to criticize Lisa's performance but to work together to improve it.

TOM: All right. One of the areas where I think you could stand some improvement, and I think it ties in with your wanting to achieve a greater closing percentage, is in handling the objections that prospects frequently raise to our product line.

LISA: (*Wrinkling forehead as Tom talks*) Handling objections? I have to disagree with that, Tom. I think I'm very good at handling objections.

TOM: (*Leaning forward*) So you're kind of surprised, then, that I'd identify that as an area where you could stand to improve?

It seems clear that Lisa's receptivity has dropped like a stone. What do you think would happen here if Tom tried to explain himself rather than listen to what she has to say?

LISA: Yes, I am surprised. I mean that's an area that I'm really strong in. In fact, I even keep a notebook on objections so I can always be coming up with better and better arguments for them.

TOM: (*Still listening attentively*) Uhm-humm.

LISA: (*Starting to wind down a little*) Uh . . . (*Now smiling*) maybe I should let you tell me what you meant.

TOM: (*Smiling*) Okay, but you really did seem surprised, maybe even a little hurt, that I said you needed to improve in an area that you think you're doing very well in.

LISA: (*Smiling*) Yes, that's pretty much how I felt. •

• Now Lisa's receptivity seems to be back up so Tom will take a crack at clarifying what he meant.

TOM: First of all, let me say that I agree with you that your arguments for the objections that prospects raise are really quite good.

LISA: (*Looking a little surprised and curious*)

TOM: And I think that you should continue to use those arguments; it's the timing of your arguments that I think could stand some improvement.

LISA: (*Looking even more curious and leaning forward slightly*) How so?

TOM: Well, when a prospect offers an objection to a product, such as it's too expensive or it's not compatible with our other furniture, I think it's awfully tempting to come back with an argument for why you think the prospect is wrong.

LISA: (*Nodding*) Absolutely.

TOM: But I think the best thing to do when a prospect offers an objection is to get more information. What I mean is, you want to draw the guy out. You want to get him talking about his objection. (*Pause*)

LISA: (*Looking thoughtful*) Hmm . . . that *is* something to think about.

TOM: It looks like you at least want to consider that as a possible strategy for handling objections?

LISA: (*Still looking very thoughtful*) Yeah. . . .

TOM: I'll tell you what. Why don't we come back to this a little later and move on now to another area. (*Pause*)

LISA: (*Nodding*) Fine.

Tom seems to have gotten Lisa interested in, but not completely convinced about, adopting a new strategy for dealing with prospect objections. Rather than push for full commitment from her on this issue, Tom has decided to let her think about it awhile. We've found that this incubation period often has a positive effect on getting people to see things our way.

TOM: Well, a second area where I'd like to see some improvement is in meeting reporting deadlines. (*Pause*)

LISA: (*Shaking her head and smiling*) I just knew those damn reports were going to creep into this conversation somehow.

TOM: (*Smiling*) I guess this is the time, huh?

LISA: (*Smiling, raising her palms to the ceiling, and shrugging*) Tom, what can I tell you? I hate those reports, and you know it. I think they're a big waste of time. I'll admit it. I'm guilty. But I just wish we could do away with the damn things altogether.

TOM: Sounds like you really find the reports unpleasant, almost as though the reports are an obstacle to getting more important things done?

The old standby, reflecting feeling.

LISA: (*Sighing*) Exactly. Exactly. That's just how I feel.

Receptivity's back up.

TOM: Well, Lisa, I must say that I don't totally disagree with you. I'm not real big on paperwork either. On the other hand, if those reports don't get in on time, it causes me and the people I work for a bunch of problems. (*Pause*)

LISA: (*Nodding*) Yes, I'm sure that's true.

TOM: I think I have a pretty good idea of how you feel about the reports, Lisa. And you seem to be pretty much aware of the problems I experience when the reports don't get handed in on time. What thoughts do you have on what we should do about this situation? •

• Here Tom has put the responsibility for a solution on Lisa by asking an open-ended question.

LISA: Tom, I'll make a commitment to you right now to get those reports in on time, all the time.

TOM: Well, Lisa, I'm really glad to hear you say that. A little later on I'd like us to talk about possible things that I can do to make this whole reporting process at least a little easier for you.

Just a word or two here on technique: Notice that Tom has chosen to take the tack of getting at least partial commitment from Lisa on each area of improvement without going into specific detail on what Lisa will be doing to improve in each of these areas. As you'll see, Tom's strategy will be to come back to each area a little later for this kind of specific commitment. This is not the only way to do it, however. You might choose to complete one area before moving on to the next. We'd recommend that you experiment before you firmly adopt any one strategy. Let's jump ahead now to the final area where Tom thinks Lisa can improve — time management. Remember, this is an area Lisa identified as one of her strengths.

TOM: Okay, why don't we move on to the last area where I think you could stand to improve — time management. (*Pause*)

LISA: Well, like I said, Tom, this is an area where I think I'm pretty good. (*Real coolness in her voice*) But I'd like to hear what you have to say.

TOM: Well, Lisa, maybe at this point it would be helpful if you reviewed for both of us the specific ways that you think you're good at time management. Then I could give you my thoughts on some additional things you could do that might make you even more effective in this area. How does that sound?

At this point it seems as if Lisa is almost challenging Tom to show her how she could improve in the area of time management. In other words, Tom doesn't have a very good audience for what he wants to say. So, he's decided to try to get Lisa talking in order to build up her receptivity. Notice also that he's never disagreed with Lisa's contention that she's good at time management. Rather, Tom has simply said that he'd like to make some suggestions that would help make Lisa even more effective in this area.

LISA: (*Softening up a little*) Okay, well, let's see. As I said, I work pretty fast and get a lot of things done in a fairly short period of time.

TOM: (*Nodding*) Uhm-humm.

LISA: I think I'm pretty well organized. You know, I can always lay my hands on pretty much whatever I want because I have good filing and record keeping systems.

TOM: Yes, you certainly do.

LISA: Uh . . . I think I'm pretty good at delegating tasks to other people in the department who can probably do them better and faster than I can.

TOM: (*Nodding*) Uhm-humm.

LISA: Hmm . . . I guess that about covers it. Okay. (*Smiling just a little*) I'd like to hear your suggestions, Tom. •

• Receptivity seems to be back up.

TOM: Okay. I think that review was helpful. I think the three areas that you mentioned—working fast, being organized, and delegating—are all important aspects of time management, and I agree that you're good at all three. (*Pause*)

LISA: (*Nodding*) That's good. But, then what are you suggesting?

TOM: I'd say that the only major suggestion I'd make for improving your time management skills is in the area of setting priorities. (*Pause*)

LISA: (*Leaning forward and looking very attentive*) Hmm.

TOM: Let me be more specific. Why don't I tell you exactly how I do it just to see what you think.

LISA: (*Still looking attentive*) Okay.

TOM: The first thing Monday morning I take a pad and write down all the tasks I'd like to accomplish by Friday at five o'clock.

LISA: (*Smiling*) I bet that's a pretty long list.

TOM: It sure is. Then I make an assumption. (*Pause*) I assume that doing only about 20 percent of those tasks will account for about 80 percent of the value of completing all the tasks on the list. (*Pause*)

LISA: (*Looking thoughtful*) Oh, yeah. I think that's called the 80/20 rule, isn't it?

TOM: Right. Once I've identified those key tasks, I really try to devote almost all of my energy for the rest of the week in getting them done. If none of the rest of the tasks on the list gets done, I don't even worry about it.

LISA: (*Still looking thoughtful and nodding*)

TOM: Okay, so that's my weekly "to do" list. I make up a similar daily "to do" list the first thing every morning.

LISA: (*Nodding*) Hmm. I like that. Yeah . . . I like that.

TOM: Well, Lisa, if you'd be willing to adopt those two habits, I think you'd find yourself making even more effective use of your time than you do now.

LISA: I think you're right. I'm sold.

Let's take a look at the progress Tom has made so far at this stage in the interview. After reviewing what he thinks are Lisa's strong points, Tom has presented his ideas and suggestions on the areas where he thinks she could improve. In the process, he's had to handle several dips in Lisa's receptivity, but she now appears to be ready to agree to make some changes in each of the four areas. Now Tom's job is to help Lisa make some specific commitments in each of these areas.

TOM: Well, Lisa, that pretty much covers the four areas that I felt you could stand to improve in. (*Pause*) Now it seems to me that our task is to try to agree on the specific things that you'll be working on over the next several months to improve your overall job performance. (*Pause*)

LISA: (*Nodding*) Okay. Makes sense.

TOM: (*Smiling*) I know I don't even have to say this, but I think the things you're going to be working on should include your own ideas and suggestions as well as mine.

LISA: (*Chuckling*) No, you didn't have to tell me that, Tom.

TOM: (*Still smiling*) Good. Okay, Lisa, why don't you take a few minutes to talk about the specific things that you'd like to be working on over the next several months given all the things that we've talked about so far. . . .

At the beginning of the chapter we said that you're trying to achieve an agreement in this stage of the interview — an agreement between you and your employee on the major areas where the employee will be attempting to improve job performance over the next several months and an agreement on the specific evidence that you would both accept as proof that the employee had actually made significant improvement in each of the areas identified.

So far in the example with Tom and Lisa, the two of them have achieved a pretty good agreement on the general areas where Lisa will be working to improve her performance. As we leave them at this point, they're beginning to get very specific about the tasks that Lisa will complete to satisfy both of them that her performance has improved in each area.

Getting down to specifics, as Tom and Lisa are about to do, is roughly the dividing line between this step, presenting your analysis of the employee's performance, and the next step, negotiating the performance agreement. So we'll get back to Tom and Lisa in the next chapter.

A QUICK SECTION SUMMARY

Before turning our attention to some possible setbacks, let's quickly review some of the most important points to keep in mind during this stage of the interview:

1. Remember that the performance analysis form is your basic guide through this stage of the interview. It's a reminder to you of the areas where you think your employee's performing effectively and the areas where you'd like to see performance improved.

2. Start with the positive. Before you give your ideas and suggestions on the areas that you think employees can improve, tell them in specific terms what you think they're doing well. We don't think we can stress this point enough.

3. Try to establish as much agreement as you can between the employee's analysis and your own. This will give the employee an accurate sense that the two of you are working as a team.

4. Always be ready to shift from a presenting mode to a listening mode to keep your employee's receptivity up. Remember how many times Tom had to do this to maintain Lisa's involvement in the performance improvement process.

5. Get your employee's reactions to your analysis after you've presented it. Give your employee a chance to think out loud about what you've said. It will also give you an opportunity to make certain that your employee has understood what you've said.

POSSIBLE SETBACKS

In the beginning of this chapter we said that the active listening skills that you've learned will help get you out of trouble if things start to go wrong at this stage of the interview. Throughout the example interview, Tom was able to keep Lisa's involvement and receptivity fairly high simply by remaining quiet and letting her talk when she seemed to be bothered by, or disagreed with, something Tom said.

However, even though the interview with Lisa was not smooth sailing for Tom, Lisa didn't cause Tom any major difficulties. Unfortunately, some employees can be a little bit more troublesome.

What we've tried to do in the last section of the chapter is anticipate some of the more difficult situations you might find yourself in with an employee when you try to make suggestions on how he or she could improve performance. After you read through each situation, we'd like you to at least imagine how you might handle it. If you feel more adventuresome, ask another person to help you role play the situation, or write your own dialogue.

After you've responded to each situation, you'll have an opportunity to compare your response with the way we would have handled the situation. Our answers certainly are not the only effective ways to handle these situations, but on the basis of a lot of practical experience, we do know that they work pretty well.

SITUATION 1:
TOUCHING A NERVE

Have you ever been in a dentist chair after your dentist has been drilling awhile and starts to clean out the cavity with a little water nozzle? Sometimes that cold water hits an exposed nerve and you just about jump out of the chair up through the ceiling.

Sometimes when you're talking to employees about how they can improve their performance, you get a similar reaction. You're calmly explaining an area where you think the employee could stand to improve, and wham, the person comes back with a very strong response that almost dazes you. Here's an example:

SUPERVISOR: Good. All right, Pat, let me move on to another area. I think another thing you could do to improve your overall performance is to take a more active part in our weekly staff meetings. I think—
EMPLOYEE: (*Interrupting and throwing hands up in the air*) Oh, that's beautiful! Really beautiful! Let me tell you. . . .

Imagine that you were the supervisor and had provoked this touched-nerve reaction from Pat. How would you handle the situation? After you've had an opportunity to think about it and respond, take a look at how we would have handled the situation.

We approach the situation with these thoughts:

☐   The issue of participating more actively in staff meetings is obviously a sensitive one for Pat.
☐   The supervisor is very unlikely to get anywhere with Pat until he responds to Pat's very strong feelings.
☐   Once Pat has had an opportunity to express these feelings, the supervisor will be in a position to get specific information on why this is such a sensitive issue and what the two of them can do to solve the problem.

For example:

EMPLOYEE: All I can say is that I have a completely different opinion than you do on that matter. (*Folding his arms and leaning back*)
SUPERVISOR: (*Calmly and softly*) You sound pretty ticked off at me, Pat.
EMPLOYEE: (*Leaning forward*) Damn right! I'd just like to remind you of something! I used to speak up all the time at staff meetings, if you'll remember. But I'm sure as hell not going to do that anymore!
SUPERVISOR: (*Remaining calm*) Something happened, maybe something I did, that changed your mind?
EMPLOYEE: (*A little softer now*) Yes. •

• Now the supervisor should start to get more specific information.

SUPERVISOR: (*Nodding*) Tell me, Pat. I'd really like to know.
EMPLOYEE: I'll tell you exactly what you used to do. *Every* time I said something at a staff meeting, you would follow up whatever I said with, "I think what Pat is trying to say is. . . ."
SUPERVISOR: And that really annoyed you?
EMPLOYEE: That's putting it mildly. I felt like you didn't have any confidence in me. Like you had to act as a translator for me.
SUPERVISOR: (*Nodding*) That must have been annoying.
EMPLOYEE: (*Now visibly calmer*) It certainly was.
SUPERVISOR: Well, Pat, I'm really sorry I used to do that. I honestly wasn't aware of it, but I want to make sure I stop doing it completely in the future.
EMPLOYEE: (*Smiling a little*) That would be great.
SUPERVISOR: You've got a deal. Okay, so if I agree to. . . .

SITUATION 2:
GIVING GROUND GRUDGINGLY

Every now and then you'll run into an employee who goes along with your suggestions, but does so in a reluctant, half-hearted fashion. For example, in response to specific suggestions that you make on how performance could be improved, the employee might blandly respond by:

- ☐ Nodding slowly with a blank expression,
- ☐ Saying, "Yeah, okay, I guess that would be all right,"
- ☐ Turning both palms upward and saying, "Why not?" and
- ☐ Saying, "Sure, whatever you say."

Let's say you're conducting a performance improvement interview with your employee and have been getting these kinds of half-hearted responses to your suggestions for the last ten minutes. What would you do in this situation to build up the employee's obviously low level of receptivity to your suggestions? After you've considered your response, take a look at how we'd handle this situation.

There are two basic strategies we'd recommend when you seem to be getting half-hearted commitments from an employee to your suggestions for improvement:

1. Reflect feeling, and
2. Use the stop, look, and listen technique.

You ought to reflect feeling immediately whenever you get a lukewarm reaction from an employee to one of your suggestions. For example, let's say you suggest that an employee's written communication skills could be improved by writing briefer and more concise memos. In response, the employee says, "Yeah. Guess that's a good idea," in a half-hearted tone of voice. You might respond by saying:

> "You don't seem very enthusiastic about my suggestion."
> "It doesn't seem as if you're completely sold on that idea."
> "You're not sure that's really something you want to do?"

Sometimes this strategy works very effectively. The employee may open up and tell you very directly why your idea doesn't seem to be a very good one. But sometimes it doesn't work. Sometimes the employee will continue to insist, but still in a half-hearted tone of voice, that your suggestion is a good one to follow. That leaves you with the feeling that something is still being held back from you.

In this situation we recommend that you use the stop, look, and listen technique:

1. Stop the interaction as soon as you see that the discussion is becoming unproductive.
2. Look squarely at the problem by describing it succinctly and objectively.
3. Listen for suggestions that you both can live with for resolving the problem.

Here's an example of a supervisor using these three points with an employee who doesn't seem to be really sold on any suggestions for improvement:

EMPLOYEE: (*Nodding half-heartedly to a suggestion the supervisor has just made*)
SUPERVISOR: I've noticed that you don't seem to be very enthusiastic about several of the suggestions I've been making in the last few minutes. (*Pause*) Several times you've shrugged your shoulders or said, "Yeah, I guess that's okay," and that sort of thing.
EMPLOYEE: (*Not saying anything but looking a little more attentive*)
SUPERVISOR: When you react that way to my suggestions, I feel confused and frustrated and as if we're not making any progress.

The supervisor has decided to stop the unproductive interaction. Then the supervisor takes a look at the problem by describing what's been happening between the two of them and disclosing her feelings to the employee.

EMPLOYEE: (*Still looking attentive but also a little surprised*)

SUPERVISOR: I'd like to hear your ideas and suggestions on how we can turn this situation around to make this a more productive session for both of us.

Now the supervisor will listen to the employee's suggestions for dealing with the problem. The supervisor has put some of the responsibility for making the session more positive back on the employee.

EMPLOYEE: (*Hesitating somewhat*) Well . . . I see what you're saying . . . but, well, there is something that has been bothering me.

SUPERVISOR: (*Nodding and leaning forward slightly*) Uhm-humm.

EMPLOYEE: (*Starting to build up a little steam*) Well, dammit, I just don't feel too great about listening to your suggestions for how I can improve after I told you about that big problem we've got down in inventory control and you didn't make any commitment to do anything about it.

SUPERVISOR: You feel as if I let you get the problem off your chest, but now I'm not going to help you do anything to solve the problem?

EMPLOYEE: (*Nodding*) That's exactly how I feel.

SUPERVISOR: Okay, I can appreciate that. How about if we set up a specific time next week to discuss that problem in depth? (*Pause*) If we agree to do that, would you agree to get more involved in what we're talking about right now?

EMPLOYEE: (*Nodding vigorously*) Absolutely. You've got yourself a bargain.

SUPERVISOR: Great. How about next Tuesday. . . .

Notice that the employee didn't come up with any suggestions on how to improve the situation. But by finding out why the employee was not being very responsive, the supervisor was able to suggest a way for both of them to get what they wanted.

SITUATION 3:
GETTING CAUGHT IN AN ARGUMENT

Every now and then even a supervisor who's a very skillful interviewer will end up getting into an argument with an employee when making suggestions on how to improve job performance. For example, let's say you find yourself in the same bind as the supervisor in the dialogue example on the next two pages.

SUPERVISOR: All right, Ronnie. Let's move on to another area where I think you could stand to improve your performance; it has to do with meeting reporting deadlines.

EMPLOYEE: (*Wrinkling his forehead and nose*) Oh, come on! I almost always get my reports in on time. Besides, I'm a lot better about it than anybody else in the department.

SUPERVISOR: (*Wrinkling his forehead and shaking his head*) Now wait a minute, Ronnie. Let's take a realistic look at this thing. I know for a fact that six of your last ten monthly reports have been at least a week late. Now—

EMPLOYEE: (*Interrupting*) I'm sorry. That's just not true. Now maybe one—

SUPERVISOR: (*Interrupting*) Now hold on, Ronnie. I've got some figures that Terry has been keeping. . . .

Well, here you are. You had no intention of getting into an argument with the employee, but now you're right in the middle of one. How would you get out of this situation? After you've considered your response, read ours and see what we would do if we found ourselves in this kind of bind.

Unfortunately, arguments are like a lot of situations in life—once you get into them, it's hard to get out of them. When you get into an argument, your autonomic nervous system—pulse, blood pressure, and adrenalin—usually goes into high gear. For a short while your ability to think flexibly and openly is short circuited, and it's pretty tough to do anything but continue to push your own point of view.

In spite of all this, however, we think you have at least two options:

1. Stop talking and start listening, and
2. Take a break.

The first option is easier said than done, but we think it's almost always worth a try. The trick here—and it's tough—is to force yourself to stop countering everything the employee says and to go back into an active listening mode. Here's an example:

SUPERVISOR: (*Interrupting*) Now hold on, Ronnie. I've got some figures that Terry has been keeping—

EMPLOYEE: (*Interrupting*) I don't care about any figures that Terry has been keeping.

SUPERVISOR: (*About to interrupt but catching himself*)

EMPLOYEE: I keep my own records, and I know when my reports are late, and I know when they're on time.

SUPERVISOR: (*Nodding and assuming a more relaxed expression on his face*) Uhm-humm.

EMPLOYEE: (*Slowing down just a bit*) I mean this is something we've disagreed on for a long time. And I just don't think you're aware of how hard I try to get those reports in on time in spite of all the other things I have to do.

SUPERVISOR: It's as if I don't see where these reports fit into the bigger picture of your whole job. Is that it?

EMPLOYEE: (*Softening some more*) Exactly. Now I realize that you have a responsibility also to. . . .

The supervisor really had to exercise some restraint to stop interrupting and to start listening to the employee. As hard as it was to do this, however, it appeared to get some results. The employee's tone was beginning to soften, and receptivity was slowly on the rise again.

We'd like to believe that this stop talking and start listening technique is always the best way to get out of an argument, but we're painfully aware that sometimes it just doesn't work. As hard as you try, you just can't listen to the employee. The impulse to find holes in the employee's argument is just too strong.

When you feel that you can't actively listen to the employee, we recommend the second option—take a break. By this, all we mean is take an intermission from the interview so that both you and the employee will have an opportunity to cool off a bit and get a little perspective on what's been happening.

Here are a couple of things to remember when you suggest to the employee that you both ought to take a break from the interview:

☐   Make your suggestion softly but firmly. If the employee is a forceful person and seems bent on winning the argument, you may run into a little resistance. You may have to repeat your suggestion several times before the employee agrees to this cooling-off period.

☐   Try to make your break long enough for the two of you to clear your heads but short enough so that you get back to the interview while it's still reasonably fresh in your minds. A break of a half hour to an hour is probably ideal. If this isn't possible because of other commitments, then you ought to schedule resumption of the interview as early as possible during the next day.

In this chapter we've gone into quite a bit of detail on specific ways to keep an employee's receptivity up while you present your analysis of the employee's work performance. In the next chapter we'll cover the climax of the interview— negotiating the performance agreement.

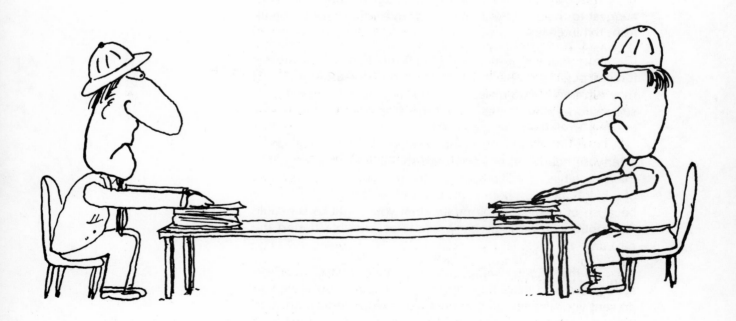CHAPTER 12 • STEP SEVEN: NEGOTIATE THE PERFORMANCE AGREEMENT

In the last chapter we noted that the dividing line between presenting your analysis of the employee's performance and "negotiating the performance agreement" is not sharply defined. With a little practice the two steps should merge so comfortably and fluidly that it's hard to tell where one ends and the other begins.

Your goal in Step Seven—the climax of the interview—is to come up with a handwritten agreement between you and the employee on:

☐ Specific tasks that the employee is going to work on during the next three to six weeks to improve specific work performance.

☐   Specific tasks that you are going to work on during this same period to help the employee improve specific work performance and to make the job less frustrating and more satisfying.

To give you an idea of what you're shooting for in this step of the interview, we'll eventually pick up Lisa and Tom where we left them in Step Six and we'll listen in as they negotiate a hypothetical performance agreement.

Here's an overview of what we'll cover in this chapter:

- Important points to keep in mind about the content and style of the performance agreement,
- The negotiating strategy for arriving at a performance agreement that both you and the employee can live with, and
- A hypothetical example of a negotiation between an employee (Lisa) and a supervisor (Tom) to reach a performance agreement.

SOME IMPORTANT POINTS TO KEEP IN MIND

As you gain more confidence and skill in conducting performance improvement interviews, they'll naturally become more your interviews and less our interviews. In other words, you'll begin to develop your own style of presentation and find techniques that work especially well for you. But in the beginning, try things our way. Use our techniques and our style as you negotiate your first performance agreement.

There are four important things to keep in mind as you approach this stage of the interview:

1. Keep the negotiating process and the language of the agreement informal.
2. Make sure the agreement has something of value in it for both you and your employee.
3. Limit the performance agreement to high-priority tasks.
4. Be specific in writing out the conditions of the agreement.

INFORMALITY

It's important for you and the employee to put the performance agreement in writing. As time passes—even a few days—it will be very easy for either or both of you to forget a given task, no matter how clearly stated, that you both agreed to verbally. A written agreement not only provides a document that you can refer back to, but the physical act of writing itself helps some people to remember things.

On the other hand, putting something in writing has a tendency to make some people a little nervous. For this reason, you should make the agreement—and how you come up with it—as informal as you can. Here are some suggestions:

☐ Handwrite the agreement on a blank sheet of paper. Don't type it.
☐ Avoid using anything that even vaguely resembles a printed form.
☐ Even though you may be tempted, don't use the word *contract*. It just makes people nervous.
☐ Assure the employee that the written agreement is for the sole use of the two of you and that copies won't be sent to the personnel department or any other organization officials.
☐ Don't be afraid to leave erasures or to scratch out items in the agreement. This will make it look less imposing and more informal.

SOMETHING IN IT FOR BOTH OF YOU

The performance agreement you reach with an employee should have significance and value to both of you. If either one of you sees the agreement as being lopsided in favor of the other person, it's a safe bet that the person who's getting the short end won't live up to his or her part of the bargain—at least not fully.

How to form a performance agreement with something in it for both of you will become clearer as you read through the chapter. However, it may be helpful to keep in mind that the agreement ought to include:

☐ Some tasks for the employee to work on based on the individual's analysis of his own performance—especially the areas where the employee feels he could stand to improve;
☐ Some tasks for the employee to work on based on your analysis of her performance and the areas where you think she could stand to improve;
☐ Some tasks for you to work on that will assist and support the employee with the tasks he'll be working on; and
☐ Some tasks for you to work on based on what the employee told you when you asked the question, "How can I make your job less frustrating and more satisfying?"

STICK TO PRIORITIES

If we've learned anything about helping people change their behavior and improve their performance, it's this: Don't bite

I still think I'm getting the 'short end' in this.

off more than you can chew! We think this is especially important to keep in mind as you negotiate the performance agreement.

Unless we miss our bet, you and your employee will have a tendency to agree to work on many more tasks than either of you has time or energy available for. If you try to do too much, you may end up accomplishing very little or giving up altogether.

Although it will be difficult, try to limit the performance agreement only to those tasks that you and the employee think have high priority. If you find it too difficult to limit the agreement to only a few tasks, then go ahead and put down a more extensive list of things for both of you to work on. But then try to pick out the most important tasks to get started on right away, with the understanding that eventually you'll accomplish all the tasks.

BE SPECIFIC

This is just a reminder from a previous chapter to avoid the use of fuzzies and to use clear, precise language in writing out the tasks for the performance agreement. For example:

INSTEAD OF SAYING:
John will be more courteous to customers.

IT WOULD BE BETTER TO SAY:
When customers come to him with a problem, John will smile at them, speak in a friendly tone of voice, read back his understanding of their problem, and ask how he can help.

INSTEAD OF SAYING:
Sally will work on her written communications skills.

IT WOULD BE BETTER TO SAY:
Sally will enroll in a company-sponsored business writing course and involve Jane (her supervisor) in giving her feedback on her homework assignments.

INSTEAD OF SAYING:
Terry will work on improving the credibility of his sales presentations.

IT WOULD BE BETTER TO SAY:
When making sales presentations, Terry will talk about how his product meets the special needs of his customer, and he will be prepared to interrupt his presentation to respond to questions and concerns voiced by the customer.

THE NEGOTIATING STRATEGY

Here's the basic strategy that we recommend supervisors use in the negotiating process:

1. Ask what the employee would like to work on. Let's assume that you presented your analysis of the employee's performance and that there's at least reasonable receptivity to your ideas. A good way to begin the negotiating process is to simply ask what tasks the employee would like to work on over the next several weeks to improve performance. While the employee is talking, take a few notes. At the same time, use your active listening skills to draw out additional ideas and to summarize them once the person has finished talking.

2. Make additional suggestions, if necessary, about what you would like the employee to work on. After you ask what tasks the employee would like to work on, you may very well receive answers that include all the areas where you would like to see some improvement. But if the employee overlooks some areas, you can suggest additional tasks.

The list of tasks you're both coming up with is probably going to be too long. Some of the tasks will have to be eliminated to keep the list manageable and to avoid overburdening the employee.

There's another important thing to remember. At this point in the interview, it's especially important to keep the employee's receptivity up. Unless you feel very strongly about it, avoid suggesting additional tasks the employee strongly resisted earlier in the interview. Here the old adage, Discretion is the better part of valor, has a lot of relevance.

3. Strike a bargain. Once the employee has talked about the tasks that he or she would like to work on over the next several weeks and you have added your suggestions, the two of you should try to agree on the tasks that will be written up in the performance agreement.

Here are a few reminders:

☐ Stick to priorities. Only tasks that are really important to either or both of you should be written down.
☐ Be specific. The more clear you make the tasks that the employee is going to work on, the greater the chances that the person will actually work on them.
☐ Muster your listening skills. You'll need them.
☐ Be patient. Sometimes good bargains take a while to work out.

4. Ask, "What can I do to help?" After you and your employee decide what tasks the person is going to work on and actually write down the tasks in the performance agreement, it's time to focus on what you can do to assist the employee in carrying out these tasks. A good way to do this is to simply ask the employee, "What can I do to help you with these tasks?"

Remind the employee to think about how he or she responded earlier in the interview to your question, "What ideas do you have on how I can make your job less frustrating and more satisfying?"

Once again, take notes and use your active listening skills to draw the person out, and read back what you have heard when the person has finished.

5. Make additional suggestions, if necessary, on things that you could work on. After the employee has finished suggesting things you could do, make some of your own suggestions.

Just as you don't want the employee to feel overwhelmed with the number of tasks, you also need to feel comfortable with the amount of work that you're committing yourself to. Remind yourself, then, that you and the employee will be eliminating some of the tasks from your list so that you can concentrate on a few things that are important to both of you.

6. Strike another bargain. Do the same thing as in item 3 (above) in the negotiating strategy, only in reverse. Instead of bargaining on the *employee*'s tasks, the two of you must try to agree on the things *you*'ll be working on.

All the reminders cited in item 3 are equally relevant here. But there is one more thing to keep in mind. Managers and supervisors tend to expect their employees to make large, even outrageous, demands on them at this point in the interview. But our experience has proven otherwise. Employees usually make small, and sometimes apparently trivial, requests of their bosses. For example, it's much more likely for an employee to ask for a friendly smile and a hello in the morning than a 50 percent increase in salary. It may be that the requests that seem the most inconsequential and easiest to fulfill are the most important ones from the employee's standpoint.

WALKING THROUGH AN EXAMPLE

In the last chapter our hypothetical supervisor, Tom, spent quite a bit of time presenting his analysis of Lisa's work performance. Tom described the areas where he thought Lisa was performing effectively and came up with some specific examples in each of these areas. Then Tom talked about some of the areas where he thought Lisa could stand to improve, and he talked rather specifically about what she could do to improve in these areas. You may remember that Tom frequently had to use his active listening skills during this process to respond to a number of dips in Lisa's receptivity.

When we left them in the last chapter, Lisa seemed pretty receptive to Tom's analysis of the areas where she could stand to improve her performance. However, Tom and Lisa had not yet written down the tasks each of them would be working on for the next several weeks to help Lisa improve her work performance.

Let's go back to where we left off in the performance improvement interview to see how Tom negotiates a performance agreement with Lisa:

TOM: Okay, Lisa, why don't you take a few minutes to talk about the specific things that you'd like to be working on over the next several weeks, given all the things that we've talked about so far.

LISA: Good. (*Smiling and shaking her head*)

TOM: (*Smiling*) What?

LISA: (*Still smiling*) Well, I was just thinking that maybe we ought to put the worst first.

TOM: (*Smiling, but looking a little puzzled*)

LISA: I mean those damn reports.

TOM: (*Guffawing*) Oh!

LISA: Seriously, Tom, like I said, I'll make a commitment right here and now to get those monthly reports in on time every month for. . . .

TOM: Say the next six months?

LISA: You've got a deal.

TOM: Great. What else? (*Beginning to make some notes*)

LISA: Well . . . I still would like to work on this problem of increasing my closing rate, especially with prospects for very large orders.

TOM: (*Nodding*) Uhm-humm.

LISA: I'm batting about 300 right now, and I'd really like to get it up close to 400, if I could.

TOM: (*Nodding and making another note*) Okay, so far we've got getting your monthly reports in on time for the next six months and increasing your closing rate for large orders from 30 to 40 percent.

LISA: (*Looking thoughtful*) Right.

TOM: (*Leaning forward slightly*) Good. What else?

At this point Tom realizes that Lisa's second task, increasing her closing rate from 30 to 40 percent, even though specific, is a very large task. Tom knows that for Lisa to achieve this goal she'll have to work on some smaller tasks such as handling objections, time management, and so forth. However, Tom won't interrupt Lisa at this point to suggest that she break the task down into smaller bites. Rather, he'll wait until they both are actually ready to write down the tasks that Lisa will be working on. Lisa is much more likely to be receptive to the suggestion at that time.

LISA: (*Pausing and still looking thoughtful*) I still would like to do a better job of getting interviews with prospects. (*Pause*) I guess what I'm saying is that I want to do a better job of selling the interview as well as selling our product.

TOM: (*Nodding*) Okay. Sounds good.

LISA: Tom, I know you already think I'm pretty good at getting leads, but it's still something I'd like to work on.

TOM: That's fine, Lisa. A little later on perhaps we can talk about how I can help you in that area.

LISA: (*Nodding*) Good. I'd like that. (*Pausing and looking thoughtful*)

TOM: (*Leaning forward slightly*) Anything else?

LISA: Well . . . you mentioned that one of the areas where I could improve is getting to know the competition better. Like I said, I really agree with that.

TOM: Good. What else?

LISA: (*Pausing for a few seconds*) I think that about covers it. I can't think of anything else.

TOM: (*Glancing at his notes*) Okay, let's see. You mentioned getting all your monthly reports in on time for the next six months, improving the closing rate for large orders from 30 to 40 percent, doing a better job of getting interviews and getting leads, and finding out more about the competition. Does that pretty much cover it?

LISA: (*Nodding*) Yes. I think that covers it.

Up to this point no real negotiation has taken place. Tom has simply used his active listening skills to get Lisa to think out the tasks she'd like to work on. Tom's been very careful not to voice any opinions, one way or the other, about what Lisa has chosen to work on. Now he'll make some additional suggestions.

TOM: Good. Lisa, before we actually write down the tasks you'll be working on over the next several weeks, I'd like to add a couple of ideas of my own. Now, before you get nervous about piling too much on your plate, let me say this: After I make my suggestions, I think our job is to pare down the list of things you'll be doing to a manageable size.

LISA: (*Smiling and looking a little relieved*) Good.

TOM: Okay. Let me make my suggestions, and then let's figure out what is actually feasible for you to do.
LISA: (*Nodding*) Fine.

Tom is really conveying two messages to Lisa. The first is fairly direct: "Don't get nervous about having too much to do; we're going to pare down the list to a workable size." The second message is a little more subtle: "Let me get my suggestions out without a lot of argument; then we can negotiate what you're actually going to end up doing."

TOM: Well, Lisa, there are only two additional areas that I'd like to mention as possibilities for you to work on. (*Pause*)
LISA: (*Not saying anything but nodding*)
TOM: One is responding to customers' objections, and the other is time management—making up daily and weekly "to do" lists to help you establish your priorities. (*Pause*)
LISA: (*Chuckling and looking a little sheepish*) Oh yeah, I guess I forgot about those.
TOM: (*Smiling but not saying anything*)
LISA: (*Smiling broadly*) It's amazing how some things are easier to forget than others.
TOM: (*Laughing*) That's very true, isn't it? (*Taking a slightly more serious tone*) Remember, Lisa, I'm not saying you have to work on these two areas. But I did want to get them down as possibilities.
LISA: (*Nodding*) Well, I'm glad you did, Tom. I guess I'm not as convinced as you are that I need to work on them, but I'd certainly be willing to give it a try.
TOM: Fair enough. Well, let's see. We've got quite a few things on the list now. Why don't we try to decide the specific things that you'll be working on and get them down on a piece of paper.
LISA: Okay.

At this point Tom takes out a sheet of paper and draws a line down the middle. On the top of the left side he writes "What Lisa is going to be working on" and on the top of the right side he writes "What Tom is going to be working on." By doing this Tom communicates to Lisa that (1) the agreement, although written, will be informal, and (2) that the focus of the agreement will be on both of them not just on Lisa.

TOM: Well, Lisa, as I said earlier I think the most important thing for us to keep in mind here is to choose a few, very specific tasks for you to work on. I think we want to avoid biting off more than you can chew.

LISA: (*Nodding and smiling*) Yeah, I think that's a good idea. I probably would have a tendency to put down too much.

TOM: (*Smiling*) Good. Let's get started. What should we put down first? •

LISA: That's a tough choice . . . but I think I'd really like to work on finding ways to get leads to new market areas.

TOM: Okay. How should we put that down?

LISA: Well, I'm not sure. But I do think it's something you can give me some help on. . . .

TOM: (*After about a fifteen-second silence*) Well, how does this sound? "Spend at least one-third of her weekly meetings with Tom talking about specific ways she can increase her leads to new market areas."

LISA: Yeah, yeah. That sounds good.

Notice that Tom gave Lisa the opportunity to state this task in her own words before he offered the wording. Tom also checked to see that Lisa agreed on the wording before moving on to the next task. Notice also the very specific way the task is stated.

TOM: All right, good. What's next?

LISA: (*Thinking for a few seconds*) I'm not sure, but I know I could work on doing a better job of selling prospects over the phone on granting me an interview.

TOM: All right. What do you think we ought to put down for that?

LISA: (*Pausing*) I don't know. But there's something I might try with you, Tom, if you're willing.

TOM: Shoot.

LISA: Well, I've got some ideas for new techniques, and it would be nice if I could sort of role play them with you, if that's all right.

TOM: (*Nodding*) Sure. What if I put down this: "Role play with Tom some new and different techniques for getting prospects to grant her an interview."

LISA: Beautiful. That's exactly what I had in mind.

TOM: Great. Well, that's two tasks. How about a couple more?

LISA: Well, what do we put down about my wanting to increase my closing rate for large orders from 30 percent to 40 percent? •

TOM: Lisa, that's a pretty broad task. But I think the first two tasks we've got down, the one on getting leads and the one on

• Once more, Tom has given Lisa the responsibility for deciding what she'll be working on.

• Here Lisa has brought up a task that Tom thinks is way too big to put down, even though it sounds specific.

getting interviews, are going to go a long way in helping you improve your closing rate. What do you think?

LISA: (*Wrinkling her forehead a little*)

TOM: You're not sure you agree with my logic?

LISA: (*Looking thoughtful*) No, I think I see what you're saying. Okay, okay. I agree. I think they will help to boost it.

TOM: All right. What's next?

LISA: (*Smiling*) Well, I guess we'd better get something down about my getting those monthly reports in on time. . . .

In the next few minutes Lisa and Tom will be finishing her portion of the performance agreement (see page 168). Notice that the agreement pretty well covers all the areas that Lisa was originally interested in working on—doing a better job of getting leads and interviews, and, indirectly, improving her closing rate. The agreement also covers two areas that are of concern to Tom—getting monthly reports in on time and learning more about the competition. So far, however, the agreement doesn't include anything on time management or dealing with objections. But we think Tom should feel very satisfied at this point. The tasks laid out for Lisa's side of the agreement are very precisely stated, and she seems quite committed to carrying them out. The fact that Tom didn't get all his stuff in there is fine. It's the natural result of the negotiating process.

Now let's rejoin them as they start discussing what tasks Tom will be working on:

TOM: Okay, Lisa, I'd say that's about enough for you to be working on over the next several weeks. What do you think?

LISA: I agree. I think it looks pretty good.

TOM: Okay. Why don't we shift gears and start talking about some of the things that I can do to help you with your tasks.

LISA: (*Nodding*)

TOM: By the way, I don't think we should forget about some of the things you said earlier in the interview when I asked you how I could make your job less frustrating and more satisfying.

LISA: (*Smiling*) No way I can object to that.

TOM: Good. Well, what are your thoughts on what we can put down for me to do?

LISA: (*Looking thoughtful*) Well, to tell you the truth, Tom, you're already plugged in to three of the tasks that we've got down for me.

TOM: (*Nodding*) Uhm-humm.

LISA: (*Pausing several seconds*) Well . . . (*Smiling and looking just a little embarrassed*) Uh, I don't even know if it's that important.

TOM: Seems like you're a little reluctant to tell me what you're thinking. I'd like to hear it.

LISA: (*Sitting up in her chair and talking in a firmer tone of voice*) Well, Tom, actually there is one thing that I'd like you to do for me.

TOM: Shoot.

LISA: Well, it really bugs me when you hold meetings with me and the other salespeople so late in the day. I must miss my train three or four times a month. •

TOM: That must be pretty annoying.

LISA: (*Looking relieved*) It really is! If I miss that train, I have to wait over an hour for the next one. It can foul up my plans for an entire evening. (*Pause*)

TOM: (*Smiling*) Well, I'm sorry, Lisa, I didn't realize I was causing you a problem. What do you think we ought to do about the situation?

LISA: How about holding the meetings a little earlier in the day?

TOM: I can buy that. What do you say we put down, "Hold sales meetings with Lisa earlier in the day so she doesn't miss her commuter train"?

LISA: If you'll agree to do that, Tom, it would make me very happy.

TOM: (*Smiling broadly*) Anything else I can do for you?

LISA: Uh . . . well, I think we already dealt with it, but (*Smiling*) it might be nice to get it down in writing. (*Pause*)

TOM: (*Looking slightly confused*) What's that, Lisa?

LISA: You know, the matter of the (*Clearing throat*) . . . *girls* in the office?

TOM: (*Shrugging his shoulders and raising his palms to the ceiling*) I guess you got me cold on that one. (*Both laughing*) How about if I write down, "Tom will no longer use the expression *girls in the office* in Lisa's presence"?

LISA: (*Half-serious, half-teasing*) Hmm. I was kind of hoping that it might read something like, "Tom will no longer use the expression *girls in the office* in *anybody's* presence."

TOM: (*Feigning outrage*) What! You do drive a hard bargain, don't you? (*Now more serious*) Well, I guess if you're going to be working on all of the things you agreed to, then that's the least I can do.

LISA: (*Smiling*) Thank you, Tom. I really appreciate it.

TOM: Don't mention it, Lisa. Anything else you can think of?

LISA: (*Thinking for a few seconds*) No, that's it. If you do those two things, I'll be completely satisfied.

TOM: Okay, I'm glad to hear that. But let me mention a couple of other things that I've been thinking about. . . .

• This is obviously a sensitive topic for Lisa, and it's taken her almost the entire interview to get it out. How Tom reacts to this may well have a strong impact on the ultimate success of the performance agreement.

Look at the final agreement that Lisa and Tom negotiated. Tom was also able to sell Lisa on the idea of trying out a daily and weekly "to do" list for the next two weeks and to having Tom show her some ways to make her monthly reporting task a little quicker and less unpleasant.

WHAT LISA (EMPLOYEE) IS GOING TO WORK ON:	WHAT TOM (SUPERVISOR) IS GOING TO WORK ON:
– Spend at least ⅓ of her weekly meetings with Tom talking about specific ways she can increase leads to new market areas.	– Hold meetings with Lisa earlier in the day so she doesn't miss her commuter train.
– Role play with Tom some new and different techniques for getting prospects to grant her an interview.	– Will no longer use the expression "girls in the office" in Lisa's or anybody else's presence.
– Submit all her monthly reports to Tom on time for the next six months.	– Help Lisa, for the next two weeks, set up daily and weekly "to do" lists.
– Meet with Tom on a quarterly basis to review what both of us have learned recently about the competition.	– Show Lisa some tricks Tom learned for getting through his paperwork rapidly.

After they completed filling out the performance agreement, Lisa and Tom agreed to meet in four weeks to discuss the agreement and the progress that the two of them had made in carrying out their tasks.

So that's it — a fully negotiated performance agreement. At this point you may be thinking, "Okay, that went very smoothly. But I can't believe that they're all going to be this easy."

We can't really argue with you on that. Some agreements will be harder to negotiate than this one was. (Some will be easier, too.) But don't forget that by now you've begun to develop some listening skills and other techniques, such as stop, look, and listen, to help you out when the going gets a little rough in any stage of the interview.

A QUICK SUMMARY

Just a reminder: The negotiating process will go more smoothly if, in addition to using your listening skills, you:

☐ Keep it informal,
☐ Make sure there's something in it for both of you,
☐ Stick to priorities, that is, don't bite off more than you can chew, and
☐ Be as specific as you can in writing down the task statements.

Now the hard work is over. In the next chapter we'll talk about how to end the interview so that you and the employee can leave this experience feeling that it was a positive one, and with the best possible chance that it will lead to improved performance for both of you.

CHAPTER 13 • STEP EIGHT: CLOSE THE INTERVIEW

You're coming down to the wire. You and your employee have agreed on the things you're both going to do in the next several weeks to move you closer to the goal of improved employee work performance. Now you're ready to bring the interview to a close.

There are four basic points you should follow to make this last stage of the interview go as smoothly as possible:

- Ask for your employee's overall reaction to the interview.
- After listening to your employee's reactions, offer some of your own thoughts and feelings on how things went.
- Schedule a specific time, date, and place for a follow-up meeting to review how well you and your employee are living up to the agreement you've just reached.
- End the interview on a positive note.

ASK FOR YOUR EMPLOYEE'S REACTION

It's not a very good idea to end any important life experience too abruptly because people often feel a strong need to talk about the experience. It's important to review and reflect on what happened.

Here's an example of how you might draw out your employee at the end of the performance improvement interview:

"Well, Pat, we certainly covered a lot of ground today. Before we close, though, I'd like to get your reactions to today's meeting. I'd be especially interested in hearing what you think we accomplished, what you think we didn't accomplish, your general feelings about where we go from here, and anything else you'd like to mention about what happened today."

A comprehensive question like this one should get the employee talking. If the person's response to the question is entirely positive ("I'm really glad we did this," or "This has been a super experience"), you're in good shape. You can say that you're glad the employee feels that way and move on to offering your reactions.

But it's very possible that the person could have a negative reaction. For example, the employee could have been upset about something you said earlier in the interview but held back from showing it at the time. Now he might say:

"I've been thinking about what you said earlier about my lack of motivation. I think what you said was unfair and untrue, especially when you compare me with the others around here."

Or the employee might have had second thoughts about what was agreed to in the performance agreement. Maybe she feels that what she agreed to do was a lot more than what you agreed to do. She might say:

"Well, I've been thinking about what we both agreed to do over the next few weeks. I don't know, it seems kind of unbalanced to me."

Think for a minute or two about how you'd respond to these two reactions. Then compare your responses to our suggestions. Our suggestions for dealing with negative reactions at this stage of the interview should sound familiar:

1. Whenever employees seem angry, irritated, or upset, give them room to talk about what's on their minds. Don't argue with them or interrupt. Don't tell them they shouldn't feel the way they do. Actively listen to what they have to say. Begin by reflecting feeling. Ask open-ended questions, probe for specificity, use encouragers, and paraphrase and summarize what they say. Then it's your turn to talk.

2. If listening doesn't do the trick, get a dissatisfied employee to come up with a solution to the problem. Ask for suggestions. Be willing to bend a little. If you can live with the employee's suggestions, make the necessary changes in the performance agreement.

3. If you and your employee have very different ideas on how to proceed, don't get involved in a win-lose struggle. Use the stop, look, and listen technique. Remember, it goes like this:

☐ Stop the interaction as soon as you see that the discussion is becoming argumentative or unproductive.
☐ Look squarely at the problem by describing it succinctly and objectively.
☐ Listen for suggestions that you both can live with for resolving the problem.

Here's an example of how these suggestions could be used at this stage of the interview:

SUPERVISOR: We've covered a lot of ground today, Lou, and before we pack it in, I'd like to get your reactions to what we've accomplished. I'd be interested in anything you have to say. (*Pause*)
EMPLOYEE: (*Hesitating*) Well . . . uh . . . I guess we made pretty good progress. Uh . . . I guess it went a lot smoother than I had expected. I don't know . . . I guess it went all right.
SUPERVISOR: (*Leaning forward*) So in some respects it went better than you thought it would. But something still seems to be on your mind, Lou. I'd like to hear anything you've got to say.
EMPLOYEE: (*Fidgeting*) Well . . . uh . . . I didn't mention it earlier, and I probably should've, but I don't think putting that agreement down in writing makes a lot of sense.
SUPERVISOR: Hmm. You're feeling kind of uncomfortable at the idea of putting it in writing?
EMPLOYEE: I guess I am. I don't know. It just seems so damned formal and legal and all. Why the hell can't we just agree to do those things and shake hands on it. I'm going to remember what I agreed to. And I'm sure you will too.
SUPERVISOR: Sounds like writing our agreement down on paper has made it seem impersonal and legalistic — very different from the informal way you like to do things?

EMPLOYEE: Yeah, that's certainly a very strong part of it. Look, I know this is your show, but . . . well, you just never know who's going to lay their hands on a piece of paper like that. I know it's not going to go in my personnel folder, or anything like that, but things like that have a way of being seen by people who have no business seeing them.

SUPERVISOR: I see. So just having a piece of paper means that there's a possibility of someone seeing it, and that makes you feel even more cautious. I'm also wondering if perhaps you may be thinking that I may show the agreement to someone else?

EMPLOYEE: No, that's not right! I believed you when you said it was just between you and me. I don't know. Maybe I'm just overreacting and taking this whole thing too seriously. But I'd still like to make it a verbal agreement. What do you think?

SUPERVISOR: (*Noticing that receptivity has gone up*) Well, Lou, I can certainly appreciate your feelings. As a matter of fact, I often get a little concerned that some of the other people I supervise will show copies of our agreements to other people. And that makes me feel uncomfortable! (*Both laugh*) As I think about it, though, I've got to say that I'd like to keep the agreement in writing. I supervise about a dozen people now, and if I don't put things in writing, I'd forget half of what I agreed to. But Lou, I want to respect your feelings as much as I can. What suggestions do you have for how we can resolve this matter of your discomfort with a written agreement and my pretty strong need to have one?

EMPLOYEE: (*Looking very thoughtful*) Hmm . . . good question. Well . . . uh . . . I don't know. (*Eyes brighten*) Well, one possibility is just scratching out our names from the top of the page. That way, if anybody did see it, they wouldn't know whose it was. But since we came up with it, we'd always know it was ours. What do you think?

SUPERVISOR: Sold! (*Erasing names*) Great suggestion! Any other reactions to what we've done today. . . .

SHARE YOUR REACTION WITH YOUR EMPLOYEE

After listening fully to your employee's reactions, you should share some of your own thoughts and feelings about how things went in the interview. What you say and how you say it will depend on how positive you're feeling about the interview.

POSITIVE REACTIONS

If you feel pleased at the end of the interview, say something positive about the experience to your employee.

"I've got to tell you that I feel very good. I think we accomplished a lot here today. To be frank, I think we accomplished much more than I had hoped. I was especially pleased with the way that you came to the interview so well prepared. You did a thorough job of examining your own work performance and had a number of very helpful suggestions for how I could make your job more satisfying. Also, I was very pleased at how we were both willing to bend a little when we had that slight disagreement on how to proceed earlier in the meeting. I'm also very happy about the things that you've agreed to do to improve your work performance. I think you've set your sights high but not too high. And, finally, I'm really looking forward to doing the things that I agreed to, because just doing those things will make me a better supervisor. Thanks for helping to make this a worthwhile experience."

NOT-SO-POSITIVE REACTIONS

Sometimes at the end of an interview you may feel that the employee hasn't been very cooperative and that you've had to take several giant steps just to get the employee to move an inch. In a situation such as this we suggest that you:

1. **Be honest about your feelings without being brutal.** You have a right to your feelings, just as the employee does. You'll feel better if you express them directly and sensitively.

2. **Don't blame the employee for anything that happened.** Don't overreact, lecture, or use emotionally loaded expressions.

3. **Stress the positive.** Try to find something the employee said or did during the interview that made you feel good.

4. **Describe the specific problem or problems briefly and objectively.** Tell the employee how it made you feel. Ask for suggestions on how the problem might be resolved in future meetings. Look for win-win solutions and be prepared to shift back and forth from presenting to listening.

Here's an example:

SUPERVISOR: (*Having just heard employee's reactions to interview*) Well, Dana, I have to admit that my reactions are also kind of mixed. Let me begin by mentioning some of my more positive feelings, and then I'll mention some that aren't so positive. (*Pause*)

EMPLOYEE: (*Looking thoughtful*) Okay.

SUPERVISOR: On the plus side, I'm very happy we had this meeting. I realize we had some trouble scheduling it and had to postpone it twice because of our bouts with the flu. So, it's nice to have it behind us. (*Pause*)

EMPLOYEE: I've got to agree to that.

SUPERVISOR: Another thing I'm happy about is the thorough job you did of identifying your strengths. You helped to make me aware of some things you're capable of handling around here that I hadn't really seen before today.

EMPLOYEE: I'm glad of that, Dana. I've been itching to get some new, more challenging assignments.

SUPERVISOR: That's another thing I'm pleased with, Dana—that you want to take on more responsibilities. (*Pause*) On the other side of the coin, I was surprised and a little disappointed when you said you couldn't think of any ways you could improve your performance. Compared to the thorough job you did of identifying your strengths, I was hoping to get the benefit of your thinking in that area too. (*Pause*)

EMPLOYEE: It was kind of unbalanced, huh?

SUPERVISOR: Well, yes it was. Now that may be because this is the first time I've asked you to do something like that. And people usually get better at it the second time around. The next time we get together, I'd like to find a way out of this problem of me identifying all of the ways you can improve and you focusing pretty much exclusively on your strengths. Any suggestions for how we might solve this problem?

EMPLOYEE: Well, that was pretty much how it went today. Uh . . . it seems like I've been focusing on my strong points and ignoring the weak ones. And maybe you've been focusing on both, but putting a little more emphasis on the things I could be doing better. Maybe . . . uh . . . maybe next time we get together, I could just focus on how I could improve and you could just focus on my strong points. How's that sound?

SUPERVISOR: That sounds good. We'll both be concentrating on an area we didn't focus on as much as we should have today. Any other suggestions for how we can make our next meeting a more productive one?

Sharing your reactions with the employee, especially if they're not all positive, means taking some risk. However, as long as you're ready to shift from a presenting mode to a listening mode to deal with any dips in employee receptivity, you should be able to manage the situation pretty well.

SCHEDULE THE FOLLOW-UP MEETING

After you and the employee have discussed your reactions to the meeting, schedule a follow-up meeting to review your progress. You should set up this meeting in the same way you set up the performance improvement interview itself:

1. Tell the employee the purpose of the meeting and briefly explain what's going to happen when you meet.
2. Tell the employee how you plan to prepare for the meeting and suggest how the employee can prepare for it.
3. Arrange a specific date, time, and place for the meeting.
4. Answer any questions the employee may have about the meeting.

Here's an example of a supervisor arranging a follow-up meeting:

SUPERVISOR: Even though we'll be talking informally on almost a daily basis, Maxie, I'd like to schedule a follow-up meeting in two to three weeks to review our progress. (*Pause*)
EMPLOYEE: Two to three weeks? Okay, sounds good.
SUPERVISOR: As I see it, the purpose of the meeting will be to review how both of us are doing in terms of the agreement we reached earlier. In that meeting, I'd like to take a careful look at how well we've both accomplished what we set out to do, discuss any problems we've run into, and talk about where to go in the future. (*Pause*)
EMPLOYEE: (*Nodding*)
SUPERVISOR: I plan to review my copy of the agreement every couple of days, just to make sure I stay on top of things. You might want to do the same. So let's plan to use the agreement as a springboard for discussion, okay?
EMPLOYEE: (*Smiling*) Okay.
SUPERVISOR: All right. Before we schedule a specific time and date, let me answer any questions you might have about the meeting?
EMPLOYEE: Hmm. Can't think of any right now.
SUPERVISOR: Fine, if you think of anything, don't hesitate to ask. (*Pause*) Okay, how about Thursday, the twenty-first, at, say, 2:00 P.M., here in my office?
EMPLOYEE: (*Looking at calendar*) Looks good to me.

The exact timing of follow-up meetings will vary from situation to situation, but they shouldn't be put off too long. They should probably be scheduled within a month of the interview. If too much time passes, there's a tendency to lose the momentum you built up in the first meeting.

END THE INTERVIEW ON A POSITIVE NOTE

Try to end the interview on a positive note. Especially if the interview had some difficult moments, you should have the employee leave your office in a positive frame of mind. Here are some suggestions:

1. Make a positive concluding comment about the interview. Here are several examples:

"I'm glad we had this meeting. I think we've made a lot of progress today."

"Well, it was a hard but productive session. I'm glad we met."

"I always seem to learn so much in meetings like these. And this one was no exception."

2. Usher out your employee in a friendly, easy manner. Stand up, smile, walk the employee to the door, and shake hands.

3. Thank the employee for meeting with you. For example, you might say:

"Thanks for working as hard as you did in today's meeting, Ted. I really appreciate the effort you made."

"Thanks for the suggestions you came up with, Helene. I'm going to start putting some of them into practice right away."

"Thanks for spending as much time on this as you did, Tim. I know the effort will be worth it in the long run."

4. Say that you're looking forward to the follow-up meeting. Don't overdo it or you'll sound insincere.

Here's an example of a supervisor ending the interview on a positive note:

SUPERVISOR: (*Standing up and smiling*) Well, that about does it for today. Barry, I really enjoyed this meeting. (*Pause*)
EMPLOYEE: (*Smiling and also standing up*) Yeah, me too! I have to confess, it went a lot better than I imagined it would.
SUPERVISOR: (*Hand on employee's shoulder, walking toward door*) A large part of the reason it went so well is that

you really got seriously involved in the process. Thanks. I appreciate it.

EMPLOYEE: Well, you certainly helped make it go as well as it did. And I appreciate that too.

SUPERVISOR: Thanks. (*Shaking the employee's hand warmly*) I'm looking forward to meeting with you again on the twenty-first. Take care of yourself, Barry.

That concludes the actual interview. You've heard your employee's reactions to how things went, shared some of your own reactions, arranged for a follow-up meeting, and ended on a positive note. Now you need to prepare for the follow-up session.

CHAPTER 14 • STEP NINE: FOLLOW UP

The interview is over. You and your employee are beginning to work on some specific tasks that you've both agreed will lead to improved employee performance.

Following up to see that these tasks get done is an important final step in the process. It will help you and the employee take advantage of the momentum you built up in the interview. Both of you will be much less likely to fall back into old habits that will tend to get in the way of completing the tasks.

We cover two types of follow-up in this chapter—informal and formal. We'll begin by describing several informal, ongoing procedures that you can begin almost immediately. Then we'll offer some thoughts on how to proceed with the formal follow-up meeting you scheduled for several weeks after the performance improvement interview.

INFORMAL FOLLOW-UP

An immediate, informal follow-up with an employee is important for several reasons:

1. Immediate reinforcement of any new behavior is important. The longer reinforcement is delayed the less likely the new behavior will become a habit. Waiting several weeks until the formal follow-up interview is too long.

2. You and your employee are likely to be very busy during the next several weeks and you might neglect your agreement. There will be lots of responsibilities, besides what's written on your performance agreement, competing for your attention. It'll be very easy for both of you to put the agreement on the back burner and concentrate on the normal demands of your jobs.

3. Changing behavior is hard work and periodic encouragement is necessary. Both you and your employee can expect to get a little frustrated and discouraged before the follow-up interview. You'll both need something to boost you up between now and then.

In the rest of this section we'll describe some specific things you can do to keep up the momentum between now and the follow-up interview:

☐ Follow up immediately and touch base periodically,
☐ Ask the employee to follow up with you,
☐ Reward employee effort,
☐ Expect to get a little discouraged, and
☐ Use other resources to support your efforts.

FOLLOW UP IMMEDIATELY AND TOUCH BASE PERIODICALLY

It's important to check in with the employee a day or so after the performance improvement interview. For example, you might approach the employee when there are no other employees around and say:

"Hilary, I just wanted you to know that I enjoyed our meeting yesterday. I think it was a valuable and productive session. I'm looking forward to working together with you on the areas we agreed on."

Following up immediately has several advantages:

1. It lets your employee know you meant what you said during your initial meeting. Since some supervisors never follow up, some employees will wait a day or so to figure out whether or not you mean business. Following up immediately shows that you're committed to improving the employee's performance.

2. Checking back with employees informally gives them a chance to ask questions that didn't occur to them during the interview. They can also clear up points that have come up since the meeting. You may even want to probe for questions or comments, saying something like this:

"Well, it's been two days since we met. Any questions you didn't get a chance to ask during our meeting? Or any thoughts that you've had since then?"

3. An immediate follow-up with the employee is good for you. It helps remind you that your responsibility didn't end with the interview. And it makes future follow-up contacts that much easier.

It's a good idea to touch base periodically with the employee after the first informal contact. There are many ways to do this. You can arrange to take a coffee break or to have lunch. You can even chat briefly in the parking lot or when you're both waiting for the elevator.

Without giving employees the feeling that you're looking over their shoulders, let them know you're ready to help them achieve their goals for improved performance.

ASK YOUR EMPLOYEE TO FOLLOW UP WITH YOU

As soon as you begin working on your part of the performance agreement, ask your employee to follow up with you. For example, you might say:

"Listen Jean, I'm going to have to work hard to live up to my part of the bargain and I'd appreciate all the support and encouragement that you can give me. You know, I'd appreciate your asking me how things are going every now and then, giving me a pat on the back when you see me doing something that I've agreed to do, reminding me of anything I might have forgotten to do, and that sort of thing. Believe me, any help will be greatly appreciated."

Involving the employee serves several purposes:

1. It establishes a two-way relationship in which you can help one another out. You're partners in a behavior change effort, and it's important to act like partners.

2. It helps make certain that the spotlight doesn't always shine on the employee. You deserve some attention too.

3. Most important, it will help you do the things you agreed to do. You don't want to be the one to fail to carry out your part of the agreement.

REWARD EMPLOYEE EFFORT

Psychologists and educators have often said that it's better to praise people for behaving as you want them to than it is to punish them for behaving in a way you don't approve of. This certainly applies to employees. Whenever you see them in the process of accomplishing something they said they would, give them some solid praise:

"That was really nice work, Terry. Good job!"
"I couldn't help but notice how you handled that situation, Dee. Nice!"
"You're really giving this an all-out effort, Al. Keep up the good work!"

When you praise people for a certain behavior, it increases the chances that they'll behave the same way in the future.

EXPECT TO GET A LITTLE DISCOURAGED

Employee progress after a performance improvement interview is usually a mixed bag. You'll see some definite signs of improvement, but you'll probably also see some areas where no progress, or even some backsliding, occurs.

It's at times like these that you should avoid the common ineffective tendencies identified earlier in the book: avoiding confrontation, complaining to other people, lecturing, and overreacting. You—and the employee—have to be prepared for some discouragement.

It's important to use your listening skills when you see the employee begin to backslide. Find out how the person feels. Ask for ideas on how to get back on track. When receptivity is up, let the employee know it's normal to see a failure or two at this point. Remind the employee of whatever good progress you have observed. Use your presentation skills to offer your own suggestions and to get the employee thinking positively again. As one of our supervisors put it, "It's like being a good coach. You accept a temporary failure and concentrate on the future. You rebuild morale and get the players to try even harder the next time."

USE OTHER RESOURCES TO SUPPORT YOUR EFFORTS

You and the employee don't have to take on this thing alone. You can take advantage of other resources:

1. Programs and supporting materials that focus on the areas where the employee is trying to improve. For example, you might want to send an employee a copy of the article "How to Get Better Control of Your Time" with a short note: "Thought you'd be interested." Or you could suggest that the employee attend a workshop on time management at your local community college. Most performance problems are quite common, so there are many programs, articles, materials, and workshops already available to help people deal with them.

2. People resources within your own organization. Many companies have training staff, employee assistance counselors, consultants, psychologists, social workers, and personnel specialists with skills to help employees. For example, you can ask a struggling salesperson to meet with a member of the training staff who's interested in sales training. You can arrange a meeting between the director of your employee assistance program and an employee whose poor performance seems related to a family drinking problem. Or you can involve the management consultant you've been using with a newly appointed supervisor who's having trouble making the transition from labor to management. In short, you can act like a matchmaker between the needs of employees and the skills of third-party resource people.

So far, we've been talking about methods of informal follow-up—the things you can do to continually support and reinforce the goals you and the employee set for improved work performance. Now let's turn to the formal follow-up interview.

THE FOLLOW-UP INTERVIEW

You and your employee scheduled a formal follow-up meeting at the close of the performance improvement interview. At that time, you explained to the employee that it would be a good idea to sit down in several weeks to review the progress that the both of you had made toward the goals laid out in the performance agreement.

In many respects, the follow-up interview is just another version of the first eight steps in the performance improvement process. Basically, the same skills and techniques apply. Here is the sequence of steps:

1. Analyze Your Employee's Performance and Your Own Performance.
2. Remind Your Employee of the Follow-Up Interview,
3. Begin the Interview,
4. Find Out How Things Are Going,
5. Review Your Progress,
6. Review Your Employee's Progress,
7. Decide "Where to Go from Here," and
8. Close the Interview.

In elaborating on these steps, we've tried to avoid repetition with earlier chapters. However, reviewing some of these chapters may be helpful as you go through the steps.

ANALYZE YOUR EMPLOYEE'S PERFORMANCE AND YOUR OWN PERFORMANCE

Just as you prepared for the initial meeting with your employee, it is important to get ready for this one too. Look over the performance agreement and review the progress you both have made over the past several weeks. As you do this, ask yourself:

☐   Has the employee accomplished the goals that were set? Have I? Which goals were accomplished and which were not?

☐   In what specific ways has the employee exceeded or fallen short of the goals that were set? How about me?

☐   If goals were not accomplished, why not? If they were, why? What factors can help to explain the employee's and my performance? What events have occurred in the past several weeks that can help to put things into a better perspective?

REMIND YOUR EMPLOYEE
OF THE FOLLOW-UP INTERVIEW

Remind the employee about the follow-up interview several days prior to the meeting. As you did when you arranged the first interview:

1. Approach the person when there are not a lot of other people around.
2. Remind your employee that the follow-up meeting is approaching and briefly review the purpose of the meeting.
3. Tell your employee how you plan to prepare for the meeting.
4. Suggest how your employee can prepare for the meeting.
5. Confirm the date, time, and place of the meeting.
6. End on a positive note.

Here's an example:

SUPERVISOR: (*Out of earshot of others*) Well, Lee, the follow-up meeting we scheduled at our performance review meeting last month is coming up next week and I wanted to remind you of it. (*Pause*)

EMPLOYEE: (*Looking surprised, but not startled*) It's coming up already?

SUPERVISOR: Yeah, I could hardly believe it either. (*Pause*) Listen, Lee, I'm going to prepare for the meeting by carefully reviewing the performance agreement that we wrote up. (*Pause*) And I'd like you to prepare by doing the same thing, okay?

EMPLOYEE: Fine. Actually, I've been looking at it on and off quite a bit this month. But I'll give it a careful look before the meeting.

SUPERVISOR: Good. My calendar shows that the meeting is scheduled for next Tuesday morning at 10:30 in my office. (*Pause*)

EMPLOYEE: I'll be there.

SUPERVISOR: Good. I'm looking forward to it.

You may run into some problems when you remind employees of the follow-up meeting, especially if they're feeling guilty about not doing what they set out to do. It may be helpful to review the strategy for asking your employee to meet with you in Chapter 2, and the listening skills in Chapter 7.

BEGIN THE INTERVIEW

You want to get your follow-up interview off to a good start. Here's how you begin:

1. Set the stage for a private meeting that will have as few distractions and interruptions as possible.
2. Make the person feel comfortable and welcome. Get out from behind your desk, give the employee a warm greeting, sit down face-to-face, and engage in a bit of chitchat before getting down to business.
3. Orient the employee. Remind the employee of the purpose of the meeting. Then give the employee a preview of what's going to happen in the meeting. Tell the employee what you hope to achieve in the meeting.
4. Respond to the employee's questions and concerns without letting them throw you off track. If you ignore the questions or emotional concerns of the employee, you'll pay the price of reduced involvement and cooperation.

Here's an example of a supervisor getting a follow-up interview off to a good start:

SUPERVISOR: (*Having just reviewed the purpose of the meeting*) There are a number of things that I'd like to cover today, Gerry. Let me just mention them briefly so you'll have an idea of what to expect in this meeting. (*Pause*)
EMPLOYEE: (*Nodding*)
SUPERVISOR: First, I'd like you to begin by telling me how things are going, in general, on the job and if you're experiencing any problems that you think I should be aware of. (*Pause*)
EMPLOYEE: (*Acknowledging agreement*)
SUPERVISOR: After that, I'd like us to discuss how well we've accomplished the things we set out to do when we met about a month ago. We can use the performance agreement that we came up with as a guide. (*Pause*)
EMPLOYEE: Okay. I brought my copy with me.
SUPERVISOR: Good. I have mine here too. When we review our progress, I'd like to suggest that we begin with a review of how well I've done and then move to an analysis of your performance.
EMPLOYEE: (*Nodding*) Sounds good.

SUPERVISOR: In reviewing each other's progress, I'd like us to be frank and open with each other. After we've reviewed each other's performance, I'd like to talk about where to go from here. We'll probably come up with another agreement about what the two of us can do in the future, much the same as the one we came up with last time we met.

The employee now has a preview of what's going to happen in the follow-up meeting and a chance to get on the supervisor's wavelength before getting down to business. For more information on getting the interview off to a good start, you may want to review how to begin the performance improvement interview in Chapter 6.

FIND OUT HOW THINGS ARE GOING

As you begin your follow-up meeting, it's a good idea to find out how things have been going, in general, for your employee since your last meeting. Here's how you might do it:

"Before we review the progress we've made, I'd like to spend a few minutes talking about how things are going, in general, on the job for you. And also about any problems that you may be having that I should be aware of. How *have* things been going for you?"

Asking how things are going at the outset of the follow-up interview serves several purposes:

☐ It eases employees into the interview by getting them to talk about things that are important to them.
☐ It gives them an opportunity to discuss problems that may be important but don't seem to have much to do with the purpose of this meeting.
☐ It gives you a chance to show once again that you're interested in what they have to say.

A couple of problems may surface at this stage of the interview. Employees may want to keep talking about how things are going or about some of the problems they're experiencing. Or they may make some critical remarks about you or the performance improvement process, possibly because they haven't accomplished what they said they would. Keep your cool and use your listening skills in this kind of situation. For a review of how to handle problems such as this, review the strategy for finding out how things are going in Chapter 4 and the listening skills in Chapter 7.

REVIEW YOUR PROGRESS

It's best to review *your* progress before taking a look at how well your employee has done. By beginning with yourself, you let your employee know that you're taking the process seriously and that you're standing behind the commitments you made. You can kick things off by saying something like this:

SUPERVISOR: All right, let's begin by reviewing my progress first. What I'd like to do is take each of the things that I agreed to last month and discuss them one at a time. I'd like to get your reactions first and then I'll offer my own thoughts. (*Pause*)

EMPLOYEE: I'm ready whenever you are.

SUPERVISOR: Okay. (*Looking at copy of performance agreement*) Well, the first thing I said I'd do is stop criticizing you in front of the other workers. What are your thoughts about how well I achieved that goal? (*Pause*)

At this point, shift into a listening mode. As your employee responds be sure that you:

☐ Use good attending behavior,

☐ Probe for more information when you hear something that's not clear,

☐ Reflect feeling and paraphrase the employee's remarks to check that you're hearing things accurately,

☐ Summarize what you heard the person say before offering your own views, after your employee has finished talking.

The employee's analysis of your performance might go as follows:

EMPLOYEE: (*Thoughtfully*) Well, I guess I'd have to say that you did pretty well.

SUPERVISOR: (*Leaning forward*) Tell me a little more, Dan. I'm not quite sure how you mean that.

EMPLOYEE: Well, I won't say that you completely accomplished your goal, but I'd have to say that you came pretty close. I can only think of one time that you chewed me out in front of the other people in the office.

SUPERVISOR: So with that one exception, you'd say that I was able to stop criticizing you in front of the others?

EMPLOYEE: Right. Except for the time when the machine got jammed and you let Hank and me know what was on your mind. But I really appreciated how you came up later and apologized to us for blowing your stack.

SUPERVISOR: (*Looking down and shaking head*) I don't

feel good about that. But my apologizing for the incident took some of the sting out of it, is that right?

EMPLOYEE: I'd say all of the sting out of it. If you hadn't apologized, I think I would have been pretty resentful. I sure as hell would've stewed over it for a while.

SUPERVISOR: I'm glad to hear that you didn't. I appreciate your comments. Any other thoughts about this area before I offer my own views on the subject? (*Pause*)

When the employee gives you the signal that you've heard things correctly, then it's your turn to talk. When presenting your own views about the progress you've made:

☐   Try to be specific and factual.
☐   Build as much as you can on the employee's analysis.
☐   When you agree with the employee, say so.
☐   When you disagree, let the employee know you have a different view of the situation without attacking or challenging the employee's view.
☐   If the employee's receptivity drops after you've said something, stop talking and start listening. When receptivity goes back up, start talking again.

When you finish reviewing your progress in the first area, summarize the discussion and then make a transition to the second area by saying something like this:

"All right, it sounds as if both of us agree that I did a pretty good job living up to my agreement not to criticize you in front of the other workers. (*Pause; employee nods assent*) A little later in the interview I'd like us to talk about what I might continue to do in this area. (*Pause*) But now I'd like to move on to the second thing I agreed to do, which was. . . ."

Discuss the goals laid out in the performance agreement one at a time. In each instance, get your employee's reactions, then give your own. When you've finished reviewing your progress on all of the goals, briefly summarize the entire discussion before moving on to review the employee's performance. Here's how you might make the transition:

"All right, that was very helpful. We've covered a lot of ground, but let me try to summarize what the two of us have said about the progress that I made living up to my part of the performance agreement. In the first area. . . ."

While you give a brief summary, carefully check to see if the employee is in agreement on all of the main points.

"Okay, I think that about does it. What would you add to what I've said before we move on to a discussion of the progress that you've made?"

REVIEW YOUR EMPLOYEE'S PROGRESS

Once again you're going to ask your employee to make a self-analysis before you present your analysis. A good way to move into a discussion of your employee's progress is to say something like this:

SUPERVISOR: Okay, now that we've finished with me, let's take a look at the progress you've made in the past month. (*Pause*) What I'd like you to do now is to take each of the goals that were spelled out in the performance agreement and tell me how well you feel you accomplished each of them. (*Pause*)
EMPLOYEE: (*Nodding*)
SUPERVISOR: After you finish reviewing your progress in all four areas, I'll offer my own views. Okay?
EMPLOYEE: Sure. That sounds fair.
SUPERVISOR: All right, let's begin with the first one. How well do you think you accomplished what you set out to do in that area?

When the employee begins to talk, actively listen. Don't argue no matter how much you disagree with what is said. Draw the person out. Encourage the person to talk more. Get the employee to make as complete an analysis as possible. When the person has finished, briefly summarize what was said to make certain that you heard it accurately. Then it's your turn to talk.

For additional help with this portion of the follow-up interview, review the strategy for asking your employee to do a self-analysis in Chapter 9.

When presenting your analysis of the employee's progress, pay attention to the presentation skills you learned in Chapter 10. Remember especially to stop talking and to start listening when you notice your employee's receptivity drop. In addition:

1. As much as you can, build on your employee's analysis. Try to establish as much agreement as you can between your analysis and your employee's analysis.

2. Start with the positive. Begin by talking about those areas where the employee met, exceeded, or came very close to the goals that were established. Be specific; use examples to back up your points. Then move on to the areas where the employee didn't make as much progress as either of you had hoped. Once again, be specific. Describe what happened; don't criticize.

3. Wait until you've presented your entire analysis before worrying about "Where to Go from Here." This will be especially hard to do if your employee hasn't made much progress. However, it's important to finish describing how much progress your employee made in each area before talking about the next steps.

4. Get your employee's reactions when you've finished. Ask for an overall reaction to your analysis. Encourage your employee to think out loud about what you've said. This will give your employee a chance to express any agreement or disagreement and will give you a chance to make sure the person has understood what you said.

Review the strategy for presenting your analysis of your employee's performance in Chapter 11 if you have any questions about how to proceed.

DECIDE "WHERE TO GO FROM HERE"

Having reviewed your own progress and the employee's, now you need to answer the question: "Where do we go from here?" In this section we'll offer some suggestions on how to answer this question depending upon three different situations:

1. Your employee has made a lot of progress toward the goals of the performance agreement.
2. Your employee hasn't made much progress but has put in a lot of effort to achieve that progress.
3. Your employee hasn't made much progress and hasn't put in much effort.

1. A lot of progress. This is what you're looking for. Your employee has lived up to the terms of the performance agreement, and you're satisfied with the person's progress. In this situation, we recommend that you and the employee agree on some new goals for both of you and set a long-range follow-up meeting to review those new goals.

The goals that you and the employee set for each other may be extensions of your original goals, completely new goals, or a combination of the two. The important point is that the two of you are off to a good start. You've set the tone for a positive working relationship. Our advice is to keep doing more of the same.

Although you may want to meet again fairly soon for another formal follow-up session, you can probably afford to schedule it as far away as six months or so. Keep up informal follow-ups; they're essential. But try to reserve most of your formal follow-ups for those employees whose progress has not been so good.

2. Little progress—much effort (or mitigating circumstances). Sometimes employees make little progress even though they put out a lot of effort. For example, let's say you're a manager working with a newly appointed supervisor who's technically skilled but rough around the edges when it comes to dealing with people. Although he's trying, he just hasn't improved very much in getting along better with his employees.

You have a number of options in a situation such as this:

☐　You can decide to simply renegotiate the same agreement for another month or so to see if the person can improve with more time. Sometimes just a little more time is all that's really needed.

☐　You may decide that you set your original sights a little high and that you'll aim for more modest goals in the renegotiated agreement. You can revise your goals and plan to review progress in about a month.

☐　Maybe you've got enough evidence that the person doesn't have what it takes to function effectively in his current job. But the person is technically skilled and motivated, and you don't want the organization to lose such an employee. In this situation, think about restructuring the person's job to take advantage of his strengths and to reduce the demand on areas where he's not so capable. We'll talk more about restructuring in the next chapter when we'll help you answer the question, "What Do I Do if None of This Stuff Works?"

Sometimes circumstances will prevent employees from making real progress, even when they try. For example, injury and sickness, company labor problems, material shortages, equipment malfunctions, and many other obstacles may interfere with an employee's progress. If this is the case, give the same performance agreement another try. Schedule another formal follow-up interview in a month. If the mitigating circumstance, for example, a material shortage, is still likely to be a problem, then renegotiate the agreement to focus on aspects of the employee's performance that are under the person's control.

3. Little progress—little effort. Sometimes employees don't make much progress or much effort on the tasks they agreed to work on in the performance agreement. This may signal the beginning of the end. Now it may be more appropriate for you to consult the next chapter, "What Do I Do if None of This Stuff Works?" Before you do, however, you may want to involve your employee in arriving at a solution to the problem. You might begin in this manner:

"Okay, let's stop for just a moment to take a careful look at the situation here. (*Pause*) About a month ago we both decided to do some things that would improve your job performance and increase your job satisfaction. (*Pause*) I think we both agreed that I carried out my part of the agreement pretty well. However, when we reviewed your progress, we agreed that you came up short in accomplishing what you set out to do, especially the goals that had to do with tardiness and the use of the telephone for personal calls. (*Pause*) I'm disappointed in the progress you've made as well as in the lack of effort you've made to resolve those problems. But I'd like to put that behind us now and come up with a new agreement that has a better chance of succeeding than this one did. What suggestions do you have about how to proceed from here? What would you do if you were me and I were you?"

Here you ask the employee to think about the problem from your point of view. Then you listen actively to the employee's suggestions and draw the person out as much as you can.

If the employee doesn't come up with any good suggestions, it's time to get a little tougher by identifying some of the consequences if the employee continues to make little effort and little or no progress. Here's an example:

SUPERVISOR: Okay, Mickey, I'd like you to put yourself in my position once again. Imagine that it's six weeks from now and that there's still no progress in these areas. What would you do then if you were me?

EMPLOYEE: I don't know. (*Pause; supervisor leans forward*) Uh, I guess you'd have a right to be upset. Maybe you could put me on warning?

SUPERVISOR: Yes, I could put you on probation by giving you a formal warning letter. As you know, that's the first step of our termination process here. Any other ideas?

EMPLOYEE: (*Hesitating*) Uh . . . maybe you could make me punch in and out on the time clock?

SUPERVISOR: Yes. I could also recommend that you don't

get an increase during the next wage and salary review period. (*Pause*) Any other ideas?

EMPLOYEE: I hope that you don't do that, but I can't think of anything else.

SUPERVISOR: Well, Mickey, I'm very serious about this whole matter. I'm prepared to take strong action if I don't see any progress within the next six weeks. . . .

Sometimes a discussion like this will get the person's attention. When faced with the prospect of termination or other negative consequences, some employees will turn around. It's at least worth a try before throwing in the towel.

To review, in this section we've identified several different ways to plan your next steps with the employee depending on the person's progress. Whichever course of action you choose, you'll come up with a second written agreement stating what you both will work on in the future.

CLOSE THE INTERVIEW

Once the performance agreement has been revised, it's time to bring the meeting to a close. Here's a guide:

1. Get the employee's overall reaction to how things went.
2. Offer your own thoughts and feelings.
3. Schedule another follow-up meeting to review how well the two of you are living up to the new agreement.
4. End the interview on a positive note, or as positive a note as is possible under the circumstances. For example, you might want to say:

"I'm glad we had this meeting, Helene. Even though we encountered a few difficult moments, I really value the opportunity to sit down to put our heads together. I'm looking forward to our meeting next month. Take care."

The follow-up interview is actually the last step in the performance improvement process. Chapter 15, although we call it Step Ten, is really a series of suggestions on what to do when you decide the employee's performance is not going to improve.

But, unless you decide that "none of this stuff works" for a given employee, there is no formal end to the performance improvement process. To be helpful to you and the employee it has to be an ongoing cycle. You've got to keep following up, formally and informally, with the employee to keep the growth process going. The goal is to continue the productive working relationship the two of you have begun.

CHAPTER 15 • STEP TEN: "WHAT DO I DO IF NONE OF THIS STUFF WORKS?"

If you skipped over some of the previous chapters to read this one, we wouldn't be surprised. Helping employees—especially the problem ones—to improve their work performance can be pretty tough. It's easy to get frustrated and to wonder if you're not just spinning your wheels.

The performance improvement process doesn't always work as well as we'd like it to. With some employees it won't work at all. But we think it's important to give the process a good solid try. Then, when it doesn't appear that you're getting anywhere, you'll probably ask, "What do I do if none of this stuff works?"

In this chapter, we'll be helping you answer these three questions:

- How do you come to the conclusion that none of this stuff works for a particular employee?
- What are your options if none of this stuff works?
- How do you choose among your options?

We'll describe four options that are available to you, and we'll also give you some practice in choosing among them. The four options are:

- Firing an employee;
- Transferring an employee;
- Restructuring an employee's job; and
- Neutralizing an employee.

First let's talk about how and when to decide that the performance improvement process hasn't worked with a problem employee.

HOW DO YOU CONCLUDE THAT "NONE OF THIS STUFF WORKS"?

When you decide that "none of this stuff works" for a particular employee, you conclude that it's no longer worth your time and energy—or that of your organization—to try to help your employee improve performance in his or her current job. But how will you know when it's no longer worth your time and effort to try to help an employee change? Unfortunately, there is no way to be absolutely certain. But considering these points should give you more confidence in making your decision.

There are four kinds of employee performance that, after at least one follow-up interview, should indicate that the process hasn't worked:

1. The employee's performance is worse than before.
2. There's been no change at all in the employee's problem behavior.
3. There's been minimal change in the employee's problem behavior.
4. The employee's performance improved but the improvement was short-lived.

THINGS ACTUALLY GET WORSE

Not too often, but every now and then, an employee's performance will actually get worse after a supervisor has conducted a performance improvement interview. Of course, you may have to take a lot of the responsibility for this outcome. It may be that you did or said something during the interview that greatly confused or upset your employee. However, the fact that the individual's performance got worse, not better, is something that you can't ignore. It will have to be a factor in your decision to stop the performance improvement process to look at other alternatives.

NO CHANGE IN BEHAVIOR

You may go through the performance improvement process with your employee without seeing any change in the person's behavior. Although this failure could be primarily your fault, it's evidence that you can't ignore.

A LITTLE, BUT NOT ENOUGH

A little change is much more likely than a change for the worse or no change at all. In fact, you may expect only a little change in an employee. You don't expect a sourpuss receptionist to become warm and effusive overnight. You don't expect a sloppy and disorganized machinist to become the picture of order and neatness right away. You don't expect a salesperson with poor presentation skills to sound like an eloquent orator in a week's time.

As time passes, however, you should expect to see some gradual improvement as the employee approaches an acceptable level of performance. If the initial small changes in performance don't eventually lead to larger and more significant changes, you may have to accept the fact that you're never going to get the kind of performance you feel you need from the employee.

A FLASH IN THE PAN

Sometimes, after a supervisor has had a performance improvement interview with an employee, the employee will make some dramatic changes almost immediately. Instead of arriving at the office ten minutes late every day, the employee shows up twenty minutes early. Those reports that were overdue for months appear neatly typed on your desk Monday morning. Instead of being a grouch on the phone, the employee does an about-face and is courteous and helpful.

Dramatic changes such as these often don't last very long. After a week or so, the employee falls back into old patterns and habits. Now your employee seems to be performing at the same level as before the interview.

This flash-in-the-pan change in an employee's performance is not always a sign that the person is no longer worth trying to help improve. But people who make these kinds of abrupt changes in their behavior usually aren't committed to changing. They're making changes for you rather than for themselves. They're willing to put a great deal of effort into making the changes you want right away. *But*, if those changes don't lead to an immediate increase in their personal job satisfaction, they return to their old habits.

Let's say you've made the decision that none of this stuff works for a particular problem employee. What are you going to do now?

Some managers are simply not aware of the options available to them. For the remainder of the chapter we'll describe four such options—firing, transferring, restructuring, and neutralizing—in detail. We'll also talk about ways to decide among the four options. Finally, we'll cover some important points to keep in mind when implementing each option so things will go as efficiently and as smoothly as possible for you, the employee, and the organization.

FIRING

Firing is the action that an organization takes to sever the relationship between itself and an employee so that the employee no longer receives payment for services rendered to the organization. The usual means of firing is for a manager to inform an employee simply and directly that the person is dismissed from the job and will not be offered another position in the organization. However, there are some termination proceedings that may be easier for you and your employee to go through than a simple dismissal. Laying off an employee is one alternative; asking the employee to resign is another.

Laying off is sometimes a euphemism for firing, and sometimes not. In large manufacturing industries, it's common to lay off workers (both union and management) when business drops. When business picks back up, these workers are rehired. The same pattern holds true for seasonal industries such as construction and tourism. During slow periods, workers collect unemployment or take hold-over jobs until they're rehired. In many situations, however, laying off does not mean that the employer has any intention of rehiring the employee. In these situations the employer decides to lay off rather than fire the person to make it easier for the worker to collect unemployment insurance benefits. An important note: This *does cost* the company money.

Asking the employee to resign is another way of making the termination process a little easier for the person being terminated. You're still firing the worker. You're just giving the individual the opportunity to do it with a little more dignity.

WHY MANAGERS ARE RELUCTANT TO FIRE PROBLEM EMPLOYEES

Anyone who has ever been a supervisor knows that firing someone is not easy. Aside from many administrative and legal obstacles to the termination process, the majority of supervisors and managers find firing an employee emotionally difficult. Below are some of the common reasons why firing is such a tough task.

1. Supervisors feel guilty. They view being fired as a shameful and embarrassing experience for an employee. Generally, the last thing they want to be is the "bad guy" who puts an employee through such an unpleasant experience.

2. The thought of sitting down with an employee to deliver the bad news makes most supervisors nervous. The prospect of looking the employee right in the eye and saying, "Pat, I'm sorry, but we've decided to let you go," is very distasteful.

3. Many supervisors engage in what we call catastrophic thinking. They immediately think of the worst things that could happen to them, such as getting involved in a protracted legal struggle, having the decision overturned by a superior, or losing the respect and friendship of other people in the organization. Sometimes they imagine the worst that could happen to the employee. They ask themselves such questions as, "Will he be able to find another job?" "What will happen to her family if she can't get another job?" "How will I be able to live with myself if this person's family has to go on welfare?"

4. Many supervisors continue to put off firing an employee because they worry they won't be able to find a better replacement. This seems to be especially true for jobs requiring a high level of technical skills. Here's what we often hear supervisors say:

"Do you have any idea how hard it is to find a skilled and experienced programmer (or systems analyst, legal secretary, machinist, tool and die maker, and so on) these days? I'll admit that this guy's not the greatest. In fact, at times he's pretty bad. But I'd rather have him than nobody at all."

Each of these reasons is understandable. Firing is an emotional topic in our society, and it's just plain hard for anybody to approach it in a completely rational manner.

POSITIVE ASPECTS OF FIRING

Although we don't ever expect firing an employee to become an easy task, on the next page we have some opinions on the issue that may help you take a more positive outlook toward the process.

1. Although being fired is often a bitter pill for an employee to swallow, it is possible to view it as an opportunity rather than as a shameful and embarrassing experience. Not only do some employees who've been fired move on to get better jobs than they had before but, as a result of new job experiences, some of them show dramatic improvement in their level of self-confidence and self-esteem.

2. Firing an employee is never easy, but it's much less difficult if you have the kinds of good communication skills that we covered earlier in the book. The presentation and listening skills that you've learned will help make the task of firing an employee a lot smoother and less painful.

3. Do not buy the argument that a problem employee (especially one with scarce technical skills) can't be fired because it will be too difficult to find a replacement. We think that the time and effort expended to replace such an employee will be overshadowed by the damage caused by your own frustration, the employee's lack of productivity, and lowered morale among other employees in your work unit that would result from not firing the person.

You may be saying to yourself, "Yes, firing somebody is an unpleasant and distasteful task for me, and I may be more reluctant to do it than I should be. On the other hand, how do I decide when it's time to fire somebody? What rules of thumb should I use?"

PERFORMANCE PROBLEMS THAT WARRANT FIRING

As we'll point out later in the chapter, there are any number of differences among organizations, employees, and supervisors that make firing, or any of the other three options, appropriate in one situation but not in another. However, we have some strong opinions on the kinds of employee behavior and performance that should lead to termination.

1. Dishonesty. There are certain kinds of dishonesty that any supervisor would agree are grounds for immediate dismissal of an employee, such as forging company checks, accepting kickbacks from vendors, stealing money or property, or selling confidential information to a competitor. But there are other kinds of employee dishonesty that, although less obvious, can be just as destructive, if not more so:

☐ Lying, especially repeatedly, about anything having to do with work;
☐ Talking behind your back, that is, making negative or derogatory remarks about you to other people, but never confronting you directly;

☐   Behaving pleasantly and congenially in the presence of another employee, but making negative or derogatory remarks about the person as soon as the employee leaves; and

☐   Saying positive things about the organization in your presence and in the presence of other managers and supervisors, but running down the organization while talking to other employees when no managerial personnel are around.

These more subtle forms of dishonesty are, admittedly, more difficult to document than more blatant forms, such as stealing property or embezzling funds. But we feel strongly that employees who behave dishonestly, whether subtly or blatantly, are destructive elements in any organization. The quicker you get rid of them the better.

2. Absenteeism. Absenteeism has been a major problem in American industry since World War II. Each year billions of dollars in potential profit go down the drain as the result of employee lost time. All of us—consumers, employers, and employees—feel the impact of absenteeism, either through the quality of goods and services we purchase or in the frustration, dissatisfaction, and drop in morale we experience on the job.

Almost no organization will tolerate frequent and continuous absence from an employee. However, most organizations wait too long to do anything about an absence problem. And they often fail to make employees suffer any consequences for further absence once a warning message has been delivered.

We think this is a mistake.

Unless there are extenuating circumstances, frequent employee absence is an unacceptably bad habit. Like most habits, unless it's arrested in its early stages, it's likely to worsen as time passes. It's important for supervisors to make it clear to employees who've just begun a pattern of absenteeism that their lack of attendance is a real problem that needs to be corrected right away. Supervisors should begin to take immediate steps toward terminating employees whose attendance remains poor after they've made a firm commitment to correct the problem.

3. Substance abuse. Employee alcoholism has been an obstacle to the productivity of organizations for a long, long time. Since the 1960s organizations have had to face a related, if less pronounced, problem—drug abuse. In the last fifteen years there has been a sharp increase in the general consumption of a variety of illegal and legal chemical substances, including marijuana, cocaine, heroin, and "upper" and "downer" prescription drugs.

To combat substance abuse and the host of other personal problems that hinder worker productivity, many organizations, especially larger ones, have set up employee assistance programs. We strongly support these kinds of programs; they're long overdue. They have the potential for making a strong impact on the pain and suffering of millions of people, as well as on the productivity of the organizations that employ them.

In spite of our strong support for these programs, we feel that managers and supervisors have to be coldly realistic about how difficult it is for alcoholics and drug abusers to overcome their destructive habits. As much as you may be willing to help an employee give up drugs or alcohol, your responsibility as a supervisor demands that you pay attention, first and foremost, to work performance. That's the bottom line.

With many employees who have drug or alcohol problems, you'll end up facing the tough fact that your efforts and the organization's efforts to help have been in vain. The employee's habit continues, and job performance remains poor, or gets worse. Finally, you're left with one choice—to fire the employee.

4. Insubordination. *Insubordination* is a word that isn't as commonly used as it once was. As it has become more socially acceptable for all of us to stand up to and disagree with authority figures—parents, bosses, government leaders—words such as *insubordination* and *disrespect* seem rather old-fashioned.

We not only think employees have a right to disagree with their supervisors and express their opinions openly to their bosses, we think employees should do these things. On the other hand, we think there's a big difference between assertive openness and downright insubordination. For example, we think it's healthy for employees to:

☐ Ask their supervisors why certain tasks need to be performed if the supervisors don't offer a reason;
☐ Offer opinions, especially in private, that differ from their supervisors' ideas, values, or philosophies;
☐ Suggest new ways of doing things even if those new ways are different from procedures instituted by their supervisors;
☐ Tell their supervisors, in private, that they are upset, embarrassed, hurt, or otherwise disturbed as a result of something the supervisors have done or said.

We definitely do not think it's good for supervisors to put up with employees who:

☐   Flatly refuse to do certain things that supervisors request;
☐   Ignore instructions to perform certain tasks and proceed with their own methods without first checking with their supervisors;
☐   Openly disapprove of what their supervisors are saying or doing in a group setting (especially if members of the group don't belong to the supervisor's work unit);
☐   Go to their supervisors' bosses to complain, without first confronting their supervisors.

Keeping an employee who is openly and flagrantly disrespectful of your authority as a supervisor is a losing proposition. Your other employees lose respect for you, and more importantly, you lose respect for yourself. It ain't worth it!

5. General lack of productivity. From the standpoint of general effectiveness and overall productivity, employees can be roughly divided into the following three categories:

☐   Self-starters and problem-solvers;
☐   People who do only what they're asked to do; and
☐   Non-doers.

When you give people who are self-starters and problem-solvers a task to do, they often get it done ahead of time and with a higher level of quality than you expected. They also anticipate tasks that need to be done and do them without being told. They're always coming to you with suggestions and ideas on how to improve things and to increase productivity in your work unit.

You have to keep pretty close track of people who do only what they're asked to do (most of the time), or their performance is likely to fall off. But, usually, you can count on them to get the job done, even if you have to "motivate" them every now and then.

Finally, there are the non-doers of the work world. Unfortunately, there are more of them around nowadays than ever before. These are employees who:

☐   Hardly ever get their work done on time;
☐   Do what they're told to do and nothing more;
☐   Frequently give you all kinds of excuses why they can't do something; they never tell you how something can be done; and
☐   Show up for work day in and day out (sometimes week in

and week out) and not do anything unless they're given a specific task to perform.

It's not worth much effort to help non-doers improve their performance. They're frustrating to work with, and often the best solution is to terminate them.

IMPORTANT THINGS TO KEEP IN MIND ABOUT FIRING

It's a lot harder to fire somebody these days than it used to be, especially if the employee is a member of a group protected by federal antidiscrimination legislation and guidelines. Employers are subject to more legal and quasi-legal actions taken by employees dismissed from their jobs.

You should also be prepared for some unpleasantness. Firing anybody is tough—there are no two ways about it. It's almost always an emotional experience.

Here are some things to keep in mind when you consider firing an employee:

1. Explore the termination options you have available with some experts. The best way to do this is to briefly explain the situation and then interview the expert (a personnel department employee, your boss, a company attorney, or a consultant) on what to do. If you do a good job of drawing these people out, you should end up with a solid array of alternatives.

2. If possible and feasible, discuss these options with the employee and ask for the person's reactions and suggestions. Your listening and negotiating skills will help you choose an alternative that's good for you, the employee, and the organization.

3. Reduce the possibility of legal action with documentation. You must be able to prove that you took reasonable steps to help an employee improve areas of work performance and that those steps did not result in substantial improvement. Documentation involves keeping records of each time you speak to the problem employee about deficiencies in work performance and subsequent actions you take to help improve the individual's performance. These records can take various forms. For example:

☐ You can write a *memo to file* stating that you spoke to the employee about a certain matter on a certain date. Note the specific actions or efforts you agreed to make and those the employee agreed to make. You should also write a memo to file whenever somebody makes a major complaint to you about the employee's performance;

☐   You can keep a copy of any performance agreement you and the employee work out and then write a memo to file on how successfully the agreement was carried out;

☐   After several unsuccessful attempts at coaching the employee, you can write a memo to the employee directly, stating you're displeased with the employee's performance, why you're displeased, specifically what you expect the employee to do to improve, and the possible consequences if there is no improvement in a reasonable period of time; and

☐   You can send the employee a warning as part of the formal termination process in your organization. It should inform the employee that he or she is being placed on a probationary status pending improvement in performance.

Whatever form of documentation you use, it's important that you try to follow these guidelines:

☐   Keep a copy of the documentation in the employee's personnel folder;

☐   Make certain that the employee receives a copy of all communications directed to him or her. (This would not include a memo to file.)

☐   In describing the employee's deficiencies, be as precise as you can be, noting specific, observable behavior;

☐   Make certain that all appropriate personnel (especially your supervisor) receive copies of all documentation. You should speak to these people in person, in addition to giving them written copies of your documentation. Unfortunately, some people have a tendency to "forget" when things get a little tight. You don't want to be left holding the bag if your efforts to terminate an employee end up in a legal battle or in unwanted publicity.

4. Be prepared to tough it out for a number of months. In large organizations and government agencies, the process is likely to take a while.

5. Be prepared for the reverse sympathy phenomenon. As the supervisor of a problem employee, you'll get plenty of sympathy from people. "I don't know how you can be so patient with him," "If I were you, I'd have fired her long ago," and other supportive statements are common fare—until you begin the termination process. Then, many of these same folks change their tune, and you—not the employee—end up wearing the black hat. If you *anticipate* this reversal it won't take you by surprise, and you'll find it a lot easier to cope with.

6. By now, you have developed a good array of listening and negotiating skills to handle anger and criticism. If somebody says, "I just can't understand why you let Terry go, especially after all he's done for you," you can reflect feeling and say, "Sounds like you're pretty upset about the whole affair." Saying something like this is much more effective than getting defensive by snapping back at the person or explaining for the umpteenth time why you did what you did.

7. Try not to take the whole process too much to heart. Firing somebody is not a light-hearted matter, but it doesn't have to be deadly serious either. The unpleasantness will pass quickly after the employee leaves. Besides, you should look at the whole process as an ultimate solution to one of your problems and an opportunity for growth for the employee.

TRANSFERRING

Transferring means reassigning an employee from one position to a new position within the same organization. As we apply the term here, transferring also means that the employee is assigned to a different work unit (section, department, or division) under the supervision of a different manager, and that the employee's new job has roughly the same responsibility and pay as the original job.

Clearly, the decision to transfer an employee is different from the decision to fire an employee. Transferring implies that you feel the employee can make a worthwhile contribution to the organization, but that the contribution should be made in a different job. Firing, on the other hand, implies that you feel the employee is not worth trying to salvage in any job in the organization.

Here are two guidelines that will help you decide whether an employee should be transferred rather than fired:

1. The employee has some especially strong or unusual skills that could be used in another position within the organization.
2. The employee's skill deficiencies probably would have little or no impact on the new position.

To help you get a feel for applying these two guidelines, we've come up with two examples of problem employees we think should be transferred.

Tony is the general manager of a large metal working plant in the Northeast. He's been in this position for about four months; before that he had worked for over ten years as a project engineer.

During his time as an engineer, Tony had very little supervisory responsibility. Almost all of his efforts were devoted to initiating production line innovations to increase efficiency and productivity. Tony was extremely effective at this and probably saved the company several millions of dollars over the ten-year period he worked in that position.

Since his promotion to general manager, however, Tony has run into a lot of problems. The supervisors who report to him are beginning to grumble and complain. They're saying such things as, "He never really comes out and says what he wants me to do," "I thought he's supposed to be the general manager, but he still acts like he's an engineer," and, "He's got all the technical knowledge in the world, but he sure doesn't know how to handle people."

Tina has worked for a large transportation company for about five years. The first four and a half years she worked as a recruiter in the employment section of the company's personnel department. About six months ago, she received a promotion to a job in the salary administration section of the department.

When she was first promoted, Tina's new boss was very excited about having her come on board. She had developed a reputation in the employment section as a first-rate recruiter, and everybody seemed to be singing her praises. But as the months have gone by, her supervisor has changed her mind about Tina. Tina is very likable and hardworking. But there's a lot of numerical and statistical work in the job, and it has become obvious that Tina and numbers don't get along too well. She's made a number of errors that Tina's boss was able to catch, but if she hadn't, the mistakes would have been costly and embarrassing.

Tina's supervisor is not optimistic that Tina will be able to catch on to the job. She's beginning to wonder if she didn't make a big mistake in promoting Tina in the first place.

Both Tony and Tina seem to fit the guidelines for transferring fairly closely. Tony has some well-demonstrated, strong skills in the area of production line innovations, and he's saved his company a lot of money over the years. Tina also has a strong track record as an employment recruiter and has gained the respect of a lot of managers within the company. In addition to being very skilled in some areas that are important to their organizations, both Tony and Tina's areas of ineffective performance in their current jobs seem limited. Tony lacks the people skills to be a good manager, and Tina lacks the quantitative skills to be a good wage and salary analyst. The important point is this: Their areas needing improvement are narrow enough so that they probably wouldn't pose a problem in many other jobs within the organization.

IMPORTANT THINGS TO KEEP IN MIND ABOUT TRANSFERRING

The most important thing to remember when transferring an employee to a new position is to be honest with and helpful to the employee's new supervisor. It's a good idea to sit down with the new supervisor and, as objectively as you can, to tell everything you know about the employee's strengths and areas needing improvement. Make suggestions that will help the two of them get off on the right foot together.

RESTRUCTURING

Restructuring is an option very similar to transferring. Transferring involves assigning an employee to a new job under a different supervisor in another section of the organization, while restructuring involves modifying the employee's current job. Both options are designed to get an employee working in a job that will maximize the employee's strengths and special skills and minimize the areas needing improvement.

Here are some examples of employees for whom it would make sense to restructure their jobs.

Georgia works as a research scientist for a research and development company that specializes in federal government research contracts in the human sciences. Georgia has been with the company for over fifteen years and has distinguished herself as an excellent proposal writer. She's also helped other researchers who have poor writing skills prepare their final reports for publication.

Georgia has had one major problem on her job over the years—face-to-face contact with government contracting officers and technical representatives. Georgia is shy, especially with strangers, and has trouble expressing herself verbally in front of a group. Georgia's shyness and lack of good presentation skills have lost the company a number of contracts that would have been won by a more outgoing and assertive research scientist.

Georgia is a good candidate for job restructuring. Because the company is continuing to expand, it wouldn't be difficult to rebuild Georgia's job so that she spent all of her time writing proposals and reports, which she loves to do, and no time dealing face-to-face or over the phone with government representatives.

Clarence is nineteen years old and has been working for about six months for a medium-sized dry cleaning operation in a large city. Clarence's boss, the owner of the operation, had strong reservations about Clarence when he first hired him. He was concerned that Clarence might have an attendance and an attitude problem. It hasn't turned out that way. Clarence hasn't missed a day of work in six months; in fact, he's usually waiting at the door when the owner arrives in the morning. He seems to be especially good with customers, and a number of them have commented to the owner on what a pleasure it is to come in and talk to Clarence.

But Clarence seems to have a problem when he's in back working on the machines. There's nobody back there to talk to, and after a while he has a tendency to get bored and make mistakes. He seems to be trying to improve, but it's difficult.

The owner is seriously considering restructuring Clarence's job to take better advantage of his people skills. The operation has a huge backlog of overdue accounts from old customers who've been extended credit. The owner thinks that it might be a good idea to cut back Clarence's time on the machines and to have him spend several hours a day on the telephone acting as an in-house bill collector. He's tried him out on a few calls, and Clarence has been able to sweet-talk everybody he's called into paying up right away.

There are clearly situations where it will be impossible to restructure an employee's job. But we think it's an option that could be used more frequently than it is in most organizations. It can be an effective way of turning a marginal worker or a problem employee into a productive and satisfied member of your work unit.

IMPORTANT THINGS TO KEEP IN MIND ABOUT RESTRUCTURING

Restructuring is the only one of the four options in which you and the employee continue to work together. For this reason we think that it's important for the two of you to sit down to have an honest discussion about how the person's job should be restructured. The basic outline for such a discussion might go something like this:

☐ Begin the discussion by mentioning that you've been thinking seriously about ways the two of you can rebuild the employee's job to take better advantage of the employee's strengths than the current job does;

☐ Pause and actively listen to the employee's reaction to this idea;

☐ Present your ideas on how the job can be restructured and use your listening skills to draw out the employee's reactions and alternative suggestions; and

☐ Use the negotiating skills you learned in Chapter 12 to arrive at an agreement with the employee on how the job can be restructured to satisfy both of you.

NEUTRALIZING

Neutralizing is an option that we frankly don't like very much. However, there are many organizations in which neutralizing may be the only sensible option for a supervisor who has a problem employee who is no longer worth the effort to try to change.

Neutralizing problem employees means restructuring their jobs in such a way that their areas of needed improvement have as little negative impact as possible on you, your other employees, and other important people, such as customers, vendors, and clients. We see neutralizing as an alternative to firing and think it should be used only if the difficulties involved in firing would be greater than the problems you'd face by neutralizing the person.

There are two kinds of organizations for which neutralizing may sometimes be a more sensible option than firing. The first is the family-owned business, where often the problem employee is a member of the immediate family or an in-law. The second is the organization in the public sector — a federal, state, or local government or government agency. As an example of the dilemma that faces a manager in this second situation, we heard about a federal civil servant who spent so much time and effort trying to fire one of his employees that his own job performance ratings suffered as a consequence.

Here are some examples of how three supervisors neutralized their problem employees:

Charles Waylon is the chief executive officer of an old and established manufacturing firm in the Southwest. Charlie's problem employee is Hank Gorsky, his sister's husband. Charlie has tried Hank out in a variety of jobs in the company with very little success. "The problem with Hank is two-fold," said Charlie. "He's very sociable and very lazy. If he weren't my brother-in-law, I'd fire him tomorrow. But I just can't do that to my sister and her kids." Charlie has since given up on trying to get Hank to change. Instead, he's solved the problem by making Hank his director of special projects. Now Hank is kept busy every day on what many people consider to be "make work" projects. But he's happy, and he's no longer in the way of employees who are making money for the company.

Ruth Bradford is a counselor supervisor for a federally funded project sponsored by the mayor's office of a large northeastern city. When she took the job, Ruth had a counselor on her staff whom she felt was emotionally unstable and had no business working with clients. Ruth immediately began termination proceedings, but she realized that it would take at least six months to get the counselor off her staff, *if* her attempt was successful. In the meantime, Ruth stopped assigning clients to the counselor and gave him the responsibility of going to the public library to research an annotated bibliography for an information resource center she was trying to build. Although the counselor was not very effective at this task, he seemed to enjoy it, and he was able to collect some useful information. Most importantly, Ruth was able to isolate him from clients to whom he might have done some real emotional damage.

Laura Haskill is a newly appointed information director for the public relations department of a large municipal government. Laura supervises a publicity officer named Bill Richford who is 58 years old and has been working for the city for 35 years.

Right after she was appointed, Laura said, "If Bill weren't protected by civil service, I'd let him go. He's gone into active retirement. He comes in on time and leaves on time, but I just can't get any work out of him. It's very frustrating."

After wrestling with the problem for a while, Laura found one thing that Bill can do well and likes to do— edit the press releases that college interns in the department have written. Laura would still like to fire Bill. At least she's found something productive for him to do.

IMPORTANT THINGS TO KEEP IN MIND ABOUT NEUTRALIZING

Neutralizing is not an option that we're particularly fond of. If it's not feasible to fire a problem employee, the following list of dos and don'ts will be helpful to you:

1. Don't harass your employee in an effort to get the person to quit or to seek a transfer. This just doesn't work well. The employee will try to strike back at you in devious ways that can be embarrassing and painful. Besides, the ultimate result of such a campaign is the undermining of morale in your whole work unit.

2. Do assign the employee tasks that are not crucial to the effectiveness of your work unit. This may seem obvious, but some supervisors tend to get a little stubborn about this and adopt the attitude, "Well, if I've got to keep him, he's going to pull his weight like everybody else." It would be nice if he would pull his weight, but all the evidence suggests that he won't. So don't ask him to do things that you know he won't or can't do.

3. Do keep trying to help your employee change. We're firmly committed to the view that people can and will change for the better if we just open the right doors for them. As hard as it is to do so with some people, always try to convey an attitude of helpfulness to the employee. Strongly reinforce any signs of positive change by praise. Let the employee know how pleased you are with the improvement. Whenever possible, ignore faults and concentrate on strengths.

4. Do enlist the aid of your other workers in coming up with ways to help the employee to make positive changes. It's a good idea to view helping the employee change as "a challenge for all of us." Don't say, "Look, we all know she's a turkey, but we're just going to have to put up with her."

HOW DO YOU CHOOSE AMONG THE FOUR OPTIONS?

To some extent, we've already talked about how to choose from among the four options. We've described each of the four options—firing, transferring, restructuring, and neutralizing—and we've talked about when each is appropriate. But, so far, we haven't given you much help in deciding how to choose an option, given that your situation and circumstances are always unique.

To make the task of deciding among the options a little easier, consider these three sets of factors:

1. Your organization,
2. Your employee, and
3. You.

First we'll describe the implications of these factors in choosing among the options. Then we'll give you an opportunity to consider these factors to decide what to do with some hypothetical problem employees.

YOUR ORGANIZATION

Organizations are like people. They have a lot in common with each other, but they also differ in many ways. How your organization differs from others in these three ways—size, policies and traditions, and financial situation—will have at least some effect on which option you choose for a particular problem employee.

1. Organizational size. From the standpoint of what to do about a problem employee, there are at least two significant ways that large organizations differ from small organizations:

☐ Except at the highest managerial levels, the impact of an employee's poor performance on the overall productivity of the organization is less in a large organization than in a small one.

☐ Larger organizations tend to have a much greater variety of specialized jobs than a small organization.

These differences have several implications for supervisors trying to decide what to do about a problem employee. In a larger organization you're more likely to have the "luxury" of working with a problem employee longer than you would in a smaller organization. Although the employee's poor performance may be equally frustrating for you, your organization will feel the impact of the employee's ineffectiveness less if it is large. The fact that larger organizations usually have a greater variety of specialized jobs than smaller organizations makes the possibility of transferring a problem employee easier in a bigger company. Most people, even problem employees, have some skills. If you're a supervisor in a large organization, your chances of locating a position where the employee's skills could be put to good use are greater than if you work in a small organization.

2. Policies and traditions. Your organization's policies and procedures are undoubtedly going to have some effect on which option you choose for a particular problem employee. If you work for a government agency, you know that the option of firing poses more problems than would exist if you worked for a profit-making concern that quickly terminates unproductive people.

You'll have an easier time restructuring an employee's job if you work for a company that allows its managers some flexibility than you will if you work for a more tightly controlled organization. There's nothing wrong with picking an option that's inconsistent with the company line. However, it's important to be realistic about the obstacles you'll encounter if you make such a choice.

Here's one way to help ensure that you're being realistic. Take a piece of paper and draw a line down the middle. At the top of the left side write, *Advantages of Choosing This Option*; on top of the right side write, *Disadvantages of Choosing This Option*. If you take the time to fill out both sides conscientiously and honestly, you'll end up with a much clearer sense of whether you still want to choose the option, especially if the option is inconsistent with the organization's policies and traditions.

3. Financial status of your organization. How your organization is doing financially may have a big effect on the option you choose. When profits are up and budgets are fat, you generally have more flexibility. During periods of austerity, your options tend to be narrower. In a time of relative prosperity, you might decide to transfer an employee, or restructure the individual's job. You might decide that firing or laying off the same employee, however, is the sensible option when the company is tightening its belt.

YOUR EMPLOYEE

As there are different kinds of people, there are also different kinds of problem employees. In attempting to choose among the four options, it's important to make a rough distinction between two categories of problem employees:

☐   Problem employees who are generally and broadly ineffective, and
☐   Problem employees who are narrowly and specifically ineffective.

Employees in the first category are candidates for firing, or neutralizing, if firing is clearly not a feasible option. Because of bad habits or a general lack of skill, or a combination of the two, these people would have difficulty performing effectively in any job in the organization.

Employees in the second category are candidates for transferring or restructuring. They're people who are in a position to make a worthwhile contribution to the organization. However, they have a specific skill deficiency or a bad habit that keeps them from making such a contribution in their current job, but that would not get in the way in a different or restructured job.

For example, employees in the first category might include those people who are absentee problems, openly disrespectful to their supervisors, constantly complaining, constantly offering excuses for why things can't be done a certain way, hampered by a drinking or drug problem, or guilty of dishonest behavior. Employees in the second category might include those people who are poor at delegating authority and responsibility, less able to effectively express their ideas, unable to handle a task related to the rest of the job, or apt to get flustered when work pressures mount up.

YOU

Probably the biggest factor in your choice among the four options won't be the organization or the employee. It will be *you*—you and your situation in the organization. Like the organization and the employee, you're unique. What's even more important, the employee and the organization and all its policies and traditions notwithstanding, is that you are the one who will be making the choice.

Here are some things about you that are worth considering.

1. Your philosophies about human behavior change. Even if you're not a psychologist or a behavioral scientist, it's likely that you have definite ideas on your overall chance of success in attempting to convince other human beings to change their behavior. You may be pessimistic, you may be optimistic, or you may fall somewhere in between.

Let's say you're pessimistic. You're probably not going to try very hard to get employees to improve their performance. You're going to conclude that that's just the way it is and that there's not a whole lot you can do about it. Your tendency will be either to put up with and accept the poor performance of problem employees, or to fire them. But you won't waste your time trying to get problem employees to change.

On the other hand, let's say you're an optimist when it comes to getting people to change. You're likely to give the performance improvement process some extra effort. You're reluctant to give up on employees until the evidence is overwhelming that they're not going to change. Even then, you may give it one more try.

If you fall somewhere in the middle between pessimism and optimism (as we do), then you're likely to make a strong initial effort to get employees to change. But you'll also be ready to cut your losses if you don't get some fairly immediate evidence of improvement.

None of these philosophies is right or wrong. But there are two important things to remember about your philosophy. First, try to be flexible enough to modify your philosophy in light of new evidence. At the same time don't behave too inconsistently with your philosophy. If you do, you'll cause yourself a lot of conflict by getting caught in the trap of second-guessing yourself, which can end up being awfully uncomfortable.

2. Your relationship with your boss. The relationship you have with your boss definitely has some impact on your choice among the four options. An entire book, longer than this one, could be written on the different types of bosses and on how best to get along with them. In terms of what to do about a particular problem employee, however, the most important characteristic of your relationship with your boss is the amount of general support and freedom given to you for the decisions you make. If your boss allows you to be independent in the decisions you make, you can rely on your own feelings and opinions in choosing an option, though you might want to use him as a sounding board. If your boss is always looking over your shoulder, it's probably best to involve her in the decision-making process from the beginning. If you don't, she's likely to challenge, or even veto, your choice of options. That's going to be very frustrating for you.

By the way, we think you'll find that many of the techniques we suggest in the book for dealing with problem employees are just as effective for dealing with problem bosses. A lot of people believe that the percentage of problem bosses exceeds that of problem employees.

3. Your chemistry with the employee. We believe in getting down to the level of specific, observable behavior in deciding why an employee is not performing effectively and what you need to do about it. However, the quality of the relationship between two people is extremely difficult to describe in behavioral terms. Because of a long history of experiences and perhaps a particular genetic makeup, you can get along famously with one person and absolutely miserably with another.

The same holds true for bosses and employees. In addition to the employee's actual performance, it's important to pay attention to how the two of you actually get along. Do you seem to enjoy each other and have a basic liking for each other? Or do you have a tendency to avoid and dislike each other? Do you enjoy each other's sense of humor? Or do you both tend to shudder when the other person makes an attempt at being funny? Is the atmosphere fairly relaxed when you're together? Or does it tend to be stiff and formal?

The answers to these and similar questions will have a lot to do with how comfortable either of you feels about the option you might choose. Let's say you work for a government agency and have a problem employee you would like to fire. If the chemistry between the two of you is pretty good in spite of the employee's poor performance, you might choose to neutralize the person rather than go through the protracted firing process. If the chemistry is bad, however, you might decide to endure the long firing process rather than to continue working with someone who causes you so much discomfort.

PRACTICE CHOOSING OPTIONS

Up to this point we've talked about the four options and the factors—the organization, the employee, and you—that will affect the one you choose. Now we'd like to get you involved in trying the options on for size. The form below and on page 218 will give you a chance to practice choosing.

CHOOSING THE BEST OPTION

Below are descriptions of hypothetical situations about four problem employees. In each case, their supervisors have decided that none of this stuff works. For each employee, decide which of the four options —firing, transferring, restructuring, or neutralizing —you'd choose.

After you've made your choices, compare your decisions with the ones we would've made.

(1) **Sam Tigner** is a senior level civil servant (GS-14) who's recently been assigned to your unit. He's about fifteen years older than you are and has been in government service for over thirty years.

Sam's reputation as a technical expert in his field is excellent. Although his level of professional activity has subsided quite a bit in the last 10 years, he's turned out lots of articles and papers that have received world-wide recognition. He still receives quite a few invitations to speak at professional conventions and conferences.

In spite of Sam's reputation, you're not very impressed with him. At staff meetings he holds forth on his ideas to the boredom and exasperation of the other members of your team. He doesn't get tasks completed on time. And when he does get them done, they don't look at all like what you expected. In the performance improvement interview you've had with Sam he's made it pretty clear that he thinks you should give him a lot more free rein so he can make better use of his real talents. When you express your side of the story, it is plain that he's not listening to you.

OPTION YOU'D CHOOSE: _____

(2) You're in the process of setting up a new sales office in the Atlanta area after having been transferred from New York City. The first person you hired when you got to Atlanta was **Caroline Robinson**, your personal secretary.

When you first hired Caroline, you were extremely pleased with her. She had superb secretarial skills in addition to being a friendly and vibrant person. But she's been on board about two months now and your estimation of her has dropped considerably. During that

CONTINUED

PRACTICE CHOOSING OPTIONS continued

period she's gotten into a shouting match with one of your recently hired salespersons when you were out of the office. Shortly after you had individual talks with both the salesperson and Caroline, you learned that Caroline had called the company's director of personnel to complain about you. When the director called you to tell you what Caroline had told him, it was apparent that she had distorted a lot of facts and had said some pretty damaging things about you. When you confronted Caroline with what you'd heard from the personnel director, she acted very charming and friendly and tried to persuade you that she was just a little upset at the time and needed somebody to talk to.

OPTION YOU'D CHOOSE: _____

(3)   You're the manager of the customer accounting department for a large transportation company. The function of your department is that of an internal bill collector. You have a staff of about twenty-five customer account representatives whose job it is to call delinquent accounts to get them to pay their bills.

Nancy Battaglia has been on your staff as a representative for about five months now. At this point you're really torn about Nancy. If you look at it one way, she's the best representative you have. She's very persuasive and has been able to close out some delinquent accounts that nobody else (including yourself) has been able to do. On the other hand, Nancy is about to give you an ulcer. She's so incredibly bad with numbers that her records are almost incomprehensible. Your boss has told you flat out that he can't put up with any more of her mistakes because he's starting to get heat from *his* boss.

OPTION YOU'D CHOOSE: _____

(4)   You're the manager of sales training for a large electrical corporation headquartered in the Northeast. One of your principal responsibilities is the supervision of young management trainees just out of college.

You took **Jim O'Rourke** under your wing about three months ago when he expressed a strong interest in sales engineering. You decided to take Jim into the sales training program primarily on the basis of his very high standing in the graduating class of a prominent engineering school.

Now that you've had an opportunity to observe Jim in a number of different kinds of selling situations, you're pretty well convinced that he's never going to make it as a salesperson. His knowledge of engineering principles and application is remarkable for someone so young, but he obviously lacks a lot of the people skills that you feel are so important for selling. In spite of several coaching sessions with him, he still doesn't smile very much, give a good firm handshake, talk enthusiastically about his products, and so on.

At this point you're beginning to wonder whether you should even go through the motions of running him through the last six months of the training program.

OPTION YOU'D CHOOSE: _____

CHOOSING THE BEST OPTION: ANSWERS AND DISCUSSION

Here are the choices we would've made for each of these employees. When you compare your choices with ours, it's important to remember that there are no right or wrong answers —just different consequences.

(1) *Fire or neutralize Sam Tigner.*

We're not 100 percent certain what we'd do about Sam. We know we wouldn't transfer him or try to restructure his job, but we're not sure whether we'd try to fire him or try to neutralize him.

Our final choice would probably come down to something like this: If Sam were really arrogant and constantly challenging our authority, we'd probably try to fire him in spite of the tremendous effort it would take to make that happen. On the other hand, if Sam were just kind of independent but not really abrasive, we'd probably be more inclined to neutralize him. Even though the choice of putting Sam off in a corner would be distasteful, it probably wouldn't be as unpleasant as the long, drawn-out process of trying to get him fired.

(2) *Fire Caroline Robinson.*

We don't have any doubts here. We'd move quickly to fire Caroline. She's given us some pretty strong evidence that she's deceitful, if not downright dishonest. We think that not getting rid of her quickly and deliberately would be courting disaster.

(3) *Restructure Nancy Battaglia's job.*

Nancy obviously has some real strengths and some areas that definitely need improvement as a customer account representative. She's very skillful at getting people to pay their bills, but she has an absolutely terrible time with figures.

We'd be inclined to restructure her job to take advantage of what she does well and to minimize the effects of what she does poorly. One way to do this would be to make her a troubleshooter—that is, restructure her job so that she's responsible for helping the other representatives with particularly troublesome accounts. This would allow her to put her persuasive skills to good use, but her lack of skill with numbers would no longer be a problem because the representative in charge of each account she worked on would be responsible for all paperwork and arithmetic.

(4) *Transfer Jim O'Rourke.*

We'd begin to think pretty seriously about a transfer for Jim. He seems to be very technically competent. In such a large organization, there are probably any number of engineering positions where his skills and abilities could be used, and where his poor interpersonal skills would not be the drawback they are in selling.

In this chapter we've tried to describe four options—firing, transferring, restructuring, and neutralizing—that are available to you when you decide that the performance improvement process hasn't worked for a particular employee. In addition, we've given you some guidelines for choosing among these options and some practice in implementing them.

We strongly hope that the first nine steps of the performance improvement process will reduce the number of times you have to come to the conclusion that "none of this stuff works." But when the conclusion is unavoidable, we hope our suggestions in this chapter will make your task a little easier.

A CONCLUDING NOTE

Being a supervisor isn't easy; you don't need us to tell you that. But we feel that it can be tremendously rewarding too. Although we're interested in helping you increase the productivity of your employees, there are some humanistic fringe benefits you'll get from using the performance improvement process outlined in this book. Perhaps the most rewarding will be watching people develop. It's a reminder of the tremendous capacity we all have for growth.

If you adopt the attitude of "How can I help unlock this person's door to growth?" with all the problem employees you encounter, you may not always find the key, but you'll feel good as a result of having tried. And your skills as a developer of people will get better all the time.

QUESTIONS & ANSWERS

Following the completion of our workshops, many participants have questions about the implementation of the performance improvement process. We've included some of these questions—and our answers—below.

My company has a performance appraisal system with a rating form that has to be filled out on each employee at least once a year. The approach you recommend is a little different. What do you think I should do?

We're strongly opposed to performance appraisal rating forms. They ask you to evaluate the employee from unsatisfactory to exceptional (the words may differ, but they mean the same) on a long series of global traits such as dependability, ability to get along with others, quality of work, and so on. They don't get at the heart of employee performance because they don't get down to specific behavior. After an appraisal where one of these forms is used, employees often end up feeling like school kids who've just received their report cards. If their marks are high, they feel pretty good. If their marks aren't so hot, they feel bad.

We think you should try to get around these forms. Here's how:

1. During the performance improvement interview, tell the employee that you don't approve of the forms, but that they have to be filled out and that you want to schedule a separate meeting to get the form out of the way.
2. When you meet with the employee, say that the purpose of the meeting is to get the form taken care of quickly because you don't feel it's a helpful tool.
3. Ask the employee to fill out the form. If you can live with these self-ratings, tell the employee that's exactly how the form will be turned in. If you can't live with them, use your negotiating and listening skills to arrive at ratings you can both agree on. (Always give the employee the benefit of the doubt.)

By the way, if you work in an organization where many managers get away with not filling these forms out, join the ranks. They're a waste of time, and we're convinced that they do more harm than good.

I'm the president of a family-owned business. Most of the people who report directly to me are relatives or in-laws. How would you modify your approach to handle this kind of situation?

We wouldn't modify it at all. Our work with a number of family-owned businesses has taught us that our approach can be especially helpful to somebody in your situation. It's informal, task-oriented, and personalized. It involves employees appropriately in the process of improving performance, theirs and yours.

221

How long should these performance improvement interviews last? And how often should they be held?

The interviews should probably last between an hour and an hour and a half. If you take less than an hour, you're probably rushing things a bit. If you take more than an hour and a half, you may be getting bogged down in one area. (It's much better to err on the side of too much time than too little.)

As you begin to interview your employees, you may find yourself taking well over an hour and a half. The main reason will probably be that your employees have a lot to say because they haven't had the opportunity to talk in this manner before. The extra time spent should be worth it.

You should hold a comprehensive interview with each one of your employees at least once a year. But more important than the formal interview is using these skills and techniques on an informal, continuing basis. You can find out how things are going in a ten-minute conversation in the hall. You can give feedback, both positive and in areas needing improvement, on an aspect of employee performance in a few minutes in your office. You can get employees to talk about problems they're experiencing over lunch.

The more you use the skills, the sharper they'll get and the more helpful they'll be to you.

I'm a manufacturing supervisor with thirty-one people who report directly to me. How can I possibly do what you recommend with so many people? I'd spend all my time in meetings.

You're right. It's impossible to do what we recommend with that many employees and still do all the other things you have to do. We suggest that either you try to reduce the number of people who report directly to you or you interview only on a priority basis.

Let's take the first option. Supervising thirty-one people violates a management principle called span of control, which states that managers should supervise between five and ten people. Supervising any more than ten people makes it very difficult to keep track of what everybody's doing; thirty-one makes it impossible.

Our solution is that you talk to your boss and ask to have four or five of the thirty-one promoted to supervisory positions in which they would report directly to you. Each of them would then have six or seven people to supervise.

If you work in an industry where profit margins are close, you'll definitely get some objections to this kind of proposal. The major argument you'll hear is, "If I promote these people to supervisors, they're not making money for us; they're an expensive overhead item." And your argument (after using your listening skills to build up receptivity) should be that productivity will go up, not down, with a properly supervised production force. →

But let's say your argument fails. The second option is to interview only workers who meet certain criteria, such as:

☐ Hard-core problem employees;
☐ The real star performers (who will probably get promoted anyway); and
☐ Workers who are new and need a lot of feedback.

Even if you have to choose this second option, don't give up on the first. Keep trying to get your supervisory load reduced.

I work in an area where there aren't really any enclosed offices, only partitions and room dividers. It's almost impossible to carry on a private conversation. What suggestions do you have?

We take a strong stand on this issue; if you want to conduct an effective interview, you've got to find someplace to do it where people can't overhear you.

If you don't have a private office, you might try:

☐ Using the conference room or some other community space where you can close the door and hold a private conversation;
☐ Asking if you can borrow your supervisor's office (or the office of some other senior person) for an hour or so. It's for a good cause, and it'll give your boss an excuse to get out of the office for a while;
☐ Coming in early or staying late to conduct the interview (give the employee some compensatory time if you use this approach); and
☐ Leaving the building if you have to. Go to a library, a quiet restaurant, or another relatively private place.

Be persistent. You'll find a solution.

I'm brand new in my job, and I'm much younger than most of the people I supervise. They haven't really accepted me yet as their supervisor. What can I expect if I begin to use this process with them?

We've found that a major complaint of older workers about younger supervisors is that these supervisors don't really value and respect the older workers' experience. They say things such as:

"I know this place inside and out, and he doesn't even know where the restrooms are yet."

"There are all kinds of things I could tell her that she really needs to know. But if she isn't asking, I'm not telling."

"He's making mistakes that are so obvious, but he doesn't pay much attention when we give him advice."

"She's got a good head on her shoulders, but she really doesn't know anything yet. I could really help her out."

The performance improvement interview is an excellent opportunity for you to show older workers that you value and respect their experience by listening to them. When you find out how things are going, you give them an opportunity to tell you all kinds of things they feel you should know about the organization, about the best ways to cut through red tape, about things to look out for, and so on. You show them—without giving up your authority as a supervisor—that you're interested in what they have to say and that you want to benefit from their experience.

What do you do when it comes to the follow-up meeting and the employee has done everything he agreed to and you haven't?

This will happen sometimes. When it does, go ahead and hold the follow-up meeting. Don't give in to the temptation to postpone it until you've had more time.

Here are some other suggestions on how to handle the situation:

1. Without feeling or sounding guilty, tell the employee why you failed to live up to your end of the bargain.
2. Without blaming anybody or making excuses, mention any special problems you had in accomplishing what you agreed to do.
3. Get the employee's view of the situation and ask for suggestions on how to improve things in the future.
4. Renegotiate a performance agreement that has a better chance of succeeding than the last one.

You first say that the performance agreement is for the use of the supervisor and employee only and that copies will not go in the employee's file. But you also say that documentation is necessary if an employee is going to be fired. Isn't that a contradiction?

This is a sensitive issue. If you tell the employee that the performance agreement is just between you and me, then it's not ethical to later use the agreement against the employee in the termination process. As a supervisor, however, you're responsible to yourself and the organization to act if the employee doesn't live up to the performance agreement — even if that action leads to firing.

Here's what we suggest:

1. Keep the original performance agreement as a confidential document between you and the employee.
2. If, in your follow-up meeting, it's clear that the employee has violated the agreement, tell the employee that any future agreements will not necessarily be kept confidential. Say that these agreements will be put in the employee's personnel file and may be used to build a case for termination.

What should you say when you ask the employee to meet with you to discuss work performance and the employee says, "Are we going to discuss my salary in this meeting?" This happened to me and I didn't know what to say.

We think there are two reasons why you should keep discussions of salary and work performance separate:

1. If you include salary in discussions of work performance, the employees will tend to focus on how much money they're going to get, not on how work performance can be improved. This is especially true when employees feel they're not getting the type of raises they deserve. No matter what you say about the positive aspects of their performance, dissatisfied individuals are likely to walk away thinking, "Well, I guess that's all they think I'm worth."
2. Although an employee's salary is certainly related to work performance, there are other factors that affect salary and salary increases, things that don't have anything to do with performance. For example: ➡

□ Budget constraints: Often it's impossible to give even a superb performer more than a small raise because of poor profits, budget cutbacks, and other fiscal problems beyond your control;

□ Job market competition: There are more and more technical areas (for example, systems analysts, electrical engineers, tool and die makers) in which the supply of skilled workers is scarce. It's often necessary to offer large salaries and annual increases to attract and to keep these workers even if their performance is average or even a little below; and

□ Internal equity: A typical problem in organizations that employ union personnel is called compression. That's what happens when the wages of hourly union employees begin to approach (or surpass) the salaries of nonunion management personnel who supervise them. To keep things equitable, organizations automatically increase the salaries of these supervisory personnel regardless of their performance.

When you have a meeting to discuss an employee's salary, a lot of the steps and techniques covered in the book will apply. The most useful skill you've learned for this kind of discussion, however, is the ability to actively listen. Employees are often dissatisfied with their pay and their raises. Give the employee an opportunity to talk about this dissatisfaction without offering all kinds of explanations and reasons why the dissatisfaction is unjustified. Just listen. They'll feel better and so will you.

When analyzing the employee's performance, I agree with you that the performance analysis form should be filled out thoroughly and completely. Is it also okay to have the employee fill out the same form?

We think it's better to keep the form for your own use. If you ask your employee to fill out the same form, the person is likely to be very curious about how you filled out your copy and will probably expect, if not ask, to see it.

This can cause some problems. The language you use on the form is likely to be somewhat blunt and straightforward on the "needs improvement" side. Unlike you, the form can't monitor the employee's receptivity. It can't stop talking and start listening if receptivity drops. And once the person has read the form and feels unfairly judged by you, it's difficult to undo the damage. It's better not to let it happen in the first place.

As an alternative, ask employees to write down:

□ The areas where they think they're performing effectively;

□ The areas where they feel they could stand to improve; and

□ Their thoughts on how you could make their jobs less frustrating and more satisfying.

We've found that employees who write these things down before the interview are better prepared for, and get more involved in, the meeting than those who are only asked to think about these things.

I'm concerned about asking the employee, "How can I make your job less frustrating and more satisfying?" Isn't that going to open up a Pandora's box? Aren't I going to get some weird requests if I do that?

This is one of the most common questions supervisors ask us during our workshops. They fear employees will make all kinds of unreasonable requests, like two-hour lunch breaks or six-week vacations.

We think your question is part of the very human tendency to expect the worst—to engage in catastrophic thinking.

In our experience employees rarely make unreasonable or irrational requests when their supervisors ask this question. When outrageous requests are made, they tend to be in jest. In such cases, the best response is to say, "Okay, anything else I can do for you?" The serious requests will usually follow.

One final word of caution. Don't avoid the question just because you expect the worst. You'll deprive yourself of some very useful information if you do.

Throughout the book you use the phrase, "areas where the employee could stand to improve." Why not just use the simpler expression "weakness"?

For a couple of reasons:

1. The word *weakness* is an emotionally loaded expression that's likely to lower the employee's receptivity.
2. It's not a very useful concept. Its focus is negative, not positive. You don't get as much useful information when you ask, "What are the employee's weak points?" as you do when you ask, "How could the employee stand to improve?"

I know that what you say about listening skills is important. But will it really work with the silent types? I've got a guy in the office who hasn't said Boo! in two years. How, all of a sudden, is he going to start talking in a performance improvement interview?

We've talked with lots of supervisors who've expressed this concern about getting workers to open up in an interview. Most of the time they come back later saying:

"It was really something. He just started talking and didn't stop."

"You know, this stuff really does work!"

"I thought she was just going to sit there and say nothing, like she usually does, but she opened up. I was surprised."

We've found that when employees don't open up, it's usually because their supervisors are not the best listeners. These supervisors tend to talk rapidly and to monopolize conversations. They often ask closed-ended questions and don't wait very long for an answer. When the employee doesn't start talking right away, they'll usually answer the question themselves and keep on talking. And they often interrupt whenever they disagree with what the employee's got to say.

If you're this kind of listener, you'll have to work especially hard to get a quiet worker to talk. Comprehensive ➔

questions are often very good with quiet people. Plan to use a lot of encouragers when they do start talking. Do the other things regarding listening skills we suggested in Chapter 7. Use good attending skills. Ask questions that give the employee plenty of room to respond. Paraphrase and summarize to make sure you understand what the employee has said.

If you listen skillfully, the employee will talk.

I not only have problem employees, I also have a problem boss. I can see the value of your approach for dealing with my employees. Do you think it could be adapted for use with my boss?

Yes. We know some people who've done it. Here's a possible adaptation:

1. Analyze your boss's performance following the same basic approach described for analyzing your employee's performance in Chapter 4.
2. Ask your boss if you can meet to talk about some ways both of you can improve the quality of your working relationship. (If he or she balks, use your listening skills.)
3. Begin the meeting by explaining:
☐ The purpose of the meeting as you see it; and
☐ Your ideas on how to proceed. For example, your boss could start off by giving you feedback on your performance and then you could give your boss feedback. Then the two of you could come up with an agreement on what you're both going to do to improve the relationship.
4. Ask your boss to give you feedback on your performance, starting with the areas where you're doing well and moving to the areas where you could stand to improve.
5. Do the same for your boss. The most important thing to remember is *stop talking and start listening* if your boss shows even a hint of defensiveness.
6. Negotiate a performance agreement if you can (preferably in writing, but don't press it) and try to arrange a follow-up meeting.
7. End the meeting on a positive note, saying how pleased you are that you had a chance to talk things out.
8. Try to follow up both formally and informally using the techniques discussed in the chapter on following up.

Even **STEP TEN**, "What Do I Do if None of This Stuff Works?" can be adapted to a problem boss. You can't very well restructure your job or neutralize your boss, but you can "*fire*" your boss by quitting or by trying to get a transfer.

And Now . . . Six Step-by-Step Guides for Dealing with Training and Performance Problems

by Robert F. Mager, internationally acclaimed trainer of trainers

1 **ANALYZING PERFORMANCE PROBLEMS, or 'You Really Oughta Wanna'** (with Peter Pipe). Some performance problems can be solved, especially those caused by our own lack of skill at applying principles of human behavior. This book is about those problems that arise because people aren't doing what someone else expects them to be doing. It explains a procedure for analyzing such problems, and helps point you in the direction of solutions that will work. 120 pages; $5\frac{1}{2}'' \times 8\frac{1}{4}''$; paperbound; #031-A138; **$5.95**

Quick Reference Checklist from **ANALYZING PERFORMANCE PROBLEMS** is available in expanded worksheet form, with space for answers to questions. This worksheet is a handy tool, especially in interview situations. Package of 25; 4 pages; $11'' \times 8\frac{1}{2}''$; #0302-A138; **$4.95**

Performance Analysis Poster of the flow diagram from **ANALYZING PERFORMANCE PROBLEMS** is available as a large ($23'' \times 35''$) two-color poster. #0303-A138; **$3.50**

2 **PREPARING INSTRUCTIONAL OBJECTIVES, 2nd Edition,** identifies ways to recognize the characteristics of well-stated objectives and prepares you to develop original objectives of your own. The practice materials will help newcomers to the field master the techniques of drafting objectives. 144 pages; $5\frac{1}{2}'' \times 8\frac{1}{4}''$; paperbound; #5601-A138; **$5.95**

3 **GOAL ANALYSIS** explains a procedure that will help you describe the meaning of the goals you hope to achieve — whether these goals deal with attitudes, appreciations, or understandings — so that you will be able to make better decisions toward their achievement and recognize progress and success. This goal analysis procedure is often critical in the development of meaningful and achievable objectives. 144 pages; $5\frac{1}{2}'' \times 8\frac{1}{4}''$; paperbound; #3476-A138; **$5.95**

4 **MEASURING INSTRUCTIONAL INTENT, or Got a Match?** shows you how to select or create test items that are "just right" for measuring the achievement of your instructional objectives. It provides step-by-step procedures, with examples and practice, for spotting the important characteristics of an objective and tells you how to test an item for its validity in assessing a corresponding objective. 168 pages; $5\frac{1}{2}'' \times 8\frac{1}{4}''$; paperbound #4462-A138; **$5.95**

5 **DEVELOPING ATTITUDE TOWARD LEARNING** shows you how to recognize behaviors that can be used as evidence of favorable (or unfavorable) attitudes toward instruction. It describes three principles you can apply to develop a more receptive attitude, and offers a way of measuring success and a technique for improving upon it. 120 pages; $5\frac{1}{2}'' \times 8\frac{1}{4}''$; paperbound; #2000-A138; **$5.50**

6 **DEVELOPING VOCATIONAL INSTRUCTION** (with Kenneth M. Beach) explains in concise, understandable language the systematic development of instruction and how it can aid you in transmitting skills and knowledge to others. Each step in the process is fully described and illustrated with practical examples. 96 pages; $5\frac{1}{2}'' \times 8\frac{1}{4}''$; paperbound; #2060-A138; **$5.50**

Save over $5.00 When You Buy All Six!

THE MAGER LIBRARY contains all six books described above and comes in a convenient slipcase. #4333-A138; **$29.50**

PITMAN MANAGEMENT AND TRAINING
a division of
Pitman Learning, Inc.
6 Davis Drive
Belmont, California 94002
(415) 592-7810

Prices subject to change without notice.